Lionel St

Lent.
1925

ATONEMENT

MACMILLAN AND CO., Limited
LONDON . BOMBAY . CALCUTTA . MADRAS
MELBOURNE

THE MACMILLAN COMPANY
NEW YORK . BOSTON . CHICAGO
DALLAS . SAN FRANCISCO

THE MACMILLAN CO. OF CANADA, Ltd.
TORONTO

ATONEMENT

BY

H. MAYNARD SMITH, D.D.

CANON OF GLOUCESTER
AUTHOR OF "LECTURES ON THE EPISTLE OF S. JAMES,"
"PRAYER," ETC.

MACMILLAN AND CO., LIMITED
ST. MARTIN'S STREET, LONDON, W.C. 2
1925

51426

COPYRIGHT

S08981

TO THE MEMORY OF

FRANK

SOMETIME BISHOP OF ZANZIBAR

WHO

LOVING THE GOSPEL OF OUR LORD JESUS CHRIST

GAVE HIS LIFE FOR ITS PROCLAMATION

THIS BOOK IS DEDICATED BY

THE FRIEND

WHO STILL HOPES FOR HIS PRAYERS

PREFACE

MANY a man, who cannot escape from the attraction of the Cross, is baffled by the doctrine of the Atonement. Face to face with the Crucified, he asks, Who is He? What do His sufferings mean? Why were they necessary? and How do they avail for me? He receives the traditional answers, but he expects them to be supported by reasons; and when he is dissatisfied with the explanations, he is apt to conclude that the answers are untrue. This is not quite logical, for we are bound to believe many things which we cannot explain; but, on the other hand, we are bound, if possible, to give a reason for the faith that is in us. So book after book has been published dealing with the doctrine of the Atonement, and there is room for yet another, because the subject cannot be exhausted, and no two men have exactly the same difficulties or the same needs.

Much has been written on the history of the doctrine, and the historians differ widely in their criticisms and appreciations, but they all witness to the fact that, until recently, the answers given to the above questions were very similar, although the arguments to prove their validity were strangely discordant.

Secondly, several books have been written by scholars for scholars about the opinions of other scholars, and such works are very necessary, for theological thought can only advance by theologians constantly reviewing one another, and correcting one another's conclusions.

Thirdly, there have been books devoted to an examination of the teaching contained in the New Testament. In the old days, men propounded a theory, and thought it established by quoting proof-texts. Next came scholars concerned with the exact meaning of words, who, ignorant of the *Koine*, wrote elaborate dissertations on the force of Greek particles. Then came literary critics who carefully distinguished between the Petrine, Pauline, and Johannine theologies; and lastly came the subjective critics, who show great ingenuity in discrediting texts which do not accord with their theories.

All these works are important to the student, but they are all preparatory to the formulation of belief in the doctrine of the Atonement, which is what the author of this book, greatly daring, has attempted.

Having been for thirty years engaged in parochial work, his interests are primarily religious and practical. For a good part of that time he preached regularly to educated people, who were interested in religion, but not specialists in theology. He believes himself to know their needs, and those of brother priests who minister to similar congregations. For them, he has written this book, and endeavoured

I. to provide rational grounds for believing in the Atonement;

II. to interpret the doctrine in relation to other articles of the Christian Creed;

III. to insist on the life that should be lived if such a belief be true.

The plan of the book is new, and the author claims to have thought out the subject for himself; but it is the result of much reading, and no doubt shows the impress which many books, read at different times, have made upon his mind. There may be nothing that is original in the book, but it is none the less an individual contribution to the subject, and shows how one person at least justifies to himself the faith that is in him. He hopes that it may help others to a fuller understanding of the mystery, and may stimulate those who disagree with him to continue their search after Truth.

CONTENTS

CHAPTER I

INTRODUCTION

The Atonement and the Modern Mind—The Atonement and Modern Needs—The Atonement and its Need of Explanation —The New Testament and resulting Tradition—The difference of Emphasis at different Times—The Truths to be preserved in discarded Theories—The Aims of the Author 1

CHAPTER II

GOD'S APPEAL TO MAN

Sin is Lawlessness—Some Results of Sin—Sin separates from God—Difficulties in Reconciliation among Men—Difficulties in Reconciliation with God; (A) The Need of Self-knowledge and Repentance; (B) The Need of a Revelation; (C) The Need of a Mediator; (D) The Need of an Example—The Story of the Cross; (A) The Revelation of Man's Sin; (B) The Revelation of God's Love; (C) The Revelation of what Man should be—The Appeal of the Cross . . . 32

CHAPTER III

OUR LORD'S VICTORY

The Old and New Covenant—Sin a Bondage; (A) Original Sin; (B) Sinful Habits; (C) An Evil Environment; (D) The Devil—Is Man a fit object for the Divine Compassion ?— Our Lord's Victory; (A) Free from Original Sin; (B) Resists all Temptation; (C) Overcomes the World; (D) Casts out the Devil; (E) Rises from the Grave and Ascends into Heaven—The Victory was won on our Behalf—How far the Victory accords with (A) Man's Expectations; (B) Our Lord's Teaching about His Death; (C) And how we are to understand the words Ransom and Redemption—The Victory is Availing, because Our Lord is (A) The New Adam; (B) The Messianic King; (C) The High Priest of the New Covenant; (D) The Conqueror of Death. 66

xi

CONTENTS

CHAPTER IV

THE ONE OFFERING

CHAPTER V

FORGIVENESS

CHAPTER VI

SANCTIFICATION

CHAPTER VII

MAN'S RESPONSE TO GOD

ATONEMENT

CHAPTER I

INTRODUCTION

I. THE ATONEMENT AND THE MODERN MIND

A COUPLE of generations ago, the man-in-the-street said : " The Story of the Cross appeals to everyone, but the doctrine of the Atonement fills me with horror." By the doctrine of the Atonement, he meant a popular Calvinism distorted by controversy almost beyond recognition.

More recently, those who shun dogma, but write about the life of Our Blessed Lord, concentrate their attention on the Galilean Ministry, and only regard the Cross as the tragic close to a beautiful life. It makes to them no compelling appeal, and has no special significance when they estimate Our Lord's life and work.

Yet, for the Disciples who knew Jesus and for the writers of the New Testament, the Cross was the wondrous fact. It was through preaching Christ crucified and risen again that the Church started on its way to conquer the world and to restore men to communion with God.

Multitudes in succeeding centuries have found salvation through the Cross, and their witness is not invalidated because they expressed it unfortunately,

B

or invented impossible theories to account for its happening.

Are we to conclude that a fact so potent in the past has now lost its value ? That is to beg the question. The Cross in the beginning was " to the Jews a stumbling-block, and to the Greeks foolishness " ; and many to-day, however unconsciously, retain Jewish conceptions of the Being of God; and many to-day restrict their speculations within the limits that are proper to natural science. Contempt for the Cross has never ceased; but modern conditions quite rightly permit a freedom of criticism which was not allowed when the Church was dominant in worldly affairs.

The Cross has not lost its power of appeal. Every street-corner preacher will assure us of that. The same testimony will be echoed from Missions in every quarter of the globe. The publican, the sinner and the harlot are still pressing into the Kingdom of God, and finding a new life and extended freedom after laying their burdens down at the foot of the Cross. It is when we come to respectable people that we find the doctrine is disregarded. It is when we enter the fashionable church that we find the doctrine is not preached. It is in the works of scholars that we find the doctrine not so much explained as explained away. An atonement, we are told, by our gifted journalists is alien to the modern mind.

What, it may be asked, is this " Modern Mind " ? It is the polite way of referring to the somewhat indefinite opinions which are effervescent in the more or less educated middle classes to which the journalists as a rule belong.

If the ordinary public school boy on the " classical

1 Cor. i. 23.

S. Matt. xxi. 31.

side " is examined in heathen mythology and Bible history, he is almost certain to acquire more marks in the former subject. The ordinary undergraduate is much more likely to pass an elementary examination in Aristotle than in S. Paul. An ordinary club man may have inaccurate knowledge on the subject of evolution, but he has none at all on the subject of the Atonement.

If the ordinary man was aware of his ignorance there might be some hope for him, but he takes his knowledge of Christianity for granted. He went to church with his nurse as a child, and was bored, because nobody tried to explain to him the service. He attended his school chapel and heard eloquent exhortations to " play up and play the game "— he understood and liked them. He occasionally attends church with his wife, and wonders at the persistence of pietistic platitude—it corresponds to nothing in his life and is relative to a plane on which he is not at home. He never reads a theological book unless it is profusely advertised as " a broad-minded and courageous attack on some Article of the Christian Faith, by a Clergyman." Then he buys it and finds that his uneasy feeling about the unreality of Christianity is justified; and he is under the pleasant delusion that he is, after all, in the van of religious progress. Christian writers take him very seriously. He is spoken of as the thoughtful man with difficulties who ought to be conciliated. Books are written to minimise the claims upon his credulity, and the Christian doctrines are restated in terms so broad and vague that they could not excite his un-reasoned tolerance. He accepts such concessions as due to his enlightenment, but remains quite

properly indifferent to a Creed which is so evanescent.
How could it possibly help him?

These respectable people lead the easy lives of the
fairly well-to-do. They have had no religious education, but they have learnt to observe a respectable
standard of conduct. Comparing themselves with
their fellows, they have no sense of sin; and, comparing
themselves with others in less fortunate surroundings,
they cannot fail to have a pleasant sensation of superiority. They have never felt called on to think things
out. Their lives have no real purpose, for they have
been taught to disregard the ultimates of heaven
and hell. When all goes well with them, they disregard God; when anything goes ill with them, they
blaspheme His Name. They are more interested
in their golf handicap than in their eternal salvation.
They drift through life, and " fleet the time carelessly
as they did in the golden world."

I do not write to condemn. These men have many
admirable virtues—an inheritance received by them
from a Christian past, and maintained by Christian
sentiment which has taken the place of Christian
thought. They are not heedless of the less fortunate,
but are ever ready to support generously any well-
advertised scheme of philanthropy. They are neither
anti-religious nor even anti-clerical. They mostly
have friends and relations in Holy Orders. But they
have no real hold on the thought of God, and no
conception of sin. They know very little about the
degrading conditions in which so many are forced
to live, of the burning hatred kindled by a sense of
injustice, of the sin, envy and discontent which
abound; of the vice, squalor and misery which hold
men in bondage. If they did know, they would be

face to face with the problem of a Good God and a
Fallen Humanity : they would be seeking for some
message of reconciliation : they would be conscious
of the awful consequences of sin, and desirous for
some hope of redemption.

But what of the clergy in residential neighbourhoods,
who should teach these kind-hearted worldlings ? They
are men of their own class who have been to the same
schools and universities. They are more serious
about life, but they are terribly oppressed with fear
of the fictitious monster called The Modern Mind.
Their predecessors had had a strictly clerical education,
and lived in a clerical atmosphere steeped in theological traditions. They were very narrow, perhaps;
they saw no need to change their explanations to
meet a widening field of knowledge; they failed to
understand either the meaning or the method of
modern Science—but they kept the faith. The new
men have a wider outlook, which is good; they are
sympathetic, which is better; they are desperately
anxious to find terms of agreement with the philosophy
and science of the day—a noble ambition; but,
scared because of past mistakes, they are timid in
assertion, and dread beyond all things being called
obscurantists. Obsessed by such fears, the clergy
of recent years have not pursued their own subject
with the same single-eyed devotion to truth which
has characterised the best scientists. Scientists have
gone forward careless of what theologians or philosophers might think, while theologians have too often
written with an apprehensive eye on agnostic philosophers and a deprecatory gesture for materialistic
scientists. This is not entirely to their discredit,
for the theologian has still cared for his brother's

soul, while the scientist has been indifferent, through not believing that his brother had a soul.

These clergy have not, like their brethren in the slums, been face to face with defiant sinners, or seen the abject misery which results from sin. They, moreover, learnt such theology as they know from amiable and learned gentlemen who had lived all their lives in "haunts of ancient peace." Such teachers find it hard to feel a horror for sin which is unreal to their experience. The Professor reads the account of a murder in his daily paper with the same thrill and the same personal detachment as he reads any other story of horror from *The Times Book Club*. He shudders for a moment as he hears the mirthless laugh of a prostitute outside a public house, but he forgets all about it as he watches the innocent gaiety of his daughters by his own fireside. He is told how a defaulting solicitor has robbed the widow and the fatherless, and sends a cheque to help them in their destitution; but he never considers how the solicitor, once as honest as himself, was first tempted to "borrow for a few days" from trust funds.

So the good man tends to be an optimist. He says, Sin is negative, it is due to regrettable survivals in the upward course of man's evolution; sin is due to ignorance; sin is due to morbid physical conditions or mental deficiencies, or indicates an unresolved complex in the Unconscious. He endorses the French belief that if we only understood all, all would be pardoned. God, he may add, understands all, and will assuredly pardon. What need is there, in consequence, of any Atonement?

We may conclude that the Atonement is alien to

the Modern Mind, because the Modern Mind is very
ill-informed on the subject. This is due to a certain
timidity in those who should proclaim boldly the
whole counsel of God. It is also due to a defective _{Acts xx. 27.}
view of sin, which implies in turn an inadequate
conception of goodness. Besides, many are unwilling
to mention so unpleasant a subject as sin in polite
ears, lest some should think that a personal reference
was intended.

II. The Atonement and Modern Needs

But if the doctrine of the Atonement is not taught,
man's need for the Atonement is everywhere felt.
The man in the trenches knew his need of God, and
for the first time realised how far he was away from
Him. The convicted felon, broken with shame,
knows his need of a forgiveness which society dare
not bestow. Thousands oppressed with a sense of
their own failure cry out in their impotence for a
Saviour. Thousands who wish to make a fresh start
are longing to know whence the power may come.
Those who see " a world lying in wickedness " know _{1 S. John v. 19.}
the need of redemption. Those bowed down with
sorrow, and tempted to be bitter, because despairing,
are still groping in darkness, because they cannot
see the light of the Cross. " Does God care ? "
asks the victim of some terrible wrong, and why has
he not been taught to listen to the voice of the Crucified saying : " Is it nothing to you, all ye that pass
by ? Is any sorrow like unto My sorrow " ? And _{Lam. i, 12.}
the sorrow of the Saviour is because we will not understand.

Those who need Him will not be comforted by being

told that the Cross is only a human drama, though perhaps the most tragic in history, and that it is efficacious in purging the emotions by pity and terror. There are plenty of sentimentalists who enjoy shedding tears at the theatre in a comfortable stall; but the people of whom I am thinking have their own troubles to weep over. They do not want a drama, they want help.

It was this help which was found in the old days. Saints and martyrs, peasants and scholars, old and young, rich and poor, of all races and all times, have confessed that somehow through Our Lord's death they have found a way to reconciliation with God and a power which has enabled them to live in communion with Him. They found in the Cross, not a human drama, but an Act of God; not a tale to excite their sensibilities, but a deliverance from sin. Surely such evidence—and it is so abundant—cannot be despised.

Secondly, if individuals are longing for a Saviour, the world is very conscious of its need of redemption. To-day it is in danger of drifting back into chaos, for lack of any real faith or any sound principles. A few are still deluded by the Victorian mirage, and look forward to the time when everyone will be happy in an earthly paradise, because supplied with every material comfort.

Multitudes, on the other hand, are full of wrath and discontent because they have so few of the good things of life, and are also full of envy because others possess them. They would destroy the very imperfect civilisation we have achieved after centuries of effort, in the hope that somehow, some day, something better may be evolved. Then there are the cool-

headed and cold-hearted men who are ready to produce
a hell upon earth in order that they may observe the
working out of their particular formulæ. They would
destroy all human freedom, so that nothing should
interfere with the scientific expression of their economic
laws. They would abolish the family and the nation,
but apparently not " the colour bar "; they would
stifle all romance and art, and blot out the knowledge
of God and heaven, in order that the automata, who
once were men, may produce cheap goods efficiently,
and enjoy the dubious blessing of compulsory work
for only four hours a day.

The Victorian optimists are a dying race, the
anarchists only wish to glut their rage in an orgy of
destruction, and the non-Christian thinkers have
nothing better to offer us than a mechanical hell.
Those who have some conception of human values
and some desire for human happiness cannot do better
than teach men once more to contemplate the Cross,
and learn from it anew the obvious lessons about the
way to social betterment.

Love alone can create : hate can only destroy.
The hate of men pursued the Lord to death, and His
love is their salvation. The world's redemption will
not be advanced by organising any Terror, Red or
White; but by being ready to suffer for others as Our
Lord suffered upon the Cross. It is not by means
of the big battalions, loud majorities or accumulated
material that human happiness will be increased,
but by the inspiration of the solitary hero, who stands
for Truth, Beauty or Righteousness, " though the
heathen rage and the earth be moved." It is not Ps. xlvi. 6.
by proclaiming the obvious lie of human equality
that men will be brought to realise their solidarity,

but by all owning One Master, and each ministering to the common good in his appointed place. There are too many reformers nowadays, ready to mind any business but their own; and there are too few ^{Rom. xii. 16;} who will " condescend to men of low estate " and be content with service. Yet the Son of God emptied Himself of His Glory that He might become the servant of all, and die on behalf of those He served. He did not talk much about His love of humanity; He was content to work, to sympathise and to suffer; but He made brotherhood a reality by His revelation of the One Father; and the Father gave His Son that all men might be united in Him. Our Lord did not promise a Kingdom which would come with ^{S. Luke xvii. 20.} observation. The strength of the Kingdom was to come from within, and the world would only be better when it was composed of better men. He promised His help, and proclaimed His power, resulting from His Victory on the Cross. If the world to-day needs redemption, there is only One Saviour. He has come, He is present, and He will do everything except compel men to accept His Salvation.

For nineteen centuries we can follow the fortunes of the Church and marvel at the miracle of her survival. All the powers of the world have tried to destroy her. Age after age she has been derided by the intellectuals, who age after age have predicted her collapse. She has been torn asunder by the self-will of her members, and disgraced by their acting in defiance of her creed. Yet she has won great victories, achieved great changes and has slowly been pursuing her mission ^{S. Matt. xiii. 33.} of leavening the world. You may say, How slow has the progress been; but that is because of the fierce and persistent opposition. You may complain:

How much remains to be done! But it can be done if men will lift their crosses and carry them after Jesus; if men believe that through His death came the triumph; if they are assured that He is still by our side. In the midst of our doubts, perplexities and sorrows, the Cross is still a rallying point for humanity, and through it men may still find the power of God unto salvation. But in order that men may be con- Rom. i. 16. vinced of this a doctrine of the Atonement is necessary.

III. The Atonement and its Need of Explanation

The Crucifixion is a fact. It happened in time, and its consequences are still apparent. For Christians it is the central fact in human history, and non-Christians cannot escape from its challenge. We estimate and interpret historical events according to their consequences, and the results of the Crucifixion demand an explanation commensurate with their magnitude and extension.

To supply one that would be adequate is indeed beyond our power. No one mind could master or arrange so vast an accumulation of evidence of such a very varied character. God, also, is still working His purpose out, and the full meaning of the Atonement will only be revealed at the end of the world, if then. Thirdly, if Our Lord died for all men and appeals to all men, no one human heart has wide enough sympathies to comprehend the fulness of that appeal. But in admitting this, the theological student is in precisely the same position as the student of natural science. The latter knows how little has been discovered in comparison with the

unexplored remainder. He does not, however, undervalue his knowledge, or deny its reality, because it
is incomplete. He still appreciates the importance
of an hypothesis if fresh advances are to be made.
He works on it, though he knows that it does not
cover all the facts, and that it will have to be revised,
or perhaps discarded, in the light of fresh discoveries.

There are many to-day who plead, " Let us rest in
the fact, which appeals to our hearts, and let us give
up reasoning about it. Nothing but confusion and
controversy have come from attempting to crystallise
a beautiful story into an ecclesiastical dogma." The
same people would approach the scientist and say,
" Nature is very beautiful; and why worry about it ?
Nature appeals to my heart, and I love to lie on a
grassy bank and indulge my fancy. Why should
you analyse the things which afford me such æsthetic
enjoyment ? " No one would interrupt the contemplation of a devout soul, or restrain the poet's imagination. It is, however, because men are rational
creatures that they cannot rest content with the
evidence of their senses, or only rely on subjective
impressions. They want in some way to account
for their experience, and they are bound to do so,
if they would relate it to other facts, and translate
it into action. What does not proceed beyond
sensation has no directive power. A fact, until it
is interpreted, has no practical value, and a fact in
isolation has no hold upon the mind. In order that
the Cross may influence conduct we are driven to
consider its metaphysical import.

But it may be said, " How futile have been attempts
to systematise beliefs about the Atonement ! After
all the labours of theologians, the Church has been

unable to define the dogma. The theories are many, some of them are grotesque, others are immoral, while all of them are, by your own admission, incomplete." But what else would you expect if the appeal of the Cross is universal, and intended for all men, everywhere and at all times? Each new generation has to accept or reject the Atonement, each has its own special difficulties to encounter, and each has its own contribution to make. Christianity is a progressive religion; its content is inexhaustible; and it is not for us Christians to deplore " the unsearchable riches of Christ."

Eph. iii. 8.

In everyday life we interpret whatever happens to us, and very often find that we have made a mistake. The fact is what it is, quite apart from what we think about it; but when we think wrongly we destroy or impair its value for ourselves. We know also the difficulties which arise from misunderstandings, and how they separate people who should be at one. There are plenty of misunderstandings in regard to the Atonement which have to be cleared up, if God and man are really to be reconciled.

Lastly, there must be a theory of the Atonement so long as there is an *Ecclesia Docens*. The Church exists to proclaim that Our Lord was " crucified for us under Pontius Pilate "; and she stands or falls by her ability to convince men of that fact. Her present weakness is not due to foes without, but to lack of faith in those within. There is a world which knows itself to be in need of redemption, blindly at war with itself and with God. There is an Atonement which has been made, which is perfect and sufficient, but it has to be accepted, if men are to enjoy its fruits. Men's hearts may be touched by the story of the Cross, but men's minds need to be convinced of the victory which was won, and their consciences need to be reassured that there is nothing inconsistent with justice in the revealed love of God.

IV. THE NEW TESTAMENT AND RESULTING TRADITION

When it was said above that Christianity was the religion of progress, it was suggested that we should hope for an ever-widening vision and a more detailed apprehension of its content. It was also implied that there was a continuing and continuous tradition, for there can be no progress unless there be a starting-point, a road and a goal. The Faith was once for all delivered, that cannot change. The explanation of the Faith and its application is always going on. There are those who explore its meaning, those who, in a provisional way, systematise results, and those who translate the teaching into practice. (1) The points on which the Church has decided are relatively few, and to deny those decisions would be to deny the Holy Ghost. (2) On most points there is a more or less dominant tradition, but no decision has been demanded, and no exact definitions can be formulated. (3) Some points, which have given rise to fierce controversies, remain open for anyone to believe as he likes. The doctrine of the Atonement in its main outline belongs to the second class, but it involves several points which belong to the third, and it is this fact which renders any systematic attempt to expound the doctrine difficult.

There is no systematic presentment of the Atone-

Jude, 3.

ment in the New Testament, and its authors evidently found that the subject was too big for the categories proper to human reasoning. But we have to remember that the Epistles were occasioned by special circumstances, and were sent to people instructed in the Faith. When S. Paul writes to the Corinthians— "I delivered unto you . . . that which I also received, how that Christ died for our sins according to the Scriptures "—he shows what was the faith 1 Cor. xv. 3. of the Church when he was baptised into it. We cannot, in consequence, doubt that this faith belonged to the original deposit.

It is not the reticence of the Apostolic writers which renders the subject difficult. On the contrary, we are embarrassed by the wealth and range of their references to Our Lord's death. For them it seemed to interpret the whole of life, so that to know Christ and Him crucified was the sum of knowledge. Some- 1 Cor. ii. 2. times they speak of the attractive power of the Cross— Gal. vi. 14. it was for them a Standard of salvation. Sometimes, Acts xiii.38. and most frequently, they tell how through it had come the great deliverance, and how by it men were justified, forgiven, sanctified and saved. It was a Rom. iv. 25; witness to the exceeding sinfulness of sin, because v. 18. on the Cross men had slain the Lord of Glory; it Acts v. 30, was evidence for the exceeding love of God, Who 1 Cor. i. 30; spared not His only begotten Son. It was the ground Heb. x. 14. for the reconciliation of God and man: nay, they 1 Cor. ii. 8. went further, and through the blood of the Cross, S. John iii. proclaimed the reconciliation of all things, whether Rom. v. 10. in earth or heaven. They announced that Our Lord's Col. i. 20. victory was over principalities and powers of evil, Col. ii. 15. that it was a mystery which angels desired to look into—an eternal fact of cosmic significance. It 1 S. Pet. i. 12.

S. Matt.
xxvi. 24.
S. Mark ix.
16.
Acts iii. 8.
1 Cor. xv. 3.
Heb. x. 1. was according to the Scriptures, and they found in it the fulfilment of prophecy and the antitype of all sacrifices. It revolutionised for them the whole of human values, and enthroned self-sacrificing Love. They reminded one another how they must live to be Rom. viii.
11.
2 Cor. v. 17. worthy of so costly an offering, and they counted the world well lost if only they might be united with Phil. iii. 8.
Col. i. 27. the Crucified. The Cross filled them with hope, for on it what seemed like a failure proved a triumph, and 2 Cor. xii. 9;
xiii. 4–9. strength had been made perfect through weakness. Knowing, as they did, of the Resurrection and Ascension, they believed that through the Cross death had been robbed of its sting and the grave of its victory. Hos. xiii. 14.
1 Cor. xv. 55. The grisly phantom, man's last terror, had been dissipated.

It was natural that those who had known Our Lord and seen Him die, or lived and talked with the immediate disciples, should be more inclined to reason from the event than to it, should be more explicit about its effects than about its cause. But the whole of the New Testament is quite clear on the point, which has so often been obscured in Protestant theology, that God's Love was the cause of the Atonement, and that the death on the Cross was the means by which the Atonement was brought about.

Very interesting critical studies have been made on the distinctive teaching of S. Peter, S. Paul, S. John, and the unknown writer to the Hebrews; but they were all in possession of the same facts, they all worshipped the same Lord, and a sane criticism regards them as complementary to one another, and not as antagonists. They were indeed very different men, and we may compare them to the four walls of that Rev. xxi. 16. New Jerusalem which stands four square. Each

wall faces outwardly in a different direction, but
faces inwardly to a common centre. There stands
the Cross towering over all, and it is the doctrine of
that Cross which they alike defend.

During the early ages there was very little controversy about the nature of the Atonement, and this
shows that there was a general agreement on the subject, and not that the doctrine was of subordinate
importance. Even the well-known differences between
Eastern and Western Fathers have been very much
exaggerated by critics who seek to be clear by anti-
thetical statements. Gradually, however, the doctrine gave rise to many questions, and some of them
were foolish : heretics also provided answers, which
were sometimes still more foolish; and the Church
condemned propositions which were fatal to her
faith; but the Church has never defined the dogma.

This does not mean that there has not been a
continuous tradition, which is all the more impressive
because it does not depend on an authorised formula.
We forget this in studying controversial writings,
because controversialists accentuate their differences,
and are sometimes eager to show that the arguments
of opponents have logical conclusions, which the
opponents do not admit.

Recent historians of the doctrine have paid too
little attention to ascetic theology, though a man's
real faith is often more apparent in his devotional
life than when he is armed for disputation. What
seems hard and unreal when expressed in syllogisms
for the schools becomes human and helpful when
applied to life. An anatomist dissects a dead body,
that by a beneficent surgery a living body may be
set right. A theologian exercises his analytical

c

reason upon a dogma, that a living truth may be proclaimed among men. If S. Anselm's *Cur Deus Homo* seems to us hard and formal, we should go on and read how the doctrine of satisfaction sounds in the fervid sermons of S. Bernard. If we revolt from the logic of Calvin's *Institutes*, we should try to understand what Calvinism really meant in the pages of *Pilgrim's Progress.* We may still dissent from the doctrine, but we shall do so in a different spirit.

Secondly, in considering the Tradition, too little regard has been given to Liturgies, and yet *Lex orandi, lex credendi* is an approved maxim. All down the ages, men, in approaching God, have prayed in the Name of the Christ Who died for us, and asked to be heard for His sake. All down the ages they have collected their prayers and summed up their worship in that Eucharistic sacrifice whereby " they show 1 Cor. xi. 26. forth the Lord's death."

Thirdly, although controversies have been fierce upon the subject of grace, there has been but little dispute on the subject of saintliness; and there has been uniform consent in attributing it to the redeeming power of Our Lord through the outpouring of His Spirit. The unsolved problems about Grace divide men into hostile camps, but the results of grace in the lives of the Saints unite men together. They are the admitted fruits of the Cross.

Returning to the theologians, we may also note that historians of the doctrine of the Atonement are apt to convey a wrong impression. As they review one author after another, they try to seize on what is distinctive in each individual, what contribution he made to the discussion, where he went wrong, and whither his arguments were bound to lead. Each chapter is apt to begin : " Leaving out what is common to all "; but it is just this that is common to all which constitutes the tradition. It would be possible to compile a very fat volume of extracts to prove how Fathers, Schoolmen, Protestants and Jesuits repeat one another, but it would be impossible to read it. We learn much more from the critical method in every respect save one, and that is in respect to the persisting tradition.

That tradition may be summed up as follows. The Son of God became incarnate for our salvation. He died upon the Cross that our sins might be forgiven. He died that we might receive grace to lead a new life, and that we by being incorporated into Him might be at one with God.

V. The Difference of Emphasis at Different Times

In the first age, when slavery was the most obvious fact in life, and many of the converts were actually slaves, it was natural that metaphors like ransom and redemption should be pressed in a very literal manner. A spiritual freedom was the outstanding experience of Christians, and they looked on the Cross as the great deliverance from the powers of evil. Arguing, in consequence, from the analogies of their everyday life, they arrived at what we consider a monstrous theory, and believed that Our Lord's Blood was a ransom paid to the Devil.

In the Dark Ages, when crimes of violence were common, men naturally thought most of Our Lord's physical sufferings. They noted how sin led to the

suffering on the Cross; and life was interpreted for
them when they believed that through suffering sin
was expiated. It was a time of awful sins and terrible
penances. Men had no idea of earning merit, but
were trying to follow in the way of Our Lord.

In the days of Feudalism no man was in theory
independent. The Pope and Emperor were said to
hold of God directly, but everyone else did homage
to someone, and received homage from those beneath
him—even the villein had rights over his child.
Secondly, everyone was responsible for those beneath
him, the lord for his vassals and the villein for his
child. It was, in consequence, natural for men to
think of Our Lord on the Cross as head and representative of humanity, offering satisfaction for the
honour of God, outraged by man's rebellion against
Him.

With S. Francis and the miracle of the stigmata
a new conception filled men's hearts. They began
to desire a mystical union with Our Lord even in His
suffering, and so to find the way of the Atonement.
They felt that Our Lord had consecrated poverty by His
life, and glorified pain by His death; that, in sympathy
with suffering, He had shared man's lot, and that
those who sympathised with Him must be ready
to suffer with the suffering members of His Body,
in the persons of His poor.

As absolute monarchies arose, and with marked
success put an end to the chaotic conditions of the
fifteenth century, men turned once more to emphasise
the unconditioned Sovereignty of God, and to answer
all questions concerning the Atonement with the
phrase, *God willed it*. To question His Will was
treason to His Majesty, and to wish for an explanation

of His inscrutable justice was an unseemly curiosity which showed lack of faith and loyalty. Man was utterly depraved and worthless, and so could deserve no salvation; but it was according to God's decrees that His predestined ones should be saved, and that the punishment due to their sins should be visited on His Son. Strange as such teaching seems to us, it did not sound so terrible to men who provided whipping boys to receive the stripes which young princes had deserved.

As constitutional government took the place of autocracy, and law became the dominant interest of men, the Atonement was once more interpreted, and this time in a legal sense. God had given men a law and provided penalties for breaking it, which for the sake of human welfare it was necessary to enforce. Our Lord had come, willing to pay the penalties, and justice was, in consequence, satisfied. By His death the supremacy of the Law had been vindicated and the damage done to the Divine Order by sin paid for. By liquidating the debt Our Lord had acquired the right to pardon the debtor.

This theory for a long time seems to have satisfied men's intellects, but it is obvious that it made no appeal to men's hearts. It was accepted by evangelicals without question, but it had very little influence on their religious life. They were individualists dominated by an emotional ideal. They sought to be justified by faith in Our Lord's saving power, and the experience of conversion was the fact which proved their success. It was a personal devotion to Our Lord and an assurance of His abiding Presence which inspired them, and not the barren theology which they had inherited from their fathers.

The discoveries in physical science and Darwinism revolutionised man's conception of the world's order and method; and books on the evolution of religion became fashionable. Christian thinkers elaborated the process by which men had arrived at their moral and religious ideas. They saw them evolving in struggle and suffering according to the strictest rubric of Natural Selection. All led up to and culminated in Our Lord's life and death upon the Cross. Through suffering, death and resurrection, He proved His survival value, and from Him the long process starts afresh for the gradual redemption of the world. As life is only possible by correspondence with environment, so eternal life is equivalent to correspondence with God—a true At-one-ment.

Lastly, we note the Humanitarian tendencies of our own age, which have led men to concentrate their attention on the example of the Son of Man. He came to save man, but His power lay in the perfection of His sympathy. His love was such that He refused to resist even the wicked men who slew Him. What we call His redemption, however, is not something which He has done for us, but something which He is doing in us, by the inspiration we derive from the splendour of His example.

All these views are one-sided and incomplete, but the most erroneous contains some elements of truth. The errors do not really arise out of the original deposit, or from the tradition of which I have spoken. They are due to the efforts of theologians to accommodate their truth with the thought of their day. We are not the first generation to be confronted with a Modern Mind. Each generation in the past has been equally confident of its own infallibility,

and equally critical of God's revelation. From the
first century onwards there have been Apologies
for Christianity, and it has generally happened that
the successful apologetics of one generation have been
a cause of stumbling to the next. Apologetics too
often tie the eternal truth in knots with contemporary
opinions, and the next generation has the irksome
task of disentangling them again.

VI. The Truths to be Preserved in Discarded Theories

Too many only regard past theories as opportunities
for present criticism. They delight in pointing out
in old theories the immoral but logical conclusions
which were not perceived by those who advocated
them. It never occurs to them that they may have
something to learn from the past; and, though they
pride themselves on being the inheritors of all the
ages, they inconsistently depreciate the value of their
inheritance.

The belief in a ransom paid to the Devil sprang quite
naturally out of the conditions of the times. It was
for centuries very widely held; it also—and this
should be remembered—was rarely emphasised and
occupied but little space in most theological writings.
One or two Fathers, with a misplaced ingenuity,
tried to justify the belief and also the corollary that
the Devil was cheated in his bargain. To the cunning
Greek there was nothing in this that was inappropriate; but the theory so expounded has caused
subsequent generations to blaspheme. We have
nothing to-day to do with such a theory, but it would
be well for us to learn from those early centuries

how very real was the power of the Devil over sinners, how awful was the conflict which Our Lord waged, and how tremendous was the victory which He won.

The modern man smiles and the modern woman sighs over the self-imposed austerities of mediæval saints, while the controversialist exults in his spiritual religion, which can be enjoyed without the least discomfort to the body or any form of self-denial. But are we quite sure that they are right? Our Lord was certainly no hard ascetic, but He was Heb. ii. 10. "made perfect by suffering." We are learning more and more about the interaction of mind upon body, and of body upon mind. It is possible that the next generation may see more clearly the connection between Our Lord's physical sufferings and His conquest of sin. We may then also discover that the irrational instincts of our forefathers did not altogether deceive them. Meantime we may note that the so-called spiritual religion, which despises fasting and mortification, has not been illustrated in the lives of many conspicuous saints.

It is funny, but not true, to say that the twelfth-century conception of God was a glorified feudal baron. Eight hundred years hence it may be just as funny, and just as untrue, to say that the twentieth-century conception of God was an easy-going Papa of the well-to-do classes. Chivalry was an imperfect ideal, but it had its merits. We need to-day to be recalled to reverence—to honour our fathers on earth and to honour Our Father in heaven. If we cultivated loyalty a little more, and criticism a little less; if we were ready to offer satisfaction, and apologise for our rude indifference to the feelings and rights of others; if we felt more responsible for the conduct of our children and dependents; if we felt more keenly in ourselves the disgrace which sin brings on our family and on our nation, and if we were eager and willing to make such reparation as was within our power, we should be better, the world would be happier, and we should understand more clearly the twelfth-century explanation of the Atonement.

To start an enquiry into the mystery of the Atonement by postulating the total depravity of the human race is, of course, absurd. If men were altogether worthless it would be irrational to save them : they could only be saved through arbitrary caprice. Yet men in the sixteenth century believed this, and found no difficulty in accepting also the doctrine that God made an equally arbitrary choice of those whom He would save. Here we have a distorted truth, which arrived at a logical consistency through controversialists attempting to justify their own exaggerated language. The truth from which they started was that men had gone very far from original righteousness, were in a very real bondage to sin, and could not by themselves escape. By no number of good works could man atone for the past, and a lifetime of well-doing would not merit an eternal recompense. Man needed a Saviour, and man needed His grace, which is a free gift of God. But here again reasoning caused men to err. They argued that, as grace was the free gift of an omnipotent God, it must be irresistible in its power and indefectible in its nature. They were not afraid of any argument which seemed necessary to secure the freedom of the transcendent God, though they destroyed even the semblance of freedom in the man who was created in His image. When men complained that their

God was a capricious tyrant, unaffected by moral considerations, they replied that God was not a man bound by laws, that what He willed was right, and that none might question His inscrutable justice. Dissenting as we do from the doctrine as a whole, it is right that we should realise the elements of truth within it. We need to-day to recover a sense of God's sovereignty, and not to be so glib about what He can or cannot do. We dare not pass a judgment on God's ways, for we do not know all, and we do not know the end to which He is working. We believe that God is good, and that He can do nothing that is inconsistent with Himself. But we cannot fathom the mystery of His moral government, and so cannot fathom the mystery of the Atonement. It is quite useless to explain the doctrine away so as to bring it into exact accord with our own incomplete morality; for we are still face to face with the facts of life, where the same difficulties are apparent. Nothing that we know to be wrong dare we ascribe to God; but about much that is mysterious we do well to be reticent, quite certain that in the end God will justify Himself.

It is easy to ridicule the legal theory, and to imagine heaven turned into a law court, where the guilty are declared to be innocent because of a legal fiction. It is an outrage on our moral sense to argue that justice must require a penalty which is more than equivalent to the crime; but that justice is indifferent to the person who suffers it. It is untrue to our experience to maintain that a just judge cannot freely pardon an offender who is penitent, for every State preserves its prerogative of mercy. On the other hand, it is well to remember that God, because He is righteous and just, must ultimately vindicate righteousness and

justice, that He must satisfy every true claim, and
set right every wrong that has been done. How
this may be done baffles our comprehension, but we
see how through injustice and death Our Lord passed
to a joyful Resurrection and a glorious Ascension
into heaven, and we may believe that the wrongs we
suffer here will be more than compensated for in the
heaven above—nay, that they may prove to have
been the necessary prelude to our particular beatitude.

We believe that the Atonement cannot be completely explained in the terms of Darwinism, but we
are grateful to Evolutionists for the new light which
has been shed on religious problems. We have
learnt to realise, as never before, that there can be
nothing capricious in God's dealings with men, that
the God of nature and the God of grace are one,
and that all things are inter-related. We have
learnt to understand better the gradual unfolding
of God's revelation of Himself and the slow process
of the world's redemption. We can no longer regard
the Cross as an isolated portent in history; it is
what it is in relation to an infinite plan; and through
the ages God is working His purpose out.

We may not assent to all the criticisms of those
who interpret the Atonement in the terms of moral
influence, but we should be grateful for their positive
teaching about Our Lord's example. They have at
least made us remember, what was sometimes
forgotten, that to estimate the value of Our Lord's
death without reference to His Life and teaching is a
mistake. The Atonement must not be conceived of
as a transaction with which we have nothing to do,
except to receive the benefits. It is an act of a Person
for persons, an appeal from God to men, and it calls

for a response from men to God. But it is just because there is a necessity for this response that we must not be one-sided in accepting Our Lord as the One Mediator. If He represents God to men, He also represents men to God. His human life did not end with the message which He brought *from* God, but by the offering which He made upon the Cross *to* God; and it is with this offering that we must identify ourselves if our response is to be made.

VII. The Aims of the Author

From the brief survey that has been made, it should be evident that many attempts to explain the doctrine of the Atonement have only failed because they were one-sided. The fact cannot be interpreted from a single standpoint, but must he approached first from one direction and then from another. We may understand this if we think of the different ways in which we see a picture and a statue. We stand still to see one, but we walk round the other. A picture is painted to be seen at a particular distance, and if it is properly composed it can be seen all at once. It has its own light and its own perspective, and neither of them changes : one photograph will preserve every detail. But if we would see, not a picture on the wall, but a statue in a great temple, we know that it will appear differently according to the direction from which we approach it; and if it stands with its back to the wall, there is one side from which it cannot be properly seen. At different hours of the day the light will change, casting shadows on the marble, revealing or obscuring particular features.

What is true of a statue is still more true of an

historical fact. It may be examined from many sides, but there is always one side, its relation to God, that is hidden. As circumstances and conditions change, one aspect or another will be prominent. And, all the time, appreciation will vary with the knowledge, temperament and taste of the person who contemplates it—though it is what it is in itself, and nothing can change it.

We may, for instance, approach the mystery of the Atonement as historians, and search out *how* everything happened, and *how* the world has been changed in consequence. Secondly, we may enquire *what* the event was in itself, which quickly leads to the psychological enquiry, *What* does it mean to me? Thirdly, we may regard it as a metaphysical problem, and concentrate our attention on *why* it was necessary, and *why* it is availing.

The historic side of the question has been much neglected by theologians, and we cannot but feel that certain dogmatic treatises would have been different had the authors written with their eyes on the Crucifix, and had they pondered the incidents of the Passion in their hearts. The Critic is now taking his revenge on the Theologian, by isolating the facts and treating them apart from faith and thought. This also is a wrong method, for the significance of a fact is known by its consequences, and the consequences determine its importance. Even an alleged fact, unlikely in itself, becomes probable if it fits into a long series, is consistent with the attending circumstances, and satisfies the mind.

The man who argues from his personal experience of Our Lord is naturally intolerant of the man who argues from some theological conception of the Godhead. He pleads that his subjective apprehensions are real knowledge, while deductions from dogmas have only a speculative value. The other replies that the emotions are delusive and cannot be verified by others, whereas history and logic can be tested and are common to all. The truth seems to be that emotional experience needs to be interpreted by reason, and can only be relied on when it corresponds with facts, while a revelation and the deductions made from it are without value to the individual until they have been verified by the response of the heart. We cannot learn of the Crucified until we have certain beliefs about Who He is, and why He came to die; but the most orthodox teaching is of little value unless our hearts go out to the Lord and our wills are surrendered to Him. It is only then that we have real knowledge of what the Atonement means.

This book, while it witnesses to the faith of the author, is chiefly concerned in showing the rationality of the Christian faith in the Atonement. The subject is not approached from a single standpoint, but from six points of view. It is hoped, however, that they will be found complementary one of another, and not inconsistent.

The first half of the book endeavours to show why an Atonement was necessary, and how it was made, the second half endeavours to show what are the results of the Atonement, and how they may be enjoyed. In the first half, sin is shown (1) to separate us from God, (2) to reduce us to bondage, and (3) to deserve punishment. Our Lord is described (1) as God coming to us with an offer of reconciliation, (2) as Man delivering us by His own victory over sin, and (3) as Man offering to the Father a reparation for our sins. In the second half of the book we consider the new life which results from the Atonement. How (1) we are forgiven past sin, how (2) we receive grace for the future, and (3) how we must live in order, at the end, to be perfectly at-one with God. We think of Our Lord as (1) eager to forgive, as (2) conveying to us the fruits of His passion, and (3) as so uniting us with Himself, that His sacrifice becomes our sacrifice :— in His victory we triumph, and enter upon eternal life.

CHAPTER II

GOD'S APPEAL TO MAN

I. SIN IS LAWLESSNESS

GOD'S laws are not arbitrary and sin is not natural. For every Christian these should be self-evident propositions; and our muddled thinking on sin and atonement results from their being ignored.

When a skilled mechanic constructs a machine, he makes it to be used in a certain way for a definite object, and it will be of service to anyone who understands the mechanism, and uses it for the purpose intended. But if an ignorant boy tampers with the machinery or tries to use it for some purpose which the mechanic never contemplated, there will probably be a smash, and it may be that the boy will suffer from what *he* will call an accident.

Gen, i. 31. This is equally true in speaking of God's creation. He creates all things and creates them very good. They only become evil when they are misused. Before anyone plays with them, he ought to understand their laws. There are endless possibilities for their adaptation and use, but "Nature is only controlled by obeying her." To disobey Nature is to court disaster and produce confusion.

The boy referred to above may be excused on the score of ignorance, curiosity or an inopportune love of experiment; but as a rule he is rightly punished, not because he has broken the machine, but because he has disobeyed a command that he was not to touch it. This further factor helps us to understand the nature of sin. Sin is not the same as ignorance, but is the result of disobedience. There is a defiant will which assumes that the law is arbitrary, and asserts that the act is natural.

Man is more than a machine, but man has also a law for his being. So long as that law is obeyed, he is free to make the most of his potentialities; but when that law is disobeyed, he impairs his own powers, damages himself, and incurs the consequences of so doing. " Sin," said S. John, " is lawlessness "; and, [1 S. John iii. 4.] we repeat, that the law is not arbitrary, nor the sin natural.

II. Some Results of Sin

Sin being contrary to nature inevitably produces disorder and confusion in the world. By it a man injures himself and corrupts his nature, so that dissolution is only a question of time. But man does not live alone : all that he is, as well as all that he does, influences the world about him. Sin, therefore, even of the most private nature, is a wrong done to our neighbours and increases the misery, pain, disease and injustice of the world. Worst of all sin is a wrong done to God, Who created man for His glory and His [Isa. xliii. 7.] joy. By sin we first spoil His work, and then blaspheme against His justice, and this is all the more heinous because He loves us and wills our good.

But it may be argued, " As God made us with the power to sin, and knew that we would sin, who is to blame but God if we exercise that power in accordance with His own prevision ? "

D

This argument, to which we shall recur later, confuses " freedom of choice " with " power to sin," and forgets that God lives in eternity and not in time. Let us put the same facts in another way. God, being Love itself, could not be content with creatures unable to offer Him a free response. He endowed them with wills able to choose the good and reject the evil, with minds free to aspire, and hearts that cannot be satisfied until they rest in Him. In *His* love He refuses to compel our obedience, for He wants *our* love, and no one can love by compulsion.

Man has not responded to God's love, and has dared to disobey Him. As God's law was only intended for man's good, the results of disobedience have been disastrous. More disastrous still has been the separation between God and man, for God is the source of all good, and in God man should " live and move and have his being."

Acts xvii. 28.

But the God, Whose love has been spurned, and Whose law has been broken still pursues after man, and would undo the damage which man has done to himself and to his fellows. God might have destroyed man, but in His Love He would save him with all his endowments, including the freedom of his will. Man is not like a machine which can be repaired, for he has a soul which needs to be converted, and his conversion can only take place with his free assent. His identity also depends on his memory, so that the past cannot be blotted out, but must in some way be atoned for, if there is to be a real reconciliation.

In this chapter we shall consider how sin separates us from God, and how the offer of reconciliation comes from Him. In the next chapter we shall have to consider how sin is a bondage, from which God, and

God alone, can redeem us; and in the fourth chapter
we shall have to consider the claims of justice and how
they may be satisfied.

III. Sin Separates from God

In order to understand how sin separates us from
God it is only necessary to consider how sin separates
us from our neighbours. An injury, a contemptuous
or spiteful word naturally causes enmity, while even a
difference of opinion often gives rise to a sinful
suspicion about the honesty of an opponent. Conflicting interests and competition may be stimulating
to exertion, but when sin enters in men are divided
into hostile camps.

Apart from overt acts, sinfulness in itself spoils the
amenity of social life. We cannot feel at ease with one
whom we have wronged even when he is unconscious
of the fact. Confidence with those whom we love is
never perfect, because of secrets which we hope that
they will not discover. We lack freedom in social
intercourse, however innocent, because of the scandal
or suspicion it may excite.

But sin more especially separates us from the good,
for we find it difficult to tolerate in others virtues
which we do not ourselves possess. We do not like
the feeling of inferiority which we experience in their
company. We prefer people worse than ourselves,
even when we "thank God that we are not as they
are."

S. Luke
xviii. 11.

It is true, we are told, that "we needs must love
the highest when we see it"; but it is only a half
truth. Hero worship is quite natural, but disciple-
ship is far less common. We admire from a distance

the hero on his pedestal; but we resent his superiority
or suspect it, if he shares our lives. All men not utterly
perverted admit the beauty of Our Lord's life, even
when they reject His claims, deny His miracles, and
explain away such of His sayings as they happen to
dislike. But the men with whom He lived either
rejected or deserted Him. " He came unto His own
S. John i. 11. and His own received Him not." He sadly admitted,
" A Prophet is not without honour, save in his own
S. Matt. xiii. country." There were plenty in those days ready to
57.
Cp. S. Luke build the sepulchres of the Prophets, but their fathers
iv. 24.
S. Matt. slew them. Men build cathedral churches to the glory
xxiii. 29.
S. Luke xi. of Jesus, but the men among whom He lived desired
47.
that He might be slain.

Pondering these facts, we understand the separation between God and man made by sin. Like Adam,
Gen. iii. 10. men hide themselves, conscious of their nakedness.
Like S. Peter, they cry, " Depart from me, for I am
S. Luke v. 8 a sinful man, O Lord." Like silly sheep they try to
S. Luke xv. escape into an ever more desolate wilderness. Only a
3-6.
good Shepherd will find them, only in His arms shall
they be restored to the fold.

IV. DIFFICULTIES IN RECONCILIATION AMONG MEN

If sin separates us from God, and the separation
is caused by man, we begin to see the difficulties in the
way of reconciliation. Reconciliation, even when
desired by both parties to an estrangement, is never
easy; and we shall understand better what it was
necessary for God to do if we first think of facts
within our own experience.

In our ordinary social life we know that many
quarrels are due to misunderstanding, and in most

quarrels there is something to be said on both sides. The friend who mediates generally finds that both parties are to blame, and though he may convince them of their faults, it is no easy matter to bring about a reconciliation. His judicial attitude is even a disadvantage. He is led to adopt the position of an arbitrator, and draw up terms by which differences may be settled. But even if they be accepted and observed, reconciliation does not result, for that is an affair of the heart, and not a question of contract. You can make terms between a husband and a wife, between a father and a son, but you don't by making terms bring them together. Reconciliation does not follow from mutual concessions, but only through mutual penitence. It is not even sufficient that the heart of each should be yearning for the other, for one must have the energy to overleap the barriers which keep them apart. The best mediator is he who can provide opportunities for meeting, and in an unobtrusive way removes stumbling-blocks, which would render the approach of one to the other too awkward for the dignity of either.

Reconciliation is still more difficult where only one is to blame. The injured person may be quite ready to pardon or remit any penalty which may have been incurred, but he cannot forgive until the offender wishes to be forgiven, and reconciliation does not always follow upon forgiveness. Most people wish to be pardoned, some wish to be forgiven, but only a few desire a renewal of intimacy, which they fear would not be possible without a continual remembrance of their fault.

Again, many men will confess that they have done wrong, if they be conscious that their neighbour has also wronged them. They find it much harder to confess, " I only have sinned, and my sin was without provocation." Though they suffer terribly from remorse, they fly from reconciliation. They cannot believe in a love which transcends self-satisfaction.

Many partings take place for no one particular wrong, but as the result of a long sequence of petty acts of selfishness and betrayal. The injured person has overlooked offences again and again, until the offender has taken his long suffering for granted, and come to regard his own conduct as natural if not right. Finally, some small incident causes a rupture and the offender nourishes a grievance. As he tells the story of the quarrel, it seems for such a little thing. He says, " Even if I were wrong, my friend was very hard and merciless." In this instance there is no hope of reconciliation unless the offender arrive at self-knowledge.

But many people drift apart without any quarrel. A young man leaves his home and goes to London. He sees life, as he says—by which he means that he does many things which he ought not to do and makes many undesirable acquaintances. At times he thinks sentimentally of his innocent boyhood and the sweet sanctities of home. When satiated with excitement and folly, he returns to his mother's house, and the mother knows nothing about how he has lived and what he has done. She notes that he is not the same, even when he tries to protest how he loves her. He finds an alteration also. He once was happy in this quiet family and he is so no longer. The estrangement becomes irksome to all, and he finally slips away, going back to the life which he knows to be evil, because he feels that he has lost his inheritance in all

that is good. The mother did not know and shrank
from enquiry; the son did not confess because he
did not believe that his mother could forgive. They
parted, though both loved, because neither could face
the pain of a mutual understanding.

For a complete reconciliation among men, each
must desire it and each must want the other. The
offender must know himself and his faults. He must
be sorry for them and ready to confess them. He
must also keep nothing back, or complete confidence
will never be restored.

V. Difficulties in Reconciliation with God

(A) *The Need of Self-knowledge and Repentance*

When we go on to consider the separation between
man and God, the difficulties in the way of reconciliation are even greater than those we have been
considering.

However well a man may think that he knows himself, he has no idea of how he appears to God, for the
separation has caused him to adopt a different standard
of values. He has been accustomed to sin, and to
live in a world of sinners. So long as he does not
provoke human law or outrage public opinion, he is
apt to take his failings for granted and conclude that
there is little amiss.

" How can ye believe," asked Our Lord of the
Pharisees, " which receive honour one of another, and
seek not the honour that cometh from God only ? " S. John v. 44.
Secure in their reputation, and conscious of their own
respectability, they compared themselves with their
fellows and were satisfied. They believed in God,
and lamented that He seemed so far away. They

would have been offended with anyone who suggested that they did not love goodness; and so they complained, "Verily, Thou art a God that hidest Thyself."

Isa. xlv. 15.

Then Our Lord came and man's sin was revealed. Ordinary men, neither better nor worse than the generality, in His presence were convicted of their meanness and littleness—of their sin. They were rendered uncomfortable in His society, strove to avoid Him, grew to hate Him, and at length, with strange unanimity, hounded Him up the Way of Sorrows. It was not fit that He should live.

But the new standard was set up. The new revelation was made. It was not only that sin separates —that was a commonplace : the Cross revealed the extent of the separation. It caused men to put the Son of God to death.

In the light of that fact we can be under no illusion about human merit. We now know that if God is hidden from us, it is only that we may not hate Him. We also know whence we may start on the way to reconciliation. It is when, standing afar off, we cry, " God, be merciful to me a sinner."

S. Luke xviii. 13.

VI. DIFFICULTIES IN THE WAY OF RECONCILIATION

(B) *The Need of a Revelation*

But self-knowledge is not sufficient. It would be quite possible to be sorry for our sins and willing to confess them. If we are to be reconciled with God, we must also know Him. The separation had lasted so long that man had forgotten what God was like. Nature indeed in its order and beauty still witnessed to Him, conscience spoke with a still small voice, and Rom. i. 20.
Rom. ii. 15. the Spirit still lightened every man who came into the world; but many were blind to beauty, hearts were S. John i. 9. hardened, and ears, attuned to siren voices, became deaf to the truth. Men turned so resolutely to the things of sense that they could see nothing except through the mists of their own lusts. They were given over, as S. Paul said, to " a reprobate mind "; and Rom. i. 28. such men can see nothing in the holiest saints except their failings, and cannot see God at all, because He has no imperfections by which He might be known to them.

Yet even the people living in darkness and degradation were still conscious that *God is,* although they only thought of Him as a ruthless and capricious Power, and tried to propitiate Him with horrible sacrifices which reflected their own wild passions. But these sacrifices witnessed to their sense of separation from God, as did also the various acts by which they sought to be purified. The purifications might be connected with the silliest tabus of some totemistic system, and the sacrifices might be such as could only placate a monster, but behind them was some consciousness of sin, and at least a desire to escape from its consequences. They show also that even the most degraded do not regard their separation from God as final and complete, for otherwise they would not submit to purifications or offer expiatory sacrifices.

Secondly, men have imagined a God Who created all things, but is too far away to be interested in the affairs of mortals—a God Who has left the world as the area where good and evil spirits contend for the mastery, or where matter and spirit are in perpetual conflict. A transcendent first cause is assumed as a concession to Reason, while the condition of the actual world is accounted for by limited beings, who can by courtesy be called Gods and worshipped. Here the separation between God and man would seem to be absolute, but there is still a longing to be on terms with the good principle, which faith generally believes will be ultimately triumphant.

Thirdly, men have identified God with the world as they know it, and ignored the distinction between good and evil, assuming that God is All, and All is One with Him; and then they have betrayed their own lack of harmony with such a Being by complaining of sorrow and pain, revealing quite clearly that it was not all one to themselves. Even they thus acknowledged that they were separate from the God of their own imagination.

In revolt from such a system, the Buddha sought a way of escape rather than a way of reconciliation. For him life was evil and pleasure was a snare. He did not seek for the peace which comes of harmony, but hoped, by annihilating desire, to find a peace where there is no longer any consciousness of pleasure or pain. His Nirvana is just a dreamless sleep from which there is no awaking. Full of compassion for human suffering, he felt the weight of the world's sin, and cried aloud, " Who shall deliver me from the bondage of this *life ?* " He wanted something which neither polytheism nor pantheism could supply. He wanted someone who would redeem the world, and despairing of a remedy counselled a renunciation.

Fourthly, Philosophers have for the most part acknowledged the existence of God. Sooner or later they have been driven to maintain that a rational order in the universe demands a rational cause, and that if there be no rational order, science is impossible and speculation vain. But their God is apt to be an abstract and absolute Being, to Whom no attributes dare be assigned. Sometimes they wax dogmatic and proclaim that their Unknown God is also unknowable—He is only a postulate for the understanding of the world and the unification of thought, and makes little or no appeal to the religious consciousness. Here and there, some mystic, full of cosmic emotion, may abase himself in adoration of the ineffable Immensity, but no sinner was ever inspired to hope, or can receive help from what, in the last analysis, is only an abstraction.

Yet, who can withhold admiration at this unwearied search for God, conducted by the highest thinkers all down the ages? It witnesses to the unproved certainty that *God is*, and that God is separated from man. The philosopher, however, like the savage, refuses to believe that this separation is final and complete. He still " feels after God, if haply he may find Him."

What then is the conclusion of the whole matter? Man cannot by searching find out God. No man hath seen Him at any time, and therefore no image can be made of Him. Man cannot ascend into heaven to draw down God from above, and no magical rite can compel His Presence, for we cannot think of Him as subject to man. One way only remains whereby man might know God, and that is if He should reveal Himself.

A revelation is not, *a priori*, improbable, for a rational man can only think of a God Who is supremely wise, while a man with a moral sense

Acts xvii. 27.

John i. 18;

Deut. xxx. 12.
Prov. xxx. 4.
S. John iii. 13.

conceives of Him as goodness personified. Accepting such hypotheses, we may argue that when we say God is good, we mean that He does good, for we cannot call any Being good who does nothing. Now our highest conception of a good Being is one who loves, and we know that Love seeks to express itself, and love is not satisfied without a response. If this reasoning be correct, it seems to follow that a good God will reveal Himself; and, being wise, will do so in a way that man can understand.

We can, of course, neither prove nor disprove what claims to be a revelation. We can only examine the manner in which it was made, and the evidence on which it rests. We must then accept or reject it, because it explains or does not explain what we otherwise know, or because it satisfies or does not satisfy our moral and intellectual needs. An act of faith will always be necessary, and certitude is the reward, not of reasoning, but of experience.

Secondly, it should be obvious that no revelation claims to make clear to finite minds the nature of infinite reality. Revelation must be conditioned by our powers of apprehension. We should therefore expect that the revelation if true would be progressive. God would teach men, here a little and there a little, line upon line, and precept upon precept, as they were able to learn.

Isa. xxviii. 10.

But here we must make a distinction if we would understand God's revelation of Himself. It is possible to know a person very well when we know very little about him. So Abraham was called " the friend of God," and enjoyed an intimacy with Him accorded to very few since his time. But Abraham knew very little about God compared with what an

S. James ii. 27.

irreligious person may know to-day. So men will learn to know God as a little child learns to know his mother. At first he can neither account for his mother, nor describe her; he cannot estimate the extent of her knowledge or her powers. But he really does know her, knows too that he ought to obey her, knows that she loves, provides for and protects him, runs to her naturally in terror and in joy, is happy in her smile and feels safe in her arms.

We Christians believe in a God Who at sundry times and in divers manners spoke in time past unto the fathers by the prophets, and hath in these last days spoken unto us by His Son, Who is not only the brightness of His Glory, but the express image of His Person, revealing to man, just in so far as man can Heb. i. 1–3. comprehend, Who God is and what He is like. For " the Word was made flesh and dwelt among us and we beheld His Glory, the Glory as of the only begotten of the Father, full of grace and truth." And why was S. John i. 14. this revelation made ? In order that men who repented of their sins might know that the God Who forgave was lovable. " God was in Christ, reconciling the world unto Himself."

2 Cor. v. 19.

VII. Difficulties in the Way of Reconciliation

(C) *The Need of a Mediator*

We have thought of the separation caused by sin, and how the reason of that separation had to be brought home if men were to repent. We have thought how necessary it was that God's goodness should be known if men were to desire a reconciliation. But it may be argued that the more highly a man conceives of God's goodness the further will he find the distance between himself and God. He will say, " His eyes are too holy to behold iniquity, the very stars are not pure in His sight. What is man, that God should be mindful of him ? Man is a thing of nought."

Hab. i. 13.
Job xxv. 5.
Ps. viii. 4.
Ps. cxliv. 4.

For a reconciliation something more is required than that a man should know himself and know God. A mediator is necessary, if God and man are to be brought together. Men have always felt this. So we read, " And they said unto Moses, Speak thou with us, and we will hear : but let not God speak with us lest we die." In the priesthoods of nearly all nations we find how general is this feeling, this longing for a Mediator, for a " daysman to stand betwixt and lay his hands on both." That, however, was just what the old priesthoods failed to do. They might in some degree represent men to God, but they could not represent God to men. They offered a multitude of sacrifices according to traditional forms, but their very multiplicity was a proof that they were unavailing. The longed-for Mediator had to be one with humanity and one with God; and all priesthoods were only typical of Him Who came as perfect God and perfect Man—able to represent manhood to the Father and able to represent the Father to His brethren—able to pray, " Father, I will that they also, whom Thou hast given Me, be with Me where I am," and able to assert, " He that hath seen Me hath seen the Father." A reconciliation then was made possible by the Incarnation, and is conceivable so long as we can believe in the two natures of the One Christ.

Ex. xx. 19.

Job. ix. 33.

Heb. x. 3.
Gal. iii. 19.

S. John xvii. 24.

S. John xiv. 9.

VIII. Difficulties in the Way of Reconciliation

(D) *The Need of an Example*

Lastly, a reconciliation to be complete must provide for renewed intercourse in the future. Man had not only to discover how far he was separated from God and why. He needed a pattern and an example of what a son of God should be. This the Mediator supplies. From the Cross, He cries to men, " Behold Me "; to the Father, He cries, " Behold in Me, My brethren." In reply the voice of God echoes down the ages, " Thou art My Beloved Son, in Whom I am well pleased." S. Mark i. 11.

The example has not only been given, but grace is also promised that we may follow in His steps. An example which we could not in any way follow would be of no value to us, neither would an example which we could easily copy. Our example makes for reconciliation because it involves a personal relationship. It is through communion and in union with Our Lord that we enter into the life of God, and He says, " No man cometh unto the Father, but by Me." S. John xiv. 6.

We are now in a position to say that for a reconciliation between God and man, man must know his sinfulness and repent of it; God must reveal Himself as one Who is willing to forgive; and a Mediator must bring God and man together.

But the actual reconciliation is not a theory of the schools but a fact of history. In the story of the Cross we find a revelation of what sin will do, and how sin separates. In the story of the Cross we have a perfect revelation of God's love; and in the story of the Cross we have the Mediator representing Who God is and what Man should be.

IX. THE STORY OF THE CROSS

(A) *The Revelation of Man's Sin*

A careful reading of the Gospels makes it quite clear how inevitable it was that, in a sinful world, Our Lord should be put to death. Perfect goodness had come among men, the light had shone forth, and men " loved darkness rather than light, because their deeds were evil." It was not by man's will, but through the over-ruling miracle of the resurrection, that the light remains and darkness did not overcome it.

S. John iii. 19.

But people who agree that the Crucifixion was the greatest of all crimes are quite happy in condemning those wicked Jews, those intriguing priests, those hypocritical Pharisees, or that poltroon Pilate. They refuse to see in the story the natural result of sins to which they themselves are prone and which society even to-day condones.

" What," they say, " I am not a murderer like Barabbas, an adulterer like Herod, or a thief like those who were crucified with Him. I have never perjured myself like the false witnesses, and, if I am sometimes a little covetous, I could never have betrayed the Master like Judas."

And yet as we read the story more attentively, we shall see how all sorts and conditions of men were in differing degrees responsible for the death on the Cross.

There was a King who was careless, an official who was corrupt, lawyers who strained the rules of their procedure, and a populace as fickle as it was passionate. There was an official priesthood of an established Church, and the Pharisees, representing the religious world of that day in its more austere and puritanical aspects. There were the learned and the ignorant for once agreed : the Zealot with his fanatical nationalism, and the Herodian anxious to maintain the existing order, acting in common. There were rich men like Annas and Caiaphas trembling for their vested interests in the Temple traffic, and poor men disappointed in one whom they had hoped might prove a revolutionary leader. There were town dwellers in Jerusalem, and the country-folk of Galilee, and pilgrims from all quarters of the then known world. There were Herod's men of war, insolent in their cups, and the disciplined legionaries of Rome, jealous for the prestige of their Eagles. There were the servants who loved to bait a superior, and the silly fools who wagged their heads, gloating over the downfall, or as they would have said the exposure, of one whom they had feared might be wiser than themselves. There were the weak good men like Nicodemus and Joseph of Arimathea, who had so much to lose, who did not consent unto His death, but missed their [S. Luke xxiii. 57.] opportunity of doing anything in His defence. And lastly, there were the Disciples, who had been set to guard Gethsemane, but could not watch with Him one hour. They had boasted of their devotion and [S. Matt. xxvi. 40.] how they would die for Him, but when the moment [S. Mark xiv. 37.] came He stood before them, saying, " If ye seek Me, let these go their way." And they all forsook Him [S. John xviii. 8.] and fled. When Peter denied Him, how can we blame others ? All were involved in the tragedy and they represented the world of men.

These men were not so different from ourselves. Their sins were our sins. They acted as they did because of what they were. Their past lives, their immediate environment, and their varying interests

E

compelled them. Should we have acted differently had we been in their places, and must we not regard the story as a revelation, at a definite moment of time, that the ultimate issue of unrepented sin is the definite repudiation of God and goodness? Will it come to us, as it did to some at Calvary, as a great surprise?

Judas, perhaps, did not think Our Lord would die. He may merely have thought, why should he not make a profit, while he put Our Lord's claims to the test, and precipitated the crisis which all foresaw. Peter certainly did not mean to deny Him, but he would not watch and pray. Self-confident and undisciplined, he was betrayed when he was cold among the unsympathetic faces seen by the flickering firelight. Pilate strove to save Him, but he tried to do it without compromising himself. The time had passed when he could adopt the *rôle* of the upright or the merciful judge. He did not wish, and few men wish, to do evil, but when he heard the covert threat that he might be delated to Tiberius, he sacrificed Jesus for his own security. Apart from the dictates of self-interest, Caiaphas was only asserting an ordinary political maxim, when he declared that it was expedient for one man to die for the people. Intrenched in privileges, glorying in their wealthy and well organised Church, identified with it, how careful those priests had to be, lest any negligence should provide an excuse for the Romans to come and take away their place and their nation. He that wills the end wills the means, so a spy upon Our Lord's movements was hired and false witnesses were arranged for; but what nation or political party in a crisis is scrupulous about the truth of its propaganda? The voice of the people was certainly not the voice of God

S. Mark xiv. 37, 38.

S. John xix. 12.

S. John xi. 47–50.

—it rarely is; but those who respond to the herd instinct generally claim to be infallible. They desired that a murderer should be granted unto them, but it Acts iii. 14. is not the last time that a man stained by every crime has become a hero of the populace because he happened to be a symbol of a social revolution which they desired. Pilate's maladroit suggestion that they should choose Jesus and set Him free sealed Our Lord's fate. What mob conscious of its privileges S. Matt. xxvii. 15–23. would not in consequence have insisted on Barabbas? S. Mark xv. 6–15. Finding that they were able to intimidate a hated ruler, S. Luke xxiii. 18. the people were reckless how they obtained their S. John xviii. 39, 40. object. "We have no king but Cæsar," they cried; S. John xix. 15. and spoke the truth. The people who talked so much about their spiritual destiny, confessed that in the last resort they were the slaves of materialism, worshipping a Cæsar who stood for triumphant force.

In any other case how many excuses we should urge, forgetting that by the excuses we assume that sin is natural. The Pharisees were full of their responsibilities as leaders of religious thought and examples of religious practice. Jealous guardians of a traditional orthodoxy, they easily believed that the teacher of new truth was a blasphemer. A sceptic like Pilate, asking, "What is truth?" could not fail to be con- S. John xviii. 38. temptuous of one who spoke with authority. The ribald voices who scoffed, saying, "Let Him come down from the Cross, and we will believe Him," were S. Matt. xxvii. 42. merely formulating the age-long challenge of the S. Mark xv. 29–32. unbelievers, who refuse to examine any evidence, but demand a sign such as they themselves propose. How many people to-day, like Herod, imagine themselves religious, because they would see some miracle and would, like him, reject a man who did S. Luke xxiii. 8.

not pander to their appetite for occult and curious excitement.

How amazing it must have seemed to the Roman soldiers that the natives should ever have thought the meek and lowly Jesus was a possible King; and with what keen malice must Pilate have written the superscription, insulting the proud priests and the national fanatics. He had scourged the Lord in Whom he found no wrong, hoping to excite the compassion of the people, and only inflamed their blood lust. Like many another he thought that he could compromise with evil, only to discover that with the first sign of weakness he was helpless. He still arrogantly asserted —" I have power to release thee "; and then washed his hands of all responsibility and delivered Jesus to be crucified. And the people who knew that they were wrong, thought, as many have done since, that somehow a wrong ceases to be so if you accept responsibility for it. So they cried, " His blood be on us, and on our children "; and the history of their race is a commentary on that cry.

Sectarian prejudice may masquerade as religious fervour, self-interest may disguise itself as patriotism, brutality may plead that justice demands an example, and the coward may dignify his sinuosities by calling them diplomatic, but in the death of Jesus all becomes clear. Sin is stripped of its draperies and is known in the horror of the result.

And yet most of those people when they rose on Good Friday morning had no idea of committing any crime. They were in bondage to their past and had not been redeemed. A thousand acts of selfishness, self-indulgence and self-will had made them what they were. A thousand small compliances with evil custom

S. John xix. 19–22.

S. John xix. 10.

S. Matt. xxvii. 24.

S. Matt. xxvii. 25.

had rendered them insensitive to what was good. In viewing the awful failure of humanity, shall we say that "in ignorance they did it"? But the ignorance was culpable, and revealed the separation from God and goodness which prevailed.

This was the aspect of the Crucifixion which was first preached by S. Peter. He harped on it, saying, "Him ye have taken, and by wicked hands have crucified and slain." "God hath made that same Acts ii. 23. Jesus, Whom ye have crucified, both Lord and Christ." "Ye denied the Holy One and the Just, Acts ii. 36. and desired a murderer to be granted unto you, and killed the Prince of Life, Whom God hath raised from the dead." Acts iii. 14, 15; *Cp.* iv. 10.

He spoke that he might win men to repentance, and we go back to the same story to-day to be convinced of our own need of penitence. That is for us the first step to understanding the Atonement. We must know our sins and feel our need of a Saviour.

X. The Story of the Cross

(B) *The Revelation of God's Love*

Looking at the story as we have done it would be easy to conclude that the sin of man was such that he could entertain no hope of reconciliation with an all holy God.

It might be argued : God is good, and a good God cannot love what is evil. Man has been proved evil, and therefore cannot be loved by God.

On the other hand, we read, "God so loved the world that He gave His only begotten Son," and "that, S. John iii. 16. while we were yet sinners, Christ died for us." If we Rom. v. 8.

believe this we are bound to believe that, however great was man's sin, he was not utterly depraved. In the worst, the God, Who knows all, saw something that He could love. The mission of the Son had indeed been futile unless there had been among men a capacity for response. The Son came with the offer of forgiveness. He came also to show us Who God is and what He is like.

And here we may note that the life and death of Our Lord would have no meaning so far as reconciliation is concerned, unless Our Lord be God, of one substance with the Father. If God became man in order that we might know Him, and accepted the consequences of so doing in suffering and in death, we have a revelation of God's nature which calls us to adoration. But if Jesus, so obviously human, was not also divine, we have only fresh evidence for asserting that God does not care, does not protect His own, and that there is no moral government in the world. Believing in Our Lord as God, we can interpret the sufferings of saints, martyrs and the victims of many oppressions in the light of Calvary; disbelieving, we have no clue to the age-long problem of why the righteous are afflicted, while the wicked flourish as the green bay tree.

Ps. xxxvii. 35.

Accepting the faith of the Incarnation, we must not be misled into " dividing the substance " of the Godhead and into contrasting the divine wrath of the offended Father with the divine compassion of the pitiful Son. If the Father be God, the Son God, and the Holy Ghost God, they must all be alike perfect, and it is impossible to conceive any disagreement in Their thoughts, wills or desires, for such disagreement would reveal in one or other Person something that was not perfect. Therefore all three Persons must exist in a unity which transcends our power of understanding. So we believe that the Father gave the Son, and the Son gave Himself in order that He might fulfil the Father's Will, and the revelation of God's love was brought home to man by the inspiration of the Holy Spirit. All three Persons co-operated in the work of Redemption as all three co-operate in creation and the sanctifying of men.

This perfect Oneness of the Godhead we formulate in the words, *God is Love ;* and while among men we find the meaning of Love is the capacity for sacrifice, so we are amazed to discover something which indicates sacrifice even within the Being of the Blessed Trinity. Just as in the late war mothers sent their sons to die for their country, so we dimly understand what we mean when we say, that the Heavenly Father sent His only Son to suffer and die for the salvation of the world. Dimly, also we understand what is implied in Our Lord's sacrifice, " Who made Himself of no reputation, and took upon Him the form of a servant, and was made in the likeness of men; and being found in fashion as a man, he humbled Himself, and became obedient unto death, even the death of the Cross." Could the love of God be more com- _{Phil. ii. 7, 8.} pletely revealed ?

" Surely," says the unbeliever, " God's good-will to men might have been shown in some other way? Forgiveness might have been by fiat, and man's obedience ensured by a revelation of God's splendour." But as it takes two to make a quarrel, it takes two to make it up. Pardon may be by fiat, but forgiveness is only possible when the offender wishes to be forgiven. Men might be awed into submission, but God

S. John iv.
8. is love : His heart yearns for sons and not for slaves. He therefore refuses to compel and pleads for a free response.

Love indeed may be shown by bounty. So St. Paul says, " God left not Himself without witness, in that He did good, and gave us rain from heaven, and fruit- Acts xiv. 17. ful seasons, filling our hearts with food and gladness." But the love is more apparent when we note that it involves something greater than the largesse of a monarch, and expresses itself in self-denying labours. Acts x. 36. Jesus went about doing good, working so hard that S. Mark vi.
31. sometimes He had no leisure so much as to eat. Such love awakens our admiration, but our hearts are only touched by sympathy, and Our Blessed Lord felt our infirmities, shared our sorrows, was Himself tempted Heb. iv. 15. in all points like we are, was hungry, weary, footsore and poor, and knew all the misery which comes of misunderstanding, unkindness, failure, contempt and spite. But Love only finds its perfect expression in an act of self-surrender, when the Lover puts himself into the hands of the beloved, and says, " I am yours and you can do as you like with me." So the God of all the world would demonstrate that He is Love Itself. From the highest heaven, Our Lord came to be Mary's little boy. He put Himself in human hands, He put Himself at human mercy. He allowed men to do as they liked with Him, even when they hammered the nails through His hands and feet, and lifted Him up upon a Cross to die.

And here it is to be noted that Our Lord's death was entirely voluntary. He says :—" No man taketh S. John x.
18. My life from Me, but I lay it down of Myself." He says again that at His call, " My Father *would* presently S. Matt.
xxvi. 53. give me more than twelve legions of angels." He

assures Pilate :—" Thou couldest have no power at all
against Me, except it were given thee from above." _{S. John xix.}
In this way His death is distinguished from that of ^{11.}
all martyrs.   There was a time when the die was cast
and they could not draw back.   There was never a
moment when Our Lord could not have come down
from the Cross, saved Himself and left the world to
perish.

He had given Himself to men, and the gifts of God
are without repentance, but if He were willing to offer _{Rom. xi. 29.}
no resistance, He never compromised with evil.   He
spoke boldly to Caiaphas, He refused to speak at all _{S. Matt.}
to Herod, He strove to invigorate the world-worn ^{xxvi. 63,}
conscience of Pilate, He reproved and won S. Peter _{xiv. 60, 62.}
with a look.   He did not minimise the crime or its _{xxii. 70.}
inevitable consequences.   " Weep for yourselves, and _{xxiii. 9.}
for your children," He said to the women of Jerusalem. _{xviii. 34–37 ;}
He saw that the same excitable temperament, the same _{S. Luke}
violence and reckless lack of justice, must end, not _{xxiii. 28.}
only in rebellion against Rome, but in horrors, when
women and children would suffer most through the
dissolution of society.

He loved men, but He was steadfast in the Truth,
and when He prayed, " Father, forgive them, for they
know not what they do," we are not so amazed at the _{S. Luke}
justice of the plea, but at the time when it was offered. ^{xxiii. 34.}
In a moment of physical agony, He could still sympa-
thise with the soldiers who crucified Him, could still
remember their past and their rude virtues, and still
allow for the fact that, with them, a public execution
was an everyday occurrence, that they were ignorant
of His person and could not understand His claims.

But when the thief, who had cursed him, repented
and said, " Lord, remember me when Thou comest into

S. Luke
xxiii. 42. Thy Kingdom," how instant was the response : Love
at last had its opportunity. Love had won its first
victory, the willingness of God to forgive even at the
very end was shown. The thief would not merely be
remembered, at some distant place, in some far-off
future, by a king infinitely above him. " To-day,"
S. Luke
xxiii. 43. replied Our Lord, " shalt thou be with Me in Paradise."

But if Our Lord's love was such that He was just
to His enemies, and eager to win fresh friends, " having
loved His own which were in the world, He loved them
S. John
xiii. 1. unto the end." All men were not to Him alike, He
knew and considered them, one by one. He was
dying that " all men might be saved, and come unto
1 Tim. ii. 4. the knowledge of the truth," but in the stress of His
agonising endeavour, He did not forget the Mother
who had borne Him, or the friend who had leaned on
His breast at supper. Speaking from the Cross He
said " Woman, behold thy son! and son, behold
S. John xix.
26, 27. thy mother." Love is not a generalised emotion.
Our Lord never talked about His love of humanity.
He proved His love for men.

He sent them away. He did not wish that His
mother should be haunted by the horror of His death;
and she went believing that He wished to be alone.
On both sides it was a triumph of love. He was left
alone and even the sense of His Father's presence
faded from His consciousness as His powers
waned. Love is so sensitive, and Our Lord, because
He was perfect, most sensitive of all. The sense of
dereliction overmastered Him, and with a loud cry
S. Luke
xxiii. 46. He gave up the ghost. Pain did not kill Him, nor
does exhaustion account for His death. He died of a
broken heart, for when the spear pierced His side,
S. John xix.
34. there came out blood and water.

He died as a criminal, deserted by all and an object of derision, and yet the Centurion who had superintended His execution and watched His agony, concluded, " Truly this man was the Son of God." What S. Matt. xxvii. 54. and how much he meant by his words we cannot tell. S. Mark xv. 39. Probably he spoke more truly than he knew; but we Christians at least believe that through the shame and sorrow of the Cross we receive our Revelation of the God, Who is Love. It is there we learn what Love 1 S. John iv. is, and what Love will do. We assent to S. John when 8. he writes :—" Herein is love, not that we loved God, but that He loved us, and sent His Son to be the propitiation for our sins." 1 S. John iv. 10.

XI. The Story of the Cross

(C) *The Revelation of what Man should be*

If man were to be reconciled to God, he had not merely to repent of his sins and know of God's willingness to forgive. He had also to be convinced that God loved him and asked for his love in return. Responding to that appeal, he was bound to face the question, What can I do for God, how can I please Him, what does He wish me to be ?

Two cannot walk together except they be agreed, Amos iii. 3. and no reconciliation can endure, if it be based on a misunderstanding. It had been useless to bring God and man together unless man had been shown quite clearly what God required of him.

Originally created in the image of God, it was man's Gen. i. 27. destiny to reflect his Maker, but the old Adam had failed to keep the mirror clean, so that the image was faint and blurred. The sense of right and wrong remained, but the good man needed to be transfigured in the light of a personal relationship with the God who is good. Deprived of the consciousness of that relationship, a man was thrown back upon himself, and his standard of conduct was the measure of his self-approbation. He had constantly to ask himself, " Is it fitting that such a one as I am should do this or that ? " Many were virtuous but they tended to be prigs.

We still go back to the Greeks for ethical instruction, but no one to-day is satisfied with their conceptions of the good man. We reject Aristotle's magnanimous being, who lived that he might fulfil his conception of his own virtue; and are not even satisfied by Plato's just man who was king over himself. We are chilled by the Stoic saint, who was so consciously indifferent to the world's opinion, and so inhumanly contemptuous of pleasure and pain. We suspect the virtue of the cultivated hedonist of Epicurus, who made the best of everyone and everything, and enjoyed temperately every sensation, nicely discriminating between their values. We seek for a conception that shall be more human, more social, more sympathetic. We want not only to admire but also to love. We know that a good man must be something more than a good statue, graceful in form and perfect in proportion. The good man must not only be but act, must not only set an example but communicate his virtue, and for this a man must have a standard outside himself. He must look up to someone who cares not only for him but for his fellows. It is only through religion that this want can be supplied. Our Lord came to teach us that God is our Father, and that all men are brethren.

The first thing that strikes us in the Gospel story is Our Lord's abiding sense of filial relationship. From early boyhood He felt the need to be about His Father's business. All through His ministry He is S. Luke ii. 49. aware of His Sonship and would convince men of the Father's love. In the Garden of Gethsemane, He prayed ever more earnestly, " Not My will but Thine be done "; and on the Cross He committed Himself S. Luke xxii. 42. saying, " Father, into Thy hands I commend My Spirit."

S. Luke xxiii. 46.

It was through this filial life that He reconciled the two virtues of independence and obedience which divide good men into hostile camps. He never spoke against the glory of freedom, for without it there can be no voluntary obedience; and the God, Who refuses to have us slaves, asks us to be His sons.

But a voluntary obedience presupposes humility, and man has always been tempted to apologise for pride, though he knows it to be the Devil's sin. This is partly because the nature of humility has often been misconceived; but Jesus showed at His trial and in His passion that true humility is compatible with dignity and self-respect. Pride leads to the desire of domination, humility seeks only to be serviceable to others, and the Lord Who washed the Disciples' feet said, " I am among you as he that serveth."

S. John xiii. 4 ff.
S. Luke xxii. 27.

Coming as a King and proclaiming His Kingdom, He put duties always before rights. Subjects were no longer to exist for the sovereign, but the King was to rule for his subjects' good, to think of them as his family, to be trained, watched over, provided for and protected. So again success in life does not depend on the multitude of things which a man possesses, but on the number of ties which he forms in love of

God and of his fellow men. Reconciliation with God implies harmony with Him. The world is God's world and men are His sons. He cares for them and so must we. The Apostle says, " Let this mind be in you, which was also in Christ Jesus."

Phil. ii. 5.

Three other points are necessary to be remembered if, through the example of Jesus, we would be reconciled with God.

The first is His insistence on spiritual sins as being more deadly than the sins of the flesh. He of unsullied purity was very tender in dealing with the fallen, and was known as the friend of publicans and sinners.

S. Matt. xi. 19.
S. Mark ii. 16.

He was stern though loving to the careless, the negligent and the rash, for He knew their need of discipline. But he denounced the proud, envious and malicious. To the liars, selfish and hypocrites, He showed no mercy. Their sins were irreconcilable with the nature of God or the harmony of God's world.

Secondly, He showed God's love for little children, for the sick, the poor, the simple and the despised. He showed His sympathy and became a little child, He lived among the poor, He praised what was simple, He endured men's laughter and scorn, He suffered pain and did not conceal His weakness. Men have rightly glorified courage, but they have tended to confuse it with fearlessness, but a man may be fearless from lack of imagination, because he is not sensitive or because his constitution is robust. Our Lord was perfectly courageous; and, knowing what would happen to Him, set His face steadfastly to go unto Jerusalem; but that did not prevent His longing for sympathy in Gethsemane, or His thrice repeated prayer, " Father, if it be possible, let this cup pass from Me." With perfect courage, He refused the

S. Matt. xxvi. 38.
S. Matt. xxvi. 39.

stupefying cup of myrrh, resolved to taste the bitter- _{S. Matt.}
ness of death for every man, but He was not ashamed _{xxvii. 34.}
_{Heb. ii. 9.}
to cry "I thirst" or to drink the reviving vinegar, _{S. John xix.}
that His work might be finished, and our very infirmi- _{28.}
ties consecrated to God.

Thirdly, in a world where much is unequal and
unjust, where disappointments are so real and failures
seem so cruel, how could we be reconciled with God,
unless we believed in a world to come, unless we
believed that, somewhere and somehow, we should
see of the travail of our souls, and be satisfied with it.
And here Our Lord encourages us. When all seemed
lost on Good Friday, when His work seemed to have
ended in complete failure, when His very disciples
had forsaken Him and fled; in the darkness and
desolation, in the bitterness of a strong man's death,
He could still say with triumph, "It is finished." His _{S. John xix.}
work was complete. "For the joy that was set before, _{30.}
He endured the Cross, despising the shame, and is set
down at the right hand of the throne of God." _{Heb. xii. 2.}

This story of Our Lord's life is not a fancy picture of
what might be, but a record of what was. Our Lord

> . . . wrought out the creed of creeds
> In loveliness of perfect deeds.

He set us an example that we might follow in His steps. _{1 S. Pet. ii.}
As the one Mediator He shows us what Life should _{21.}
be, if lived in reconciliation with the mind of God.

This life, moreover, was not lived under ideal conditions, for the blameless Utopians are never convincing and are generally not even attractive. The
perfect life was lived in an alien and adverse environment. It began in a stable and ended on a Cross.

But, if we naturally contrast it with the ordinary

lives of men, we have to remember it was in no sense lived apart. He worked in the carpenter's shop, he shared the dangers of rude fishermen. He loved the country side and wild flowers; and understood the cares of the shepherd and work on the land. He was at home in cities and interested in the courts of kings and movements of armies. He dined with rich and poor, with the Pharisee and the Publican. He attended alike a marriage feast and a funeral. He took part in man's worship, man's work, man's feasting and man's mourning. He knew all about the children's game of make-believe. Neither did He wish His disciples to abstain from social life. For them He prayed not that they might be taken out of the world, but that they might be kept from its evil.

S. Matt. xi. 16, 17.
S. Luke vii. 32.

S. John xvii. 15.

His whole life illustrates how " God so loved the world," how God would be reconciled with the world, and how much happier the world would be if more responsive to the mind of God.

S. John iii. 16.

XII.   The Appeal of the Cross

The separation between God and man is due to man, who first sinned and then fled, went out of his way, was lost and knew not how to return.

The offer of reconciliation comes from God, Who pursues after man calling on him to return, to repent and to be forgiven.

The One Mediator has come to reveal the wonder of God's love, and also the possibilities of a restored humanity.

1 Tim. ii. 5.

He was indeed lifted up upon a Cross, but He draws all men unto Him.

S. John xii. 32.

Even the wicked and the unrepentant cannot ignore Him. His arms are stretched out wide in their appeal to humanity. He pleads with bowed head and sorrowful eyes.

He cries to the unconverted—" Be ye reconciled with God."

2 Cor. v. 20.

CHAPTER III

OUR LORD'S VICTORY

I. THE OLD AND NEW COVENANT

THAT God was ready to forgive was no new truth for the Jews, for God could say, " Since the day that your fathers came forth out of the land of Egypt unto this day, I have sent unto you all my servants the Prophets, daily rising up early and sending

Jer. vii. 25. them." By the mouth of Isaiah, God pleaded with His people, " Come now, and let us reason together . . . though your sins be as scarlet, they shall be

Isa. i. 18. as white as snow." The Psalmist knew that " a

Ps. li. 17. broken and a contrite heart God would not despise "; and Ezekiel, in the Name of God, asks his fellow-captives : " Have I any pleasure at all that the wicked should die . . . and not that he should

Ezek. xviii. 23. return from his ways, and live ? " Joel declares that God " is gracious and merciful, slow to anger, and of great kindness, and repenteth Him of the

Joel ii. 13. evil "; and Daniel is assured that " To the Lord Our God belong mercies and forgivenesses, though

Dan. ix. 9. we have rebelled against Him."

It is needless to multiply instances, and the History of Israel confirms the teaching of the Prophets. It is the long record of a merciful and pitiful God dealing with a stiff-necked and rebellious people. It is the record of how a nation was trained by the logic of events to understand in part the moral government of the world.

In the life and death of Our Lord there is no change in God's attitude towards men and no new appeal. It is the old appeal, emphasised as never before, the old promise of forgiveness sealed and guaranteed. The Prophets had after all been servants, who could not fully represent GOD, so in the end God sent His Own Son, His well-beloved, claiming our reverence. The moral government of God knows no change, but in the Old Testament men recognised His judgments as those of a Being, sitting serene above the water floods, a King for ever : in the New Testament we learn that He is no aloof Divinity; God became man ready to suffer with and for His people; Jesus is Our Emmanuel, God with us. It is idle to argue whether God could S. Matt. i. 23. or could not have redeemed the world by fiat; in the Story of the Cross we have only to consider what was most beneficial for man; and we recognise that the revelation of His self-sacrificing love is of infinitely greater value than any manifestation of autocratic power, however benevolent in intention.

Again the idea of a covenant between God and man was for the Jews no new truth; but the Old Covenant was only disciplinary—the Law was a schoolmaster to bring us to Christ. The Old Gal. iii. 24. Covenant also had come to be construed in too legal a fashion—it had been graven on stone, it was Ex. xxiv. 12. Jer. xxxi. 53. hard and external. The new Covenant was to be 2 Cor. iii. 3. written on the fleshly tables of men's hearts; and the Prophets had anticipated the outpouring of the Spirit.

But both Covenants, old and new, are not mere casual agreements, they are the results of what has happened and conditioned by facts. The magnitude of the facts constrains the parties. In human life we are more bound by our past, by what has been already accomplished, than by any hopes of the future. So the first Covenant was made after a great deliverance—when Israel came forth from the land of Bondage; and the new Covenant was made after a still greater deliverance, for Jesus redeemed us from the power of sin by the Victory of the Cross. Both covenants were ratified by the shedding of blood, and neither deliverance was merited by the virtues of those who were saved. Salvation is not merited. It is due to a Saviour. It is because God pities men.

So having learnt in the last chapter God's willingness to forgive, we pass on to consider "a world lying in wickedness" needing to be redeemed, to think of men enslaved desiring enfranchisement, to contemplate the deliverance won by Our Saviour, and the new Covenant which results from His Victory.

1 S. John v. 19.

II. Sin a Bondage

(A) *Original Sin*

People sometimes argue that all we need to know is that God in His love is ready to forgive. They rejoice that God in Christ has revealed to us the possibilities of humanity. They recognise that we should all be happier if we only lived in correspondence with God and in conformity with our true nature. They acknowledge that Sin had separated man from God, but they maintain that God has sent His Son to break down the wall of separation between us and Him. The way of return they see is open and they wonder that more men do not accept the forgiveness so freely offered.

But in the last chapter we noted that forgiveness was not all that was required to bring about a reconciliation. We started by defining Sin as lawlessness, and we should not be surprised to discover that the law breakers are in chains. In the last chapter we thought of how sin separates God from men, and men from one another. In this chapter we must consider how sin is a bondage from which we cannot by our own efforts escape. 1 S. John iii. 4.

The origin of evil is a problem, and we have not at present sufficient data for its solution. Long before man was created there was evil in the world; and if evolution has been in an upward direction, it has not been an orderly movement, but represents progress in spite of conflicting forces. What is true of nature is equally true of man, his progress and his civilisation. Before man sinned, according to Genesis there was not only a serpent to tempt, but also a tree of knowledge of good and evil: so the author believed that sin, like evil, is anterior to man. Believing, as we must, that God created all things and made them very good, we can only conclude that evil results from the misuse of the things that are made; and we can partly verify this conclusion from our own experience, for we know of many things, useful in themselves, which may be made into engines of destruction. This misuse of nature suggests an evil agent or agents; and we are probably right in affirming, that there is nothing really evil except an evil will. But then we are forced to acknowledge that all wills are the creation of God, and we have only moved our problem a stage Gen. iii. 1. Gen. ii. 7.

further back. However, we recognise in the freedom of the will, limited though it is, God's highest gift, and if we were bound to choose between freedom with all the chances of misery it may bring and an existence as conscious automata carefully protected from mischance, there is no doubt about our decision. Moreover, we cannot even conceive of a freedom which would not permit us to choose wrong, or to act in defiance of law. We are probably not the only creatures endowed with this freedom : and most objections to God's righteousness and moral government would be removed by a belief in free spirits beyond our ken, of wills more powerful than our own both for good and evil, with whom God is long-suffering as He is with us, overruling their acts and pursuing His own purpose to an end which will be His complete justification.

Gen. iii.
Few people to-day regard the story of Adam and Eve as a literal account of something that occurred. The Church has never pronounced on its historicity, and from the time of the Fathers onwards there have been those who regarded it as a parable, or as a fact told in Oriental fashion largely through metaphors. For the present we will not dwell on the story except to emphasise the truth that the God Who made all things good, made man good; and that man, however far he may have advanced beyond Gen. ii. 25. the state when he was naked and unashamed, has none the less failed to be what he might have been, has fallen from a state of grace, forgotten to live in harmony with God, and endured much pain and many disappointments in consequence. For this fall we do not need the story of Genesis which illustrates it. It is proved by the otherwise unexplained facts

of shame and remorse. Secondly, experience confirms the truth that the sins of the fathers are visited upon the children, not merely because of the environment into which they are born, but because of the mental, moral and spiritual equipment with which they start. We need not take a side in the scientific controversy on the transmission of acquired characters, or in the theological controversy between Creationists and Traducianists, in order to believe in what is known as Original Sin. It is obvious that the offspring of two imperfect beings cannot be perfect. We may go on and say that as everyone is in some sense a result depending on a sinful past, so everyone from birth is naturally predisposed to actual sin. By original sin is intended a weakened nature with bad tendencies; actual sin alone is culpable, and only culpable when it is voluntary. But to both original and actual sin, in a world where everything is interrelated, is due the bondage from which man needs deliverance.

Ex. xx. 5.

III. SIN A BONDAGE

(B) *Sinful Habits*

That sin leads to bondage hardly requires proof. We can sin because we are free, and we limit our freedom by sinning. By decisions on matters which seem of small moment, constantly confirmed, habits are formed; and while a good habit increases our effectiveness, a bad one restricts our power. Bad habits are like chains which are very hard to break.

Curiosity impels men to taste of forbidden fruit, and when their eyes are opened they are sick with

Gal. v. 1.
Rom. viii. 15

shame. They may resolve never again to indulge such an appetite; but the temptation recurs, and they find that their powers of resistance have been weakened. Slowly they become the slaves of some lust from which they have ceased to receive even a momentary thrill of pleasure.

How often some act of imprudence in youth determines a man's whole life. He cannot undo the past and he cannot escape the consequences. There seems something inevitable in a degradation where folly succeeds folly, and crime leads to crime.

There is no going back and often no chance of reparation. The bad son stands by the deathbed of the mother whose heart he has broken. He is full of remorse, but what can he do? Ever afterwards the memory will cloud his life, the spirit of evil will suggest despair. The light of self-knowledge, now within him, reveals for him no way. It is not light at all, but darkness visible.

It is true that some sinners become contented with their slavery. They take their failings for granted, plead that they are natural, and then refuse to worry about them. Worse men even gild their chains and by a perverted hypocrisy claim some merit from the display. Many again sigh like Ovid, "Video meliora proboque : deteriora sequor," but in fatalistic calm they have ceased to struggle. The best, however, will never acquiesce in their bondage and will always be conscious that they were born to be free. They may have to confess like S. Paul, "The good that I would I do not : but the evil which I would not, that I do"; but they remain true to the inner light that is in them, even when compelled to cry, "O wretched man that I am ! who shall deliver me from

Rom. vii. 19.

the body of this death ? " They look for a Saviour, Rom. vii. 24. and they want not merely forgiveness, but deliverance. They need redemption from the power of sin.

IV. SIN A BONDAGE

(C) *An Evil Environment*

If habits are like chains, a world lying in wickedness is our prison house; and before Christ came there was no way of escape but by the gate of death.

Men indeed dreamed of Utopias, and thought out ethical systems. It was not from lack of intelligence, nor from lack of ideals, that the world was perishing, but from lack of moral power. An evil environment is all the more felt to be a tyrant's stronghold when we know how fair are the fields of freedom whither we would escape.

Had we entered Rome in the first century we should have been first amazed by its splendour and then disgusted by its corruption. We should have found that the majority of the people were slaves from every nation under heaven, and that those nominally free were conscious of a very real servitude. In the past they had known the dangers of a democracy, when loud-voiced demagogues appealed to the cupidity of the least intelligent. They knew also the misery which comes when oligarchs quarrel —factions, confiscations and civil war. They had submitted in despair to a despot, generally inspired by enlightened self-interest, who gave them order and security, whose caprice only injured the few, though they might be the best. Aristocrats fled for refuge to the precepts of Stoicism, and cultivated the interior life. By contemning the world, they strove to preserve the freedom of their own souls; and then despaired because they could not preserve their children from contamination in their huge insulæ peopled with slaves. Outside in the streets, porticoes and fora—in the theatres, baths, amphitheatres and temples, evil walked unashamed and unrebuked. The poor were living in idleness on doles, and being debauched by bloody spectacles. How could such a society be reformed? How could a man be good in such an environment? How could he escape from such a prison?

Rom. i. 20. S. Paul points out that Natural religion was sufficient light, and ought to have preserved men from such corruption; but society was organised without reference to God, and in disregard of God they had disregarded also the laws of their true nature. Political power, social custom, education and public opinion were all evil, and, like four walls, closed men in. Rebels there were, and have always been—men at issue with their environment; but Society is very strong to enforce its will. Those who sank below its standard were called criminals and if possible suppressed; those who rose above its standard might be called heroes and saints after they were dead, but they were even more certainly suppressed.

Setting aside definitely Christian literature, if we were to collect the highest works of genius we should only have a few volumes of tragedies; and we cannot recite the roll of heroes and saints without thinking of persecution and death. Pessimists gloat over such facts; but an Æschylus or a Shakespeare can appraise the survival value of moral effort, and look forward to a new day. The world has to be redeemed by suffering. Can we see in the Cross a victory, the starting point for a new order, a conquest, whereby, under new conditions, a kingdom of God may be?

V. Sin a Bondage

(D) *The Devil*

If man was in chains, and the world his prison-house, was there a gaoler? Can we believe that all this organised and interrelated wickedness can exist apart from a directive will. S. Paul answers, "We wrestle not against flesh and blood, but against . . . spiritual wickedness in high places"; and Our Eph. vi. 12. Blessed Lord seems to have had no doubt about the activity of the Devil or his power.

It is strange that, in an age like our own, men should doubt the validity of His spiritual perception and prefer their own imaginations. Scientists who smile at any belief in a devil will patiently examine the evidence of a Medium, will believe in her Controls and cock-and-bull stories purporting to emanate from another world. That Mediums should be controlled seems to them natural, when demoniac possession seems to them absurd. Everyone knows how a stronger will dominates a weaker one; we are learning more and more about the power of mind over matter, and the importance of suggestion is recognised by all. There is no *a priori* reason for supposing that men are the only beings in this vast universe endowed with free will, or that, among such beings, men alone can have sinned. You cannot indeed prove the existence of purely spiritual creatures by physical experiments, because physics can only deal with matter; but, assuming the truth of revelation, we can see how it accounts for much that is otherwise inexplicable in the rationally ordered universe created by a good God.

Think of the Crucifixion! In the last chapter we noted how men of all sorts and conditions were betrayed by their individual sins into being in some degree responsible for the death of Our Lord; but surely behind them there must have been a directing and co-ordinating power. Pilate did not wish to crucify Jesus, the soldiers did not know what they were doing, and the mob was more determined to intimidate a Roman governor than to put Our Lord to death. His real enemies, the worldly priests, the hypocritical Pharisees, the nationalist fanatics, and the Herodians pledged to Rome, were all at bitter variance with one another, and on any other issue would have taken different sides. Yet all for different reasons desired one thing, and we see the forces of the whole world's evil marshalled for a decisive conflict. Was it a chance combination, or was Our Lord right in saying that the Prince of this world had come, and that for an hour the power of darkness would seem to be triumphant?

S. Luke xxii. 53.
S. John xiv. 39.

Does a belief such as this land us in the hopeless dualism of Zoroastrians and Manichæans? No! the story of the Crucifixion is the answer to any such suspicion. God may have created Spirits able to will good and evil. Spirits there may be who have become evil. God may permit them to act, but He overrules their efforts. Devils and wicked men conspired to slay Our Lord, but they could not make Him sin; and the Redemption of the world is the outcome of their malice.   What the great Tragedians had hoped for, in spite of all evidence to the contrary, what heroes had devoted themselves for, in spite of all the arguments derived from common sense, that the Resurrection and Ascension of Our Lord proves and guarantees to all who will accept His gospel— the ultimate triumph of good.

VI. Is Man a Fit Object for the Divine Compassion

But here we are face to face with an objection which we noted briefly in the last chapter.   If man's condition is such as you describe, is he a fit object for the Divine compassion?   And the answer once again is, *Yes*.

Man created in the image of God has never quite forgotten his origin.   When most certain that he is Gen. i. 27. a prisoner and cannot save himself, he remains a prisoner of hope.   He struggles on with the evidence Zech. ix. 12. of failure all about him, essays to do great things, scales hills of difficulty, and falls from precipices which he has dared.   Even when he wallows in mire, he still clings to some rag of honour, which he waves as a tattered symbol, that he has not altogether surrendered and renounced the freedom of his soul.   The very worst know in their hearts that in humanity there is something which is divine.   So the coward thrills at some tale of heroism, his blood quickens, and as a brother he salutes the brave.   The lazy man praises the splendid energy of others, and seeks excuses of health or opportunity to account for his own indolence.   The ignorant man respects knowledge, and there is something pathetic

in the attempt of all men to appreciate what is
sublime in art. Even the selfish and self-indulgent
shed sentimental tears over an act of devotion or
self-sacrifice. All recognise in a common humanity
somewhat of glory in the midst of shame, and the
God of love remembers what is good as well as what
is evil.

We pity one another; how much more must the
good God pity us! And do we not need His pity?
Think of the hero betrayed by some secret frailty,
of the great achievement which was unrewarded
because of some petty jealousy, of the poet's vision
fading in the light of common day, of the kindly
man growing cold and callous having been led away
by the heat of his lusts, of the good man's imperfect
sympathies, and of the forbidding character of much
that is called virtuous! Are we not constrained to
cry, " Will no one retrieve so much that is true,
beautiful and good, from the dirt and disfigurement
which comes of sin? " And God answers our cry—
He sends His Son to be our Redeemer. He comes
Rev. vi. 2. conquering and yet to conquer, He comes as man
that we may share His triumph; He comes as King
to establish a realm of righteousness.

VII. Our Lord's Victory

(A) *Free from Original Sin*

We have now to consider how Our Lord as man
escaped from being in bondage to sin, how He
triumphed over temptation, and reveals the nature
of true manhood—manhood in accord with the mind
of God.

First of all we believe that He was free from that depravity of our nature which we call original sin, for otherwise He would not have been perfect, nor could Humanity in Him be redeemed. We confess not only that He is true man, but also new man, the second Adam; and in Him the long entail of sin is cut off. Secondly, we believe that Our Lord, so truly human, committed no actual sin, but otherwise was like us, sharing our experience from the womb to the grave. Thirdly, we believe that He was "born of the seed of David according to the flesh," and yet is the pre-existent Son of the Father. _{Rom. i. 3.} _{Col. i. 15, 16.}

All who believe in the Incarnation acknowledge these amazing facts; and, like His holy Mother, we are constrained to ask, "How may these things be?" Holy Scripture replies with the story of the _{S. Luke i. 31.} Virgin Birth, and those who deny this doctrine have no better solution to offer in its place. And yet many theologians interested in Science find in this doctrine a stumbling-block; although it is no stumbling-block to many scientists interested in theology, for one miracle more or less makes no difference in their acceptation or rejection of the Christian faith.

We have already noted that the offspring of two imperfect beings could not be perfect. This is confirmed by all experience. So if Jesus was born in the ordinary way we are face to face with miracle. Secondly, the offspring of a man and woman is always in our experience a new personality, so we are driven either to deny Our Lord's pre-existence, or to postulate another miracle. So those Scholars who believe in the Incarnation, but would simplify the faith, ask us to accept two miracles for which there is no evidence, in order to escape from one, which is, after all, attested.

Even those who deny the Incarnation tell us that in all human history Our Lord's life and character are unique. But surely such a result must have a cause to account for it, and Christians can at least explain "there was a difference in His birth." If they are pressed to explain why such a difference should have such a result, they are in no worse case than the Scientist who has made some natural discovery. He knows that a new factor makes a difference, but he does not know why. All things go out into mystery, and as S. Ignatius says, "The child-bearing of Mary is a mystery for proclamation, which was wrought in the silence of God."

We conclude therefore that Jesus does not represent the love which Joseph had for Mary, but the love which God had for the human race. Our Lord was born [1] "not . . . of the will of man, but of God." Mary, with whom God was well pleased, was the fitting instrument of the Divine purpose that "the seed of the woman should bruise the serpent's Gen. iii. 15. head," and that man should be redeemed by man. Our Lord did not abhor the Virgin's womb, but derived from her His humanity, and is through her related to all mankind. But free from the inheritance of sinful depravity, humanity in Him has a new start. Lastly, in strict agreement with all we know of the world's evolution, the new start took place in the old environment, there was no break of continuity or reversal of method, no revolution or destruction of what went before. God

---

[1] S. John i. 13. This is, I believe, true and would have been admitted by the Evangelist, but it seems that the received reading is correct, which also expresses a truth.

redeems, reforms, restores, for God is love, and His
purpose through the ages does not change, nor can
it be ultimately frustrated by the malice of devils
or the rebellion of men.

VIII. OUR LORD'S VICTORY

(B) *Resists all Temptation*

If Our Lord came like the first man into the world
without the taint of sin, He enjoyed no other advantage. The first man, being in Paradise, sinned and
fell; Our Lord in the midst of evil overcame temptation, overcame the world and conquered the Devil.

As we read the Gospel Story, we understand how
He " could be touched with the feeling of our infirmities," and how He " was in all points tempted
like as we are, yet without sin." In His own account, Heb. iv. 15.
for it can have come from no one else, of what
happened in the wilderness, we note that He was
susceptible to temptation from the flesh, the world
and the Devil, for otherwise the whole story would S. Matt. iv.
be unreal. He knew the craving for food, the desire 1-13.
for a dominion easily achieved, and the subtle suggestion that He should impose Himself on men by
an act of self-assertion. Those days of prayer and
retreat were days of intense trial. Our Lord knew
what temptation can be, for He withstood it to the
very end, while most men succumb at its first approach
or after a brief resistance. He conquered by " the
sword of the Spirit, which is the Word of God," and Eph. vi. 17.
in those long forty days mastered Himself, before
He went out to do battle with the world.

His life ever after was a conflict. With such a

G

happy nature, and such a capacity for enjoyment, such a zest for life, He experienced one trial after another, so that the Gospel story may be summed up in the two words—He suffered.

He knew by experience the temptations of the poor, the hungry and thirsty folk. He knew what it was to be footsore, to be over-worked and weary. He, who so loved men, knew the dangers of popularity, and hid Himself from those who would make Him

S. John vi. 15.

king. He who was so compassionate must have felt the temptation to condone sin, but never did so. He Who was so affectionate knew the bitterness of being misunderstood by those He loved best—His

S. Matt. xii. 46.
S. Mark iii. 21, 31.
S. John vii. 3–5.

Mother, His Brethren and Disciples. He was betrayed by one whom He had called His friend, and was denied by one whom He had chosen as His chief Apostle. He knew what failure means to those who plan largely, work strenuously and feel acutely. He knew all the horrors of physical pain, and the agony of anticipating it. "When He was reviled, He

1 Pet. ii. 23.

reviled not again; when He suffered He threatened

S. Matt. xxvii. 56.
S. Mark xiii. 65.
S. Luke xxii. 63.
S. Matt. xxvii. 26.
S. Mark xiv. 15.
S. Matt. xxvii. 28.
S. Mark xv. 17.
S. John xix. 1, 2.
S. Matt. xxvii. 35.
S. Mark xv. 24.
S. Matt. xxvii. 38.
S. Mark xv. 27.
S. Luke xxiii. 32.
S. John xix. 18.

not." Men spat in His face and buffeted Him with their hands : men scourged Him with whips loaded with lead : men mocked Him in His pain, clad Him in purple and placed a crown of thorns upon His head. He did not even walk proudly to His death, but, according to tradition, fell beneath the Cross He carried. Degraded, He knew the shame of being stripped of His clothes, and of being crucified between two thieves. Suffering from injustice, deserted by all, He knew the last dread temptation of despair, the blackness of the soul consciously bereft of God. But He still cried " My God, My God," and died commending Himself into the Father's keeping.

Long before He had challenged His opponents, asking, "Which of you convinceth Me of sin?" and to-day He still challenges the world with the same question. He as man had faced all temptations, trials, and sufferings, and died Master of Himself in bondage to no sin. Man had at last won the great victory. It was won in the Way of the Cross.

S. Matt. xxvii. 46.
S. Mark xv. 34.
S. Luke xxiii. 46.
S. John viii. 46.

IX. OUR LORD'S VICTORY

(C) *Overcomes the World*

Our Lord came into the world and did not despise it. He was sensitive to its beauty, attracted by its glories, and interested in its manifold ways. He who told the Parables to the listening crowds was not indifferent to Nature, or to the lives of men. For Him the world was God's world, alienated by sin. He came to reconquer it for God and to dispute the Devil's claim to its possession. When that Devil offered Him the kingdoms of the world and the glory of them at the price of homage to himself, the Lord said : "Get thee behind Me, Satan," and the boastful Being, notwithstanding his pretensions, had to go.

S. Matt. iv. 10.
S. Luke iv. 8.

But the Devil's power was real enough, and the world as organised apart from God suffered from his usurped tyranny. He had persuaded men that he was irresistible, and even since Our Lord's victory, all those who plead that sins are natural do homage to the Devil. Better men believed that the world was subject to a Good and an Evil God, or they drew a distinction between matter and spirit, and maintained that the former was evil in its essence. This led the best to renounce as far as possible the things of sense and the life of action; and led the worst to wallow in vices, pleading that what happened to the body was of no consequence.

Then Our Lord came in the body to redeem it from contempt. He lived a social life and sanctified its activities and innocent pleasures. He taught His highest truth by reference to material objects, and vindicated the moral unity of the world under the One Creative God.

But the society of the wicked always arrogate to themselves the title of *The World*, and with this World Our Lord was always at variance which ended in a struggle to the death. At the beginning of His ministry, in the Sermon on the Mount, He announced the Beatitudes, which revolutionised the World's standard of values. He proceeded to criticise its morality and maxims, and taught a new view of life.

S. Matt. v. 3–11.

But the World is ever ready to compromise with the good and expects a like tolerance in return. Our Lord, however, refused to compromise with evil, declaring that "No man can serve two masters. . . . Ye cannot serve God and Mammon." He refused the secret adhesion of Nicodemus, for His Disciples were to witness on His behalf. He refused the half-hearted, for His Disciples were to be ready to forsake all and follow Him.

S. Matt. vi. 24.
S. Luke xvi. 13.
S. John iii. 1–13.
S. Matt. viii. 18–22.
S. Luke ix. 57, 62.

Secondly, the World is ever ready to seduce the good and corrupt with its favours. Men came to Him saying, "Good Master"; Herod was ready with his patronage, Pharisees asked Him to dine, Pharisees, Sadducees and Herodians tried to entangle Him in His talk; but Our Lord knew what was in man and did not commit Himself unto them.

S. Mark x. 17, 18.
S. Luke ix. 9.
S. Luke xxiii. 8.
S. Luke vii. 36.
S. Matt. xxii. 15–40.
S. John ii. 24, 25.

Thirdly, the World ever tries to make use of the good for its own purposes. The World was ready to acclaim Our Lord as the Messiah, if He would play the *rôle* which they desired, and be the Messianic King whom they expected. The crowds who were fed in the wilderness were ready to follow Him if He would continue to distribute like favours, but they went back from following Him when He talked only of the heavenly food. Revolutionaries hoped that He might lead them against the Romans, but they had no use for one who taught men to render unto Cæsar the things that are Cæsar's.

S. John vi. 26, 27.

S. Matt. xxii. 21.

Fourthly, when the World can neither corrupt, nor use the good for its own purposes, it tries to intimidate and to subdue. Our Lord knew that the Jews sought to slay Him, but He none the less steadfastly set His face to go to Jerusalem. He refused to plead before Caiaphas, He refused to amuse Herod by working a miracle, He reproved Pilate to His face. He was unconquered up to the end. In imposing the death penalty, the World acknowledged its defeat. The death penalty is always an acknowledgment by society that it cannot control.

S. Matt. xxvi. 62.
S. Mark xiv. 60.
S. John xviii. 20, 21.
S. Mark ix. 32.
S. Matt. xx. 17.
S. Luke xviii. 31.
S. Luke xxiii. 8, 9.
S. John xviii. 36, 37.
S. John xix. 11.

All the powers in which the world believes were ranged against Him, money, public opinion and the big battalions; but He said in anticipation of death, " Be of good cheer; I have overcome the world." The World crucified Him and thought they had made an end of their enemy; but on the third day He rose again in the very body which they thought they had destroyed. The world was overcome.

S. John xvi. 33.

X. Our Lord's Victory

(D) *Casts out the Devil*

We have speculated on the Devil's activity in bringing about the crucifixion of Our Lord, but we are on firmer ground in trying to estimate Our Lord's victory over Satan, for we have His own account of what happened in the wilderness after He had been S. Mark i. 13. alone for forty days with the wild beasts.

He tells us first how the Devil came to Him with S. Luke iv. the suggestion that He should work a miracle on 1-13. S. Matt. iv. His own behalf and make stones into bread; secondly, 1-11. how the Devil offered Him the kingdoms of the world and the glory of them for a single act of homage which would have been an acknowledgment of the Devil's previous rights; and thirdly, the Devil suggested that He should by an act of self-assertion, convince men of His claims, and demonstrate His own trust in the promises of Scripture.

The Devil, we may assume, was ignorant of the Incarnation, which even angels only desired to look into; but the Devil saw in Our Lord the possible Messiah and Saviour, and knew the expectations of the Jews. Some believed that the Son of Man would be a semi-divine person, and Satan hoped to tempt such a one to work miracles for his own sustenance, and so lead Him from a spiritual purpose to think first of material needs. Most Jews expected a warrior Christ, who would lead them against the Gentiles and establish a throne on Sion, and he hoped that such a Messiah, by accepting his aid, in gaining the whole world, might lose his own soul. Some Jews again looked for an apocalyptic Christ, who would descend with signs from heaven, dissolve the world order and establish a new kingdom. Might not such a Being be led through presumption into rebellion against the will of God, and become like himself—a second Lucifer that fell from heaven? Isa. xiv. 12. S. Luke x. 18.

Our Lord, however, knew who He Himself was, and the purpose of His mission. He had indeed come to be the Son of Man, the Representative of true humanity. He had come to be the warrior Christ, but His warfare was of a spiritual nature and could only be waged with spiritual weapons. He was S. Matt. xxiv. 30. S. Mark xiv. 62. coming some day in the clouds of heaven, but only at the appointed time. First, He was to be the suffering servant of Jehovah described by Isaiah, for the world could only be won by suffering, and men could only be redeemed by self-sacrificing love. Isa. liii. liii.

If this be true, it may be argued that the Devil's suggestions were no temptations to Our Lord, but this is to confuse the design of the Devil with the effect which his suggestions may have had for Our Lord's mind. A man may see quite clearly that a certain suggestion is altogether foreign to his purpose, and yet see that the suggestion is attractive in itself. He may pause to reconsider his purpose, or weaken his resolution by asking, " Is it worth while? " He may at least wonder why lower objects should be attained in a way so much more easy and pleasant, and resent the fact that the high way he has chosen involves so much hardship.

We must remember that with perfect insight into men and things, the human mind of Jesus was under no illusions about His fate. In His perfect manhood He was peculiarly sensitive to physical pain and all unkindness. How awful, in consequence, must have been His anticipations, and how resolute His will that He would not dwell on them. It was not until the end that His " soul was exceeding sorrowful even unto death," and that He prayed ever more earnestly, " Father, if it be possible let this cup pass from Me." He, who sweated great drops of blood in His anguish, was not impervious to a temptation that an easier way might be found for the World to be won without the Cross. And the way seemed so obvious. Our Lord had indeed limited Himself to feel as a man, to work with a human brain and exercise a human will, but He was conscious of His Deity. It was just because He was so conscious that the temptation was so strong, " Why maintain the limitation ? " And yet had He invoked powers on His Own behalf which we do not possess, He would have ceased to be our example. He had become man in order that as a man He might free manhood from servitude, and we may dimly estimate the self-abnegation of One Who could have demonstrated His power and compelled men to believe, but did not; of One Who so loved man and so desired a free response, that He resolutely refused an easy triumph, which would have given Him slaves instead of sons. Had He assumed His power as God, He would have conquered the world, but manhood in Him would have been conquered—manhood would not have been redeemed.

The temptation we can therefore think was very real. Our Lord, however, triumphed and the Devil had to leave Him, but S. Luke significantly says, " he departed from Him for a season." The same struggle had to be once more endured in Gethsemane, and all through Our Lord's life we note the Devil's

S. Mark xiv. 34.

S. Luke xxii. 44.

S. Luke iv. 13.

activity, speaking by the lips of others. There were those who demanded miracles, seeking a sign from heaven; there were His unbelieving brethren, who desired Him to do great works in Jerusalem; and there was S. Peter, who turned and rebuked Him when He spoke openly of His death. Our Lord recognised at once the source of the Apostle's inspiration, and said, "Get thee behind me, Satan . . . for thou savourest not the things that be of God, but those that be of man." Even at the very end the same temptation made itself heard, when His enemies laughed beneath the Cross—"He saved others; Himself He cannot save," and when they cried to Him, "If Thou be the Son of God, come down from the Cross . . . and we will believe Thee."

S. John iv. 48.
S. Matt. xii. 38, 39.
S. Matt. xvi. 1.
S. John viii. 3.

S. Matt. xvi. 23.

S. Matt. xxvii. 40–43.
S. Mark xv. 29–31.
S. Luke xxiii. 35.

But as we read the Gospel we see other evidence of the Devil's attempts to thwart Our Lord. Very early in S. Mark's Gospel, we are told how those who were possessed saluted Him as "the Holy One of God"; and it was this dubious testimony, no doubt, that seemed to justify a suspicion, that after all He might be in league with Beelzebub and the infernal powers.

S. Mark i. 24.
S. Mark iii. 11.
S. Mark v. 7.

We note also the Devil's tactics when he struck at Our Lord through His disciples. Satan entered into Judas, and desired to sift Peter. These were the hidden wounds that He received in the house of His friends.

S. Luke xxii. 3.
S. John xiii. 2.
S. Luke xxii. 31.
Zech. xiii. 6.

Lastly, is it fanciful to think of the Devil in the darkness brooding above the Cross and whispering despair? Was it his last hope that at the very end Our Lord might curse God and die? And are we to see the ultimate victory in the words, "Father, into Thy hands I commend my Spirit?" Satan had done

Job ii. 9.

S. Luke xxiii. 46.

his worst and been overthrown, the Prince of this world was cast out.

XI. Our Lord's Victory

(E) *Rises from the Grave and Ascends into Heaven*

After a struggle so terrible, and a victory so unique, we are bound to expect consequences commensurate with their cause. Sin corrupts and is the cause of dissolution; "the wages of sin is death": but we should not expect a sinless body to see corruption, and in the body of His humiliation Our Lord rose again. Sin is a bondage here in this world, and it would be foolish to expect that death of itself would set the spirit free; but the sinless Lord had never submitted to bondage in this world, and so neither the grave, hell nor Satan could confine One who had broken every chain. His Blood had been poured out, but by that very fact His Life had been set free. The Risen Lord was no longer restricted by time and space. He, Who had descended into hell, also ascended into heaven, and is seated in His glorified manhood at the right hand of the Father. It is the Son of Mary Who is on the throne of Deity. It is the God from everlasting Who is Man for evermore.

Rom. vi. 23.

XII. The Victory was Won on Our Behalf

Our Lord's death issued in a personal victory over sin, the world and the Devil; but it was a victory won on our behalf. It was for us men and for our salvation that He came down from heaven, suffered and died. Otherwise the story would not profit us. We should only admire Him and despair of ourselves.

It was not for His own sake God came, for He could not add to His own perfection. If He became man it was that He might save men. If in Him manhood triumphed over evil, it was that, through Him, men might escape.

It would have been unworthy of God that He should have come among us merely to display His own goodness. The death on Calvary viewed only in this light would seem to us unreal and a little theatrical. It would be an incidental drama and no part of the history of the world. As a story for edification it might have occurred any time, and people would soon say it was just as good a story if it never occurred at all. But we cannot read the New Testament without being aware that for the authors something happened on the Cross, and because of the Cross, which changed man's relation both to God and the Devil. The world was redeemed and we still experience the benefit.

It is, of course, quite right to insist on the subjective values. The penitent thief was won by the royal dignity and patience of Our Lord to believe in His Kingdom, asked to be remembered, and received [S. Luke xxiii. 42, 43.] a promise which exceeded all that he had hoped for. The people who saw Our Lord die " smote their [S. Luke xxiii. 48.] breasts, and returned "; they had seen strange things that day, and we may well believe that the memory did not fade, and led to their conversion. The Centurion, who had probably seen many a [S. Matt. xxvii. 54.] crucifixion, confessed, " Verily, this was the Son of [S. Mark xv. 39.] God." Perhaps his superstitious mind was shaken [S. Luke xxiii. 47.]

by the earthquake; but he at least recognised that he was face to face with the supernatural. He had heard the angry cries, " He made Himself the Son of God." He had seen the heaven dark at noonday, he felt the shock and was convinced. In after days he no doubt learnt what his words implied. Nicodemus and Joseph of Arimathæa, who had been ashamed to join Our Lord openly when He was the darling of the unlettered multitude, now when it seemed too late and all was lost, went boldly up into the presence of Pilate, and craved His body that they might give it honourable burial. The new life stirred within them when Our Lord gave up the ghost.

All down the ages men have been drawn to the Cross, and learnt from its contemplation a saving message for their souls; but we must not restrict Our Lord's victory, or only think of its subjective value for those who contemplate it. That is not only to limit His work, but also to divorce it from its central place in history. Our Lord was once asked, " Are there few that be saved ? " and refused to answer the question; but those who hold merely subjective views on the Atonement are compelled to answer, *Yes*. According to them the death on the Cross can only help those who hear of it, and then only avails for those gifted with sufficient historical imagination to enter into its meaning.

In considering the objective view, let us first note three facts connected with the Passion. (1) " The veil of the Temple was rent in twain from the top to the bottom." This must have been the outer veil hiding the Holy Place from the Court of the Israelites. We are told about it, in order that we

S. John xix. 7.
S. Matt. xxvii. 45, 51.
S. Luke xxiii. 44.

S. Matt. xxvii. 57, 58.
S. Mark xv. 43.
S. Luke xxiii. 56, 58.
S. John xix. 38–40.

S. Luke xiii. 23.

S. Matt. xxvii. 51.
S. Luke xxiii. 45.

may understand that the Old Covenant with its mediatorial priesthood was superseded by the New Covenant in the Blood of Jesus. (2) "The earth did quake and the rocks rent; . . . and many bodies of the saints which slept arose, and . . . went into the holy city and appeared unto many." The text S. Matt. xxvii. 52–53. is here suspect, and we have a confused tradition, but that does not mean that there is no truth behind it. It is evidently recorded in order that we may learn how the death of Christ was for the living and the dead. (3) "One of the soldiers with a spear pierced His side, and forthwith came there out blood and water." To the mystical mind of S. John this S. John xix. 34. seemed significant of Him, Who came "by water and by blood." We are led to think of the cleansing 1 S. John v. 6. stream which washes away sin, and of the blood, which is the life, that is communicated to the sinner. Some readers will say : "The rending of the Temple veil was a coincidence, the rending of the graves is an unsupported tradition of dubious historicity, and even if we accept the testimony of the fourth Gospel we are not bound by the allegorising tendencies of the author." Supposing such readers to be right, they cannot escape from the fact that the Evangelists attributed objective results to the death of Christ.

Until recently Christians, with very few exceptions, believed that Our Lord by dying won a real victory over evil in which others shared. His death we may believe had a retrospective as well as a prospective value, and will prove availing for those who shall say at the Day of Judgment, "We never knew Thee." Believing this we see no force in Darwin's S. Matt. xxv. 37–40. objection to Christianity—that so few had heard of the death of Christ; for their salvation will depend on what He did for them, and not on what they felt about it.

We confess in the Creed—He descended into Hell. S. Peter tells us that Our Lord went "to preach unto the spirits in prison; which sometime were disobedient; when once the longsuffering of God waited in the days of Noah." S. Paul says Our Lord "having spoiled principalities and powers, He made a show of them openly, triumphing over them." But we can only understand such statements very imperfectly.

1 Pet. iii. 19-20.

Col. ii. 15.

The Crucifixion occurred in time, but Holy Scripture views it from the standpoint of eternity. Our Lord, in the Apocalypse, is "the Lamb slain from the foundation of the world." The Epistle to the Hebrews speaks of an "Eternal Redemption." History is for us a sequence of events. We can only trace them back a certain distance, and we do not know what is coming; but we have a sense of relation and unity, which no philosophy of history has yet been able to establish. Outside time, we may imagine, the whole History can be taken in at once—a picture perfect in its composition. Could we attain to it we should see Our Lord on the Cross as the central fact and all else in relation to Him.

Rev. xiii. 8.

Heb. ix. 12. Cf. v. 9.

Again we have to acknowledge our ignorance of the economy of God, and cannot explain definitely why the death of Our Lord should have had such far-reaching results. We know that sin is a bondage and that through His death comes enfranchisement, that sin is a disease and in the Cross there is the remedy, but this can only be verified by experience. The sick man knows the remedy which eases pain, but cannot account for its virtues.

But if we cannot at present fathom the mystery, we may explore it in many directions; and there is no lack of evidence for His triumph. He is the Captain of our Salvation, bringing many Sons unto glory. He has led captivity captive and given gifts to men. ^{Heb. ii. 10. Eph. iv. 8.} He is the conqueror, holding in His hands the keys of hell and death. To understand this, we must first ^{Rev. i. 18.} see the preparation in history for Our Lord's coming and then what was His own teaching about His death. ^{Rom. v. 14–18.} We can then go on to understand from His victory ^{1 Cor. xv. 22, 45.} how He is the New Adam and head of the race of the redeemed, the Messianic King establishing His Kingdom, the Priest of the New Covenant sealed in His own blood, He Who brought life and immortality ^{Heb. ix.} to light through His gospel. ^{2 Tim. i. 10.}

XIII. How Far the Victory Accords with Men's Expectations

Men knew their bondage, and knew that deliverance could not come from within. They looked to God and expected a Saviour. By divers ways we find in the Old Testament the long preparation. More confusedly we find in the Ethnic religions dim hopes, and in the Mystery Religions various conceptions of a Redeemer God.

First of all men were naturally more concerned with the results of sin than with the nature of sin in itself. The cruelty of life and the inevitable consequences of misdoing made them long for an escape. Actual slavery or the fear of devastating enemies made them turn to God for salvation. The Israelites very early ^{Deut. xxx. Judges ii.} connected their national misfortunes with their neglect of the Law, and perceived a judgment of God in what befell them. So their history as told by themselves is one of rebellion and repentance, and throughout runs the thought that they could not help themselves. They could not control nature, but God could avert disaster. They were a weak people with mighty enemies round about, but God could save by many or by few. So "they cried unto the Lord in their trouble and He delivered them out of their distress." "The Lord ransomed Jacob and redeemed him from the hand of him that was stronger than he."

Ps. cvii. 6.

Jer. xxxi. 11.

But there was also the sense of personal shame which led men to deeper views about sin, and revealed a need which no merely external deliverance could effect. "Blessed is he whose transgression is forgiven, whose sin is covered," says the Psalmist; and he recognises the paradox that it will not be covered so long as he remains silent, and can only be forgiven when it is confessed. Something more than forgiveness is needed. It is only God who can "create a new heart" or "renew a right spirit." It is "to the God of my salvation" that the appeal is made.

Ps. xxxii. 1, 5.

Ps. li. 10.

Ps. li. 14.

During the captivity, this desire for salvation was more individual and spiritual, and with the revival of national hopes, it assumed a more political character. The two ideas, however, reacted on one another, and a nation triumphant in righteousness is a splendid ideal. It was when national aspirations were disappointed, when the wicked seemed to flourish as a green bay tree and the righteous were oppressed, that the salvation looked for was more and more of an other-worldly nature. Men despaired of this life, and looked for a new heaven and a new earth, appealed

Ps. xxxvii. 35.

to a future judgment, and speculated on the ultimates of heaven and hell.

Throughout their history there is an expectation of the Messiah. He is the prophet Whom the Lord shall raise up like Moses to effect an even greater [Deut. xviii. 15.] deliverance. He is the warrior king of the seed of [Ps. cxxxii. Isa. ix. 7.] David, Who shall conquer even a wider empire. He [Jer. xxx. 9, 10.] shall bring peace to the world, so that all nations shall [Ezek. xxxvii. 25.] come to Mount Zion, from which the law of righteous- [Isa. lxii. 1, 2.] ness shall go forth. He shall come saying, " The Lord hath anointed Me to preach good tidings unto the meek; He hath sent Me to bind up the broken-hearted, to proclaim liberty to the captives, and the opening of the prison to them that are bound; to proclaim the acceptable year of the Lord, and the day of vengeance of Our God." He is the apocalyptic [Isa. lxi. 1, 2.] Christ, Whom Daniel saw in the night visions when " there came with the clouds of heaven one like unto a Son of Man. . . . And there was given Him dominion, and glory and a kingdom, and all the peoples, nations, and languages should serve Him : His dominion is an everlasting dominion, . . . and His kingdom that which shall not be destroyed." [Dan. vii. 13, 14.]

These conceptions, apparently so different, were often held concurrently. Sometimes one and some-times another predominated; but the salvation expected tended to become more universal in its scope, and to the minds of the greatest prophets it was clear that the redemption must be spiritual. The [Jer. xxxi. 33. Ezek. xxxvi. 25–27.] law had to be written in men's hearts, and the Spirit [Joel ii. 28.] had to be poured out on all flesh. But the second [Isa. liii. 1.] Isaiah might well ask, " Who hath believed our report ? " when he describes the suffering servant of Jehovah and concludes—" It pleased the Lord to

H

bruise Him; He hath put Him to grief; when Thou shalt make His soul an offering for sin, He shall see His seed, He shall prolong His days, and the pleasure of the Lord shall prosper in His hand. He shall see of the travail of His soul, and shall be satisfied : by His knowledge shall my righteous servant justify many; for He shall bear their iniquities. Therefore will I divide Him a portion with the great, and He shall divide the spoil with the strong; because He hath poured out His soul unto death : and was numbered with the transgressors; and He bare the sin of many, and made intercessions for the trans-

Isa. liii.
10–12.

gressors."

XIV. How Far the Victory Accords with Our Lord's Teaching about His Death

It was then as a Saviour that Our Lord came into

S. Matt. i.
21.

the world. The angel told S. Joseph "He shall save His people from their sins." An angel announced to the Shepherds "A Saviour who is Christ the

S. Luke ii.
11.

Lord." The Blessed Virgin rejoices in "God my

S. Luke i. 47.

Saviour." Zacharias regards his son as preparing the way for Him Who shall "give knowledge of salvation unto His people for the remission of their

S. Luke i. 77.

sins," and Simeon prophesies that the infant Jesus

S. Luke ii.
32.

will be " a light to lighten the Gentiles, and the glory of Thy people Israel."

People may dispute about the sources from which these texts come, and their historicity. But their Aramaic and early origin is undeniable. They at least witness to the persistence of the expectation of a Saviour who should come.

We have now to consider Our Lord's own interpretation of His mission; and it is clear that He
came to save, that He foretold His death, and asserted
that by dying He would redeem mankind. He said
that He had come " to seek and to save that which
was lost." He cared for men's bodies as well as for _{S. Luke xix.} S. Luke xix.
their souls. He healed the sick and raised the dead; 10.
He cast out devils and forgave sins. If He preached
the necessity of repentance, it was that the Kingdom
of Heaven was at hand. He preached a gospel of S. Mark i. 15.
hope, saying, "I have come that they might have life, S. John x.
and that they might have it more abundantly." S. John v.
But while claiming to have life in Himself, He was 26.
very definite about His own death. As soon as He
had led His Disciples to believe in Him as the Messiah,
He began to interpret His Messianic mission in the
terms of death. No sooner had S. Peter confessed
" Thou art the Christ, the Son of the Living God," S. Matt. xvi.
than He began to teach them how the Son of Man 16.
must suffer . . . and be killed and after three days
rise again. On the first occasion S. Peter dared S. Matt.
to rebuke Him. On a second occasion, we are told S. Mark viii.
that the disciples did not understand and were afraid 32.
to ask questions. On a third occasion, they followed S. Mark ix.
and were afraid, shrinking from a mystery which S. Mark x.
seemed only horrible. But while He insisted that 32–34.
His sufferings would be caused by the Chief Priests
and Scribes who would deliver Him to the Gentiles,
He was equally clear that His death was a voluntary
act. He said " I am the good shepherd : the good S. John x.
shepherd giveth His life for the sheep. . . . There- 11.
fore doth the Father love Me, because I lay down
My life, that I might take it again. No man taketh
it from Me, but I lay it down of Myself. . . . This S. John x.
17.

commandment have I received of My Father." He tried on another occasion to explain the result of this death by a parable, saying—" Except a corn of wheat fall into the ground and die, it abideth alone : but, if it die, it bringeth forth much fruit." Again He said how He came " to give His Life a ransom for many." And then at the Last Supper, He took bread into His venerable hands and brake it, saying, " This is My Body, which is broken for you . . . also He took the cup . . . saying, This cup is the New Covenant in My blood." The Body was broken on the Cross and the Blood poured out for us. And afterwards on the way to Emmaus He asked, " Ought not Christ to have suffered these things, and to enter into His glory ? And beginning at Moses and all the Prophets, He expounded unto them in all the Scriptures the things concerning Himself." On the Mountain of the Transfiguration Moses and Elias had appeared to be talking with Him; and S. Luke tells us " they spake of His *exodus* which He should accomplish at Jerusalem." All that went before was preparatory to this death, and through this death men have been redeemed.

S. John x. 19.

S. John xii. 24.

S. Mark x. 45.

1 Cor. xi. 24, 25.

S. Luke xxiv. 26, 27.

S. Luke ix. 30, 31.

XV. The Meaning of Ransom and Redemption

We have spoken of man being in bondage to sin, the world and the Devil, and it should be recognised at once that our language is metaphorical. We have gone on to speak of Our Lord as the Redeemer, of ransom and redemption—hereafter we shall have to speak of Him as the Sin Offering and satisfaction for our sins—and it should be obvious that we are only pursuing similar lines of thought and multiplying our metaphors.

Words when not the names of things are chiefly metaphors, and even abstract nouns ending in -ation and -osity have a history which ends by connecting them with what can be seen and heard. We have no celestial language, and a very poor vocabulary to express our spiritual experience, and we must be careful not to be misled into treating a word which illustrates or symbolises a fact as if it were the fact itself.

This is a necessary caution when thinking of the Atonement, for it has led men into elaborating theories which have been ultimately stigmatised as immoral.

A Ransom is a sum paid to free a prisoner of war; Redemption set free a purchased slave; while Satisfaction suggests the Law Courts and the wiping out of debt. These metaphors have led men to discuss the Atonement in terms proper for an armistice between hostile commanders, or as a commercial transaction, or as a legal fiction by which innocence is imputed to the guilty. In consequence, those who restrict their views to the subjective value of the Cross have been wont to claim for their own theory the title of moral; but morality has to do, not merely with sentiments, but with the rules that mitigate warfare, with the honesty of the market place, and with justice in the forum; and so the reaction against " commercial " or " forensic " theories may go too far. At present, I am only anxious that our metaphors should not be pressed. We have not to think of any bargain between God the Father and God the Son, or between God the Son and the Devil. We have not to assess the sum total of the world's sin and discuss whether the sufferings of Our Lord were more than an equivalent for them. We have not to ask ourselves to whom the price of ransom was paid, or search the resources of legal chicanery to discover how the guilty were spared for the sake of the innocent. We have to remember that the New Testament is neither a commercial contract nor a legal document, but literature, and its words have to be construed according to literary usage.

A man to-day might write—" England has preserved her freedom, but she has had to pay for it. It has cost her the life-blood of thousands. Through the death of her young men she is free." How surprised such a writer would be if somebody was to ask, " How many dead soldiers are necessary for the preservation of freedom ? " or " You talk of freedom being preserved at the price of blood : Was this price paid to the Kaiser, and why had he a right to exact it ? " This, you will say, is ridiculous, but similar questions have been asked about the Atonement, and can only be answered with a smile. We can say that Our Lord gave His Life as a ransom for many without asking the question, " To whom was the ransom paid ? " The result was the redemption of the world, and we believe in that as an objective fact in just the same way as we believe our victory over Germany is an objective fact. God forbid that we should undervalue the inspiring examples of the known and unknown warriors who lie buried in Gallipoli and France. But we must likewise remember that what they did was not in vain. They saved England and it cost them their lives.

XVI. Why the Victory is Availing
(A) *The New Adam*

It is now necessary to indicate how Our Lord's Victory is also our victory, and how we share in its fruits.

It is a commonplace to speak of the endless chain of events, though the progress of the world rather resembles a carpet, where many strands are interwoven. But at present it is sufficient to insist on the fact that every cause known to us is the effect of something that went before, and that consequences result which we may compare with the ripples in ever widening circles when a stone is cast into the water. Very early the Jews learnt " that the sins of the fathers are visited upon the children unto the third and fourth generation." But what is true of evil actions is _{Ex. xx. 5.} equally true of good ones, so we may argue that the Death of Our Lord vibrates through the world to-day, and is operative even where His story is unknown.

This brings us to S. Paul's argument in the Epistle to the Romans. For after speaking of the death of Christ, he goes on to argue, " For if, by the trespass of one, death reigned through the one ; much more shall they that receive the abundance of grace and of the gift of righteousness reign in life through the one, even Jesus Christ. . . . For as through the one man's disobedience the many were made sinners, even so through the obedience of the One shall the many be made righteous." _{Rom. v. 17–19.}

But S. Paul goes far beyond those who would maintain that all this happens by virtue of Our Lord's example. For him, Our Lord is the New Adam and head of the race of the redeemed. For him, Our _{1 Cor. xv. 22.}

S. John xii.
24.
Lord's parable had come true—The corn of wheat had fallen into the ground, had died, and produced much fruit. The life set free on the Cross is potentially ours. "We were buried . . . with Him through baptism into death : that like as Christ was raised from the dead through the glory of the Father, so we Rom. vi. 4.
Cp. Col. ii.
12. also might walk in newness of life." This new life is only possible for us through sharing in Christ's nature, His perfected humanity. Incorporated into Him by the Holy Spirit we are the sons of God. For S. Paul says again, "Ye received not the spirit of bondage again unto fear; but ye received the spirit of adoption, whereby we cry Abba, Father. The Spirit beareth witness with our spirit that we are children of God : and if children, then heirs; heirs of God, and joint-heirs with Christ; if so be that we suffer with Him, that we may be also glorified with Rom. viii.
15, 16. Him."

XVII. Why the Victory is Availing

(B) *The Messianic King*

Our Lord was not simply a good man who suffered unjustly and set us an example of dignity and patience. He was ever conscious of His high vocation and felt straitened until He had accomplished the work which His Father had given Him to do.

He came announcing the Kingdom of Heaven, and in parable after parable He taught what the Kingdom S. Matt. xiii. would be like, and from the first He spoke with authority. He said Come unto Me, Learn of Me, S. Matt. xi.
28, 29. Follow Me, Take My yoke upon you, and if ye love Me keep My commandments. He claimed priority S. John viii.
58. to Abraham, He revised the Law of Moses, He claimed

to be greater than Solomon, greater than the prophets. ^{S. Matt. v. 21, 27, 33, 38, 43.} Of S. John the Baptist He said—" Of them that were ^{S. Matt. xii. 41, 42.} born of women there hath not arisen a greater ; but he that is least in the Kingdom of Heaven is greater ^{S. Matt. xi. 11.} than He." ^{S. Luke vii. 28.}

As a king He entered into Jerusalem amid the ^{S. Matt. xxi. 9.} Hosannas of the people, and as a King He was delated ^{S. Mark xi. 9.} to Pilate. He told Pilate indeed, " My Kingdom is ^{S. Luke xix. 38.} not of this world : if My Kingdom were of this world, ^{S. John xii. 13.} then would My servants fight, that I should not be delivered to the Jews ; but now is My Kingdom not from hence. Pilate therefore said unto Him, Art Thou a King then ? Jesus answered, Thou sayest that I am a king. To this end have I been born, and for this cause came I into the world, that I should bear witness unto the Truth. Everyone that is of the truth heareth My voice." As a king He was mocked by ^{S. John xviii. 36—37.} Herod and the soldiers, as a king He was crowned with ^{S. Luke xxiii. 11.} thorns, and as a king He died, for the superscription above His Cross was " Jesus of Nazareth the King of the Jews." It was written in Hebrew, Greek and ^{S. Matt. xxvii. 37.} Latin, an advertisement to the whole world. And ^{S. Mark xv. 26.} when He had overcome death and burst the bonds ^{S. Luke xxiii. 38. S. John xix. 19.} of the grave, it was as a king that He appeared to His disciples, saying, " All power is given unto Me in Heaven and in earth." Immediately He put that ^{S. Matt. xxviii. 18.} power into commission, saying—" Go ye therefore and discipline all nations." But they were not to start ^{S. Matt. xxviii. 19.} on their mission until they were " endued with power from on High." He ascended up into Heaven to sit ^{S. Luke xxiv. 49.} upon His Throne. Thence He sent gifts to men. He, ^{Acts i. 9, ii. 33.} the Mediator, through His death established the ^{Eph. iv. 8.} Mediatorial Kingdom, and He must reign until He hath put all His enemies under His feet. As a King ^{1 Cor. xv. 25.}

S. Matt.
xxvi. 64.
Phil. ii. 9, 10.

He will come again in the clouds of Heaven to vindicate His authority, for the day must come when in the
name of Jesus every knee shall bow, and every tongue
shall confess Him to be Lord.

Here on earth through nineteen centuries we can
trace the progress of the Church which bears the Cross
boldly before in its endless procession. It is the
Church of God which Our Lord " purchased with His
own blood."

XVIII. Why the Victory is Availing

(C) *The High Priest of the New Covenant*

Ps. cx. 4.
Heb. v. 6.
vii.

Our Lord's kingdom is a church, and He is the
Priest-king after the order of Melchizedek. We are
called on to obey Him, the glorified Man upon the
throne. But He would bring us into communion
with the Godhead; and He says, " No man cometh
unto the Father, but by Me."

S. John xiv.
6.

S. John xvii.
S. Luke
xxiii. 34.
S. Luke
xxiii. 46.
S. Luke
xxiv. 19–21.
S. Luke xxiv.
31.

It was as a Priest that He prayed for His friends
before entering Gesthemane, and as a Priest He prayed
for His murderers on the Cross; as a Priest also He
offered Himself to the Father, and into the Father's
hands commended His spirit. The disciples on the
road to Emmaus confessed their hope that Jesus of
Nazareth would be He who should redeem Israel, but
as their Priest and their Redeemer they knew Him in
the Breaking of Bread. As the great High Priest He
appeared later in the Upper Chamber, conveying
to His Church the power of priestly absolution,
saying, " Whose soever sins ye forgive, they are forgiven." As a Priest He sent them forth to preach
repentance and remission of sins in His Name. As a

S. John xx.
23.
S. Luke
xxiv. 47.

Priest He commissioned them to baptise; and in the S. Matt.
xxviii. 19.
act of Priestly Benediction, He ascended into heaven,
from whence He fulfilled His promise in sending the S. Luke
xxiv. 51.
Holy Ghost.

All these powers belong to the New Covenant, and
He connected that New Covenant with His death,
saying, " This is My Blood of the Covenant which is
shed for many." The words carry us back to the S. Matt.
xxvi. 28.
story in Exodus, and we read of how the blood of the
offerings was sprinkled on the altar and the people,
and Moses said, " Behold the blood of the Covenant,
which the Lord hath made with you." Both Cove- Ex. xxiv. 8.
nants were ratified in blood; but the superiority of
the New Covenant is seen when we consider, God
" spared not His own Son, but delivered Him up for
us all." A covenant so confirmed cannot pass away. Rom. viii.
32.

Although we cannot understand it, we conclude
from the New Testament that through the Death on
the Cross we enter into a new relationship with God,
and through the shedding of blood has come the
remission of sins.

XIX. WHY THE VICTORY IS AVAILING

(D) *The Conqueror of Death*

Lastly, we believe that Our Lord's victory is our
victory, because He brought life and immortality to
light through His Gospel. We read in the Epistle 2 Tim. i. 10.
to the Hebrews, " Forasmuch then as the children are
partakers of flesh and blood, He also Himself took part
of the same; that through death He might destroy
him that had the power of death, that is the Devil,
and might deliver them who through fear of death were
all their lifetime subject to bondage." Heb. ii. 14,
15.

The fear of death holds many in thrall, for death, the most certain of events, seems to most men unnatural. Rom. vi. 23. " The wages of sin is death," says S. Paul; and there seems to be something penal both in the suffering which precedes it, and in the disruption of soul and Rom. iii. 23. body. We have all sinned, and the only Sinless One died by violence, so we cannot tell how sinless beings would pass out of the world, but judging from many Christian deathbeds it would seem that the passage might be joyous and not terrible.

Death, as we know it, is spoken of in Scripture as the kingdom of the Devil. It is a result of sin and no part of the divine order. Our Lord faced the facts in their true proportion when He said, " Be not afraid of them which kill the body, but are not able to kill S. Matt. x. the soul." He Himself faced the worst in the very 28. fullness of His human life, and " tasted death for every Heb. ii. 9. man."

Even if we cannot fully explain why His death is efficacious, we know that if He had not died He would not really have shared our lot or borne the burden of our sins; and we should not have been redeemed from the fear of death. As it is, we look forward to a joyous resurrection.

Physical death remains, but it is swallowed up in 1 Cor. xv. 54. His victory; and, since He died, Death is accepted by those that are His as discipline and not vengeance. To understand that victory we must believe with S. Paul, " Now is Christ risen from the dead, and become the firstfruits of them that slept. For since by man came death, by man came also the resurrection of the dead. For as in Adam all die, even so in Christ shall 1 Cor. xv. all be made alive." 20–22.

Before He came, men had speculated uneasily on

the subject. Is death a complete end, or does the soul survive in a shadowy existence to remember and regret? Is there a dread possibility of a reincarnation, and are we now in bondage to a past we can neither remember nor escape from? Is there a judgment hereafter; and before a righteous judge, who can hope to escape punishment? But for those who believe in Our Lord's Victory, life is one and continuous. " There is now no condemnation to them that are in Christ Jesus." They can say, " O death, where is thy sting! O grave, where is thy victory! The sting of death is sin; and the strength of sin is the law. But thanks be to God, which giveth us the Victory through Our Lord Jesus Christ."

Rom. viii. 1.

1 Cor. xv.
55–57.

His victory is our victory, and the Cross is the sign of our salvation.

CHAPTER IV

THE ONE OFFERING

I. GOD'S CLAIM TO HONOUR

HITHERTO we have thought of God's love in sending His Son with a message of reconciliation; and of Our Lord's Victory, won on our behalf, over sin, the world and the Devil. But we have spoken of Our Lord as the Mediator and must not forget that a Mediator represents both sides in an estrangement. God's side as well as man's side has to be considered if we would grasp the full significance of the Atonement. We cannot leave God's honour, God's sovereignty and God's purpose out of account, so long as we pray "Hallowed be Thy Name. Thy Kingdom come. Thy Will be done in earth, as it is in heaven."

S. Matt. vi. 9, 10.
S. Luke xv. 11–32.
S. Matt. xviii. 23–34.

The conditions of forgiveness may be learnt from the Parables of the Prodigal Son and The Unmerciful Servant, and the problems of forgiveness will be discussed in the next chapter. Man's redemption we have seen is due to the Victory of the Cross, and in Chapter VI we shall have to consider how the power which flows from the Crucified is appropriated by us. But before we can profitably do this, we must consider what we mean when we say, at the most solemn moment in the central act of our worship, that Our Lord's Death is "a full, perfect and sufficient sacrifice, oblation and satisfaction for the sins of the whole world."

There are many to-day who dislike these words. They say, God has manifested His love and desire to be reconciled with us, and therefore it is clear that He does not require to be propitiated. If God delights to forgive, it is obvious that God forgoes satisfaction; while the idea of an expiatory sacrifice is abhorrent to those who know that God is Love. Men think of God as a Being of infinite good-nature, kind and tolerant, Who understands all and will therefore pardon everything, Who is probably rather amused than otherwise by our naughty behaviour. This is an extreme reaction from a belief in the Sovereign Deity of awful holiness, Who, though merciful, loving and compassionate, will by no means spare the guilty.

The God of Good Nature is no doubt pleasing to the Sentimentalist, living an easy life and not wishing to be worried; but does such a Being call for our service or our worship, does such a Being even merit our respect? That God should tolerate sin may sometimes be a comfortable thought to the sinner, but it will not lead him to repentance or amendment. Such a God will afford no consolation to the one who is sinned against; and there are many appeals for justice and vindication presented before the throne in heaven. Can we really believe that a good God can look down with an indulgent smile, when the sins of men culminate in disasters like the recent war or the Russian Revolution? When we think of the injustice and cruelty in the world, of the lies and cheating, of the ruined men, the wronged women and the outraged children, are we content to worship a God Who is so good-natured that He does not punish?

If we go back to our Bibles, we find it a stern book.

Our Lord uttered terrible threats, and showed more than once His moral indignation. In the Bible we are taught to believe in a God Who hears our cries and enters into our sorrows, Who is terrible in His wrath Ex. xxxiv. 7. because divine in His compassion, Who, far from being indifferent to sin, came down from heaven to suffer, agonise and shed His Blood that sin might be remedied and men might have a chance of salvation. Such a God regards sin seriously and must Himself be seriously regarded.

If we think of God in this way we shall begin to understand that we have not only to be reconciled with God, but God has also to be reconciled to us. The well-known phrase, that God hates sin but loves the sinner, is at best a half truth. For sin proceeds from a will and you cannot at once reprobate a result, and at the same time approve the person who deliberately caused it, whatever excuses may be pleaded on the score of folly or ignorance. If there is nothing that is really evil but an evil will, and if we cannot separate a man's will from himself, God in condemning the sinful act must in some degree condemn the sinful agent.

It is true that God is ever ready to forgive us when we turn to Him and repent, but we should not forget that in a true repentance we are overwhelmed by the thought of God's love and goodness, and full of sorrow for having slighted and defied Him. We cry with the Psalmist, " Against Thee, Thee only, have I sinned, Ps. li. 4. and done this evil in Thy sight," even when a neighbour has been injured, for the neighbour was dear to God. Such a repentance includes a desire to make reparation, and no theory of the Atonement can satisfy the penitent which does not in some way vindicate

God's honour, affirm His sovereignty and manifest the necessity of obedience to His Will.   Men need not only forgiveness for their sins, not only redemption from the power of evil, but they desire communion and to be at one with God.   For this His Kingdom of Order must be restored, and right relations established, relations not only between God and ourselves, but also between us and our fellow men.

II. SIN REGARDED

(A) *As a Debt*

We have thought of sin as lawlessness and of some of the results which follow.   We have thought of how sin separates us from God and also from one another.   We have thought of how sin is a bondage from which we cannot by ourselves escape.   We must now think how sin constitutes us as debtors, and reduces us to be bankrupts who cannot pay.

In using this metaphor we have the authority of Our Lord, for it was He Who told us the Parable of the Unmerciful Servant, and taught us to pray, " Forgive us our debts, as we forgive our debtors."   The idea is quite obvious, and the fact that lies behind it is certain.

S. Matt. xviii. 23–34. S. Matt. vi. 12.

The God Who made all things and made them very good, made them for His glory and His joy.   If we think of men as God's servants, they owe Him service ; if we think of them as His sons, they owe Him reverence.   Because He has been bountiful, we should be grateful.   He pleads for our love and we should grant Him some response.   That the world, as we know it, is not what God intended is due to the fact that we have

I

been unmindful of our obligations, have wasted our Master's goods, and cheated our fellow servants. We have rebelled against our Father's authority, and deserted His Home. We have shown no gratitude for His kindness, His protection and His mercies. We have denied Him His meed of praise, and when we have endured the consequences of our own bad acts, we S. Matt. xxi. 33–39. S. Mark xii. 1–12. S. Luke xx. 9–19. have striven to saddle Him with the blame. We have been like the wicked husbandmen in the parable, and refused to pay the Master His share of the vintage. We have done worse, for having spent what was not our own, we cannot, even if we would, restore Him what is His.

But our debts are not only due to sins of commission. The God, Who does nothing foolish, has created us because He had something for us to do. We are part of His eternal purpose which embraces the entire 1 Cor. iii. 9. universe. But we are free to be fellow labourers with Him or to be idle. We may work with the assiduity of the man who makes ten talents, or we may despise the solitary talent which we have received, and think that our debt is satisfied if at the end we can say, S. Matt. xxv. 25. " Lo, there Thou hast that is Thine." But God regards us not merely as napkins to retain His gifts, but as labourers bound to use them, and He will take account with His servants at the end. If we may S. Luke xvi. 19–31. S. Luke xix. 12–27. S. Matt. xxv. 14–30. S. Matt. xxv. 1–13. S. Matt. xxv. 41. S. Matt. xxv. 45. judge from the Parables of Dives and Lazarus, the Pounds, the Talents and the Ten Virgins, sins of omission are not easily pardoned. In the picture of the great Assize, " Depart, ye cursed," is said to those who failed to do their work. " Inasmuch as ye did it not to one of the least of these, ye did it not to Me."

When we awake to the thought of our debts towards God, we also realise that we have no means of paying them. We cannot undo the past, and we can do but little to avert the consequences. Moreover, as it is our duty at all times to serve and worship God, our debt would not be diminished if we turned over a new leaf and were dutiful ever after. We should still be unprofitable servants. But every debtor also knows _{S. Luke} how his debts are embarrassments, and hinder his _{xvii. 10.} work. Old debts are a handicap even when we are not contracting new ones. They take the heart out of our endeavours, they are a burden which bears us down. Our only hope is that we may be forgiven and permitted a fresh start. In the next chapter we shall see how our burdens may be laid down at the foot of the Cross, and our debts may be cancelled. In this chapter we must concentrate our minds on the fact that something was owing to God, which He ought to receive. He created man for a purpose which we have not fulfilled. Has God failed and will He be eternally disappointed in man? That is inconceivable if God be God. What then? Does God find in the death of Our Lord as man His sufficient satisfaction?

III. Sin Regarded

(B) *As a Dishonour Done to God*

Sin is not only a debt which we acknowledge by implication every time we pray, " Thy Will be done in earth, as it is in heaven "; but sin is also a dis- _{S. Matt. vi.} honour done to God, which we repudiate when we pray _{9–10.} " Hallowed be Thy Name."

Not only do the Heavens declare the glory of God; _{Ps. xix. 1.} but the earth is the Lord's and all that is therein; _{Ps. xxiv. 1.} _{Ps. cxv. 16.} and the earth He has given to the children of men.

But Nature complains of man's destructiveness, and the whole animal creation complains of man's cruelty: Job xxxviii. 7. we have betrayed our trust. At creation " all the Sons of God shouted for joy," and cannot we imagine the sorrow of the angels as we disfigure and deface what God meant to be beautiful in its season? As the smoke from our great cities hangs like a pall between us and the sun; so has God's glory been hidden by the clouds of sin. The clouds must be dissipated if all the works of the Lord are to praise Him.

Then think of man's complaints against his fellows, who were " created in the image of God," and should reflect somewhat of His radiance. Think of the cynic's contempt for humanity, think how the satirist lashes man's foibles and man's meanness, think how the pessimist despairs of man's future, and how to all there comes the ultimate and inevitable question, " Why has God made us, and made us thus? "

Men go on seeking their own ends, heedless of God's purpose and in defiance of His law. Then comes the inevitable crash in a great domestic sorrow, in the terrors of war or the horrors of a revolution; and men do not repent, but ask, " Why does God permit it? " So all the piled up agony of the world is laid at the door of God. We excuse ourselves in accusing Him; and we excuse ourselves as Adam did when He said, " the woman whom *Thou* gavest to be with me, she Gen. iii. 12. gave me of the tree, and I did eat." Think of the ruined man, the man in pain, the man who has suffered from some great injustice. His whole being is in revolt against the world. He cries to God, " How long, O Rev. vi. 10. Lord, how long! " but he has ceased to believe in God's intervention, he has ceased to believe that God cares.

As we listen to the man who has been wronged, we

indorse with burning hearts his plea for justice; but do
we not also sympathise with the man who has injured
him, if we overhear him beseeching God's forgiveness
for the wrong which he cannot undo.   We lift up our
hearts to heaven and think of God's honour, for neither
the sinner nor the one sinned against has hallowed
His Holy Name.   We feel a terrible darkness en-
folding us and we cannot see our way, and then
out of the darkness comes a voice from Calvary—
" Behold Me !   Is any sorrow like unto My sorrow ? " _{Lam. i. 12.}

Is it the voice of God, Who came down from Heaven
to suffer with us in our sins ?   Yes, it is.   But it is
also the voice of man making His perfect act of
reparation to the dishonoured Father on behalf of the
family which had disgraced Him.   Our Lord, we say,
is perfect God and perfect Man, but do not let us
forget that He is One Christ.   When we think of
Him as saying, " Is any sorrow like unto My sorrow ? "
He is speaking as the Mediator in the hearing of God
and men, and His words have a meaning Godward as
well as manward.   We think not only of His suffering,
but of His sorrow for our sins.

Our Lord, Who had identified Himself with men,
yet without sin, acquiesced in the mystery, which we
cannot fathom, of God's moral government of the
world, by enduring patiently what man in his sin
caused Him to bear.   In some sense the solidarity of
mankind is a fact, and therefore the consequences of
sin fall alike on the innocent and the guilty.   This was
taken for granted in the old world, when the individual
was of no account, but it is a stumbling block in these
days of rampant individualism.   It may, however,
be suggested that the greatest deterrent to wrongdoing is the knowledge that it involves others beside

ourselves; and the final test of comradeship is our willingness to suffer with those whom we love, when we have not been partakers in their iniquities.

IV. Sin Regarded
(C) *As Deserving Punishment*

We owe God service and should hallow His Name; and, inasmuch as we have not done our duty, we deserve to be punished. God's justice is vindicated when He forgives some and punishes others directly or indirectly. His severity and mercy alike proceed from a heart of love; and we must believe in both or in neither. Forgiveness has no meaning for those who refuse to believe that their sins deserve to be punished, for had no punishment been deserved, no forgiveness had been necessary. This must be insisted on, for most theories of the Atonement have broken down through wrong views on the subject of punishment.

Some would confuse God's punishment of men with the inevitable consequences of our actions, and try to interpret the moral government of the world in accordance with the laws of physical science. Others, who admit that punishment always involves a person who punishes, would attribute its prevalence in the world to the instinct of self-preservation. Others, again, see that no punishment can be morally justified without considering the person punished. In consequence, they argue that punishment should be remedial. It should correct the offender or deter him from repeating the offence, or should be exemplary—a warning to others who might commit the same crimes.

But punishment is not to be confused with consequences, for sin is not merely the breaking of a law, but disobedience to a lawgiver, and punishment is not merely the automatic result of lawlessness, but involves the moral judgment of the person who has been disobeyed. To emphasise this fact, the State does not attempt to make the punishment fit the crime. Only barbarians rely on the *Lex Talionis*—an eye for an eye and a tooth for a tooth. Every civilised community decrees its penalties in such a way as to express its moral indignation.

Ex. xxi. 24.
Lev. xxiv.
20.
S. Matt. v.
28.

Secondly, although sin is destructive of social life, punishment does not arise from the lower instinct of self-preservation, but from that higher instinct, which we may call the conscience of the community. That conscience may indeed be very ill-informed, but when the populace clamour for punishment, it is nearly always because they are convinced that it has been deserved.

Thirdly, all good men hope that the punishments they inflict may have salutary results, and wise men will not decree penalties which will hinder the reformation of the criminal; but, at the same time, we must remember that punishment is only awarded because of something which has been done. Its primary reference is to the past and not to the future.

Our conception of punishment, therefore, may be summarised as follows. It is a penalty inflicted by a person on a person. It is inflicted to express moral indignation for something which has been done. And punishment, strictly considered, is an end in itself— it provides a recompense.

At once it will be asked, How is it to be distinguished from revenge? We reply that a man by revenging himself perpetrates an equivalent or greater wrong for one he has received; and it is obvious that he does not abominate the evil, but is angry because he has suffered from it. Human nature being what it is, no man should be the judge in his own cause, and no man may take the law into his own hands. We do, however, allow a father to chastise his disobedient child, trusting in the father's love; and it is because we trust in the love of the All Father that we welcome His declaration—" Vengence is Mine, I will repay."

Deut. xxii. 25.
Rom. xii. 19.
Heb. x. 30.

However sentimentalists may rail at retributive justice, it accords with instincts deep down in the hearts of men. We know that we are moral beings and therefore responsible for our acts. We can only be responsible to a person, and if punishment be a personal act we can believe also in mercy and pardon; but if we substitute consequences for punishment, there is then no room for forgiveness. Nature, as we know it from scientific report, is inexorable.

Secondly, the idea of desert runs all through life and gives it a meaning. We form judgments and desire judgments. Our work merits praise or blame, and when praise and blame are translated into action they become rewards and punishments. A person who is indifferent to evil or acquiesces in its triumphs cannot be good; and every healthy-minded man says, " Serve him right," when some cruel brute, who has tortured others, receives his deserts.

Thirdly, most children do not resent punishment when they feel it is just, but they resent bitterly any reference to their sin afterwards. By enduring the punishment, they feel that they have expiated the offence, the account is closed. It is clear that they regard punishment as an end in itself.

Conscious, however, how imperfect human justice is, men seek for God. In the Old Testament they are

told of One " great in counsel and mighty in work,
Whose eyes are open upon all the ways of the sons
of men : to give everyone according to his ways, and
according to the fruit of his doings." In the New _{Jer. xxxii. 19.}
Testament, Our Lord asks, " Shall not God avenge His
elect, which cry to Him day and night, and He is longsuffering over them ? I say unto you, that He will
avenge them speedily." _{S. Luke xviii. 7, 8.}

So men cry to God for justice, and are confident that
in the end He will right every wrong. He is full of
compassion for those who are oppressed; and will be
terrible to those who make His little ones to stumble. _{S. Mark ix. 42.}
Sin is lawlessness and He is the God of order. Sin
is selfishness and He is the God of Love. His laws
are not arbitrary for He is righteous. In the interests
of His whole creation, He demands obedience. He is
" the God of Knowledge, and by Him actions are
weighed." _{1 Sam. ii. 3.}

But, when we pray to God for justice and the vindication of His law, we condemn ourselves, for we have
all sinned and come short of what we were meant to _{Rom. iii. 23.}
be—we worthily deserve to be punished. However, to
approve of punishment in the abstract is one thing and
to endure it willingly is another. That requires
courage and a spirit of submission which is not
possessed by all.

And yet the desire for expiation is much more deeply
rooted than many modern moralists suppose. Men,
moved by remorse, have inflicted horrible punishments
upon themselves. They have committed suicide, like
Judas Iscariot. Such instances of self-torture and self-
destruction are sometimes attributed to the desire of
propitiating some divinity; but they are really an
acknowledgment that sin deserves punishment; and

men endure self-imposed pain because they cannot forgive themselves.

Such people will not be helped by being told to believe in an evolutionary process through which good will ultimately prevail, for they know that they are in bondage to their own past, and they are convinced that some expiation must be offered. The only hope for them is to find God, the God Who knows their sin and hates it, Who knows why they sinned and feels with them in their shame, Who in spite of all loves them. When they find such a God they will know that it is for Him to punish and for them to submit, that He is inspired by love, and that a new life is possible.

So the penitent man thinks not only of punishment by God, but also of forgiveness. He longs to be restored to God's favour and communion. This desire is common to all religious minded men of all ages; but they are perplexed as to the way. They desire that their debt to God should be paid, and that reparation should be offered to God for the dishonour they have done Him, and that they themselves, notwithstanding their past, should become worthy of being His sons. But how dare they approach Him? The answer comes from the four quarters of the world, through sacrifice; and then comes the terrible doubt, is any sacrifice adequate for the purpose? Man cannot save himself, still less can he save his brother Ps. xlix. 7. or make any agreement with God for him. He wants a perfect sacrifice that will be availing, not only for himself, but for a sin-laden world. We Christians believe in "the Lamb of God Who taketh away the S.John i. 29. sins of the world"; but before we can understand such a faith, we must be clear about the ideas underlying the sacrificial system.

V. Man's Approach to God in Sacrifice

When we think of the difference between the creature and the Creator, we know that man can only approach God in worship. Secondly, if God be good and man a sinner, man knows that in his sin he cannot be accepted by God, and strives in some way to free himself from guilt. Thirdly, he would not only worship God afar off, but desires to have communion with Him, to enter as far as possible into His thoughts, share His life, and experience the fruits of His love. Communion with God is the end of life. It means being at one with the Author and Ruler of all. It means being at one with oneself, and, in a unified existence, enjoying the peace which passeth all understanding.

Wherever such ideas and such desires exist they must find some outward expression. Man has a body as well as a soul; and both belong to God. Man, moreover, is a social being; and, if God be the Father of all, it is in the family that He must be worshipped. Man can only express himself through the body and by means of material things, if he would be intelligible to his fellows, or even intelligible to himself. So in all ages and in most religions there has been sacrificial worship. It arises out of very simple ideas, it is capable of endless complexity and adaptation, it can be explained in a variety of ways, and is subject to horrible perversions. Everything really depends on the worshipper's conception of God and his own moral attitude towards Him. Two men bring an offering to God, one intends it as an act of Homage, a sign of his submission to the Sovereign will, the other hopes by his offering to purchase God's favour and so get his own way in the world. Two men agree that they should offer to God what they consider best and is most costly, but the conception of God that one has is so low that he thinks He will best be pleased with what entails the most exquisite tortures to the victim Micah vi. 7. and perhaps to the worshipper also. One man will bring a sin offering as an expression of his penitence and as an act of self-denial to show his desire to make some reparation; another will bring the same offering with the desire of averting punishment and with the thought that God may be bought off. Men may believe that communion with God is possible through sacrifice, but the character of the worship will depend on the God Who is worshipped, and there is little connection between a Passover Feast and orgiastic ecstasies or Bacchanalian frenzies. One man may believe that sacrifice works of itself, and that the worshipper has only to be careful about the correctness of the ritual; another will know that God looks not so much on the gift as on the giver, and that moral dispositions are of primary importance.

We have no space to discuss heathen sacrifices, and we should learn from them but little towards understanding Our Lord's sacrifice of Himself; for though in many cases the ritual of Jew and Gentile was identical, yet, to the writers of the New Testament, 1 Cor. x. 21. pagan altars were only " the tables of devils." We will restrict ourselves to the Old Testament as it was received by those who wrote the New, and this will free us from any necessity of determining the dates of particular texts, or the historical development of Jewish ritual. The altar forms and sacrificial terms used by New Testament writers were derived from a living system, which they believed to be ordained by God Himself. In the Old and New Testament alike it is God Who appeals to man; it is God Who proposes the Covenant between men and Himself; and it is in accordance with God's will that sacrifice is offered.

VI. Man's Approach to God in Sacrifice

(A) *The Burnt Offering*

To bestow a gift is the obvious thing which occurs to everyone who loves or reverences another. For an Oriental it is also the recognised way of approach to a superior. The gift may indeed be thought of as tribute, but it always implies his homage, and testifies to his submission. The earliest of all sacrifices were probably honorific in character. Men approached God as they would an earthly superior, and their hands were not empty when doing so. The gift in a pastoral community came naturally from the flock or the herd. The Whole Burnt Offering might consist Lev. i. of a bullock, a ram, a goat, a pair of pigeons, or even a little meal, according to the wealth of the worshipper —the value of the gift was of no consequence; everything depended on the willingness of the giver. The offering, however, had to be his own, for no one dare give to God what had cost him nothing. It had to be 1 Sam. xxiv. 24. without blemish, and given without reserve. If the 1 Chron. xxi. 24. offering were an animal, the worshipper had to kill, flay and cut it up himself, for it was to be his act. The beast was to be killed as mercifully as possible, and there was apparently no significance attached to its death; but the blood was sprinkled by the priest about the altar, so there was in the ceremony something to symbolise a dedicated life. The priest made the offering at the altar, and the whole sacrifice was Lev. i. 11, 12.

Lev. ii. 1 ff. burnt. It was offered with fine flour, oil and incense, and the smoke from the sacrifice ascended as a sweet Lev. i. 17. savour unto the Lord.

Such was the Burnt Offering, and it suggests why S. Paul writes, " Christ . . . gave Himself up for us, Eph. v. 2. an offering and a sacrifice to God for an odour of a sweet smell."

VII. Man's Approach to God in Sacrifice

(B) *The Sin Offering*

It is a joyous thing to offer a gift to someone whom you love, and to think of the pleasure with which it will be received. It is a pitiful thing to remember that there is someone whom you still love, but who is rightly offended with you. You dare no longer appear in his presence with the offering of your affection, for you know yourself to be unworthy, but perhaps he will allow some offering, which has caused you pain and self-denial, to represent your penitence. It will at least show your desire to make amends. That is the idea which lies behind the Sin Offering.

Lev. iv. The Sin Offering for the High Priest or for the whole Lev. iv. 3, 22, 27. congregation was a bullock, for a ruler was a kid and for ordinary men was either a kid or a lamb. The Sin Offering, unlike the Burnt Offering, could not be multiplied, so there was no excuse for thinking that so much sin could be compensated for by so many sacrifices. There was only one offering for sin. The Num. v. 7. sinner was instructed to confess his sin over the head of the victim, which was in some way thought to represent himself. The beast was slain and if the offerer were a priest, or a priest officiating as the representative of the whole congregation, the blood was applied to the horns of the golden altar within the Holy Place, poured out at the foot of the altar, and sprinkled seven times before the veil, because the atonement had to be made for those who were consecrated to serve within the sanctuary. In ordinary Lev. iv. 7. cases the blood was sprinkled on the worshipper and then applied to the horns of the brazen altar in the outer court, where the laity worshipped. Certain Lev. iv. 30. specified parts of the victim were solemnly burnt; and, if a priest offered the sacrifice, the rest was burnt without the camp, symbolising the discrimination of God, Who can still accept what is good even in sinners, though what is evil is doomed to destruction. If a layman offered, the same parts were offered to God on the altar with the same intention, but the rest became the food of the priests, who were commanded to consume it within the precincts, for in feeding on the sacrifice over which confession of Lev. vi. 26. sin had been made, they were reminded of their mediatorial position. They not only offered for sin but were in some sense sin bearers.

Lastly, it is well to remember that these sin offerings Num. xv. 27. were for sins of physical and ritual uncleanliness, for sins of inadvertence or ignorance; but for pre- Num. xv. 30. sumptuous sins deliberately committed there was no Deut. xvii. 12. atoning sacrifice. The wages of such sin was death. The whole elaborated system was for what we should now call venial sins, and was designed to bring home to the people how heinous was all sin to God, Whose eyes were too holy to behold iniquity. But we shall Hab. i. 13. have to go on and consider how "Christ was once offered to bear the sins of many." He was the true Heb. ix. 28. sacrifice for sin; and "by one offering He hath perfected for ever them that are sanctified." Heb. x. 14.

VIII. MAN'S APPROACH TO GOD IN SACRIFICE

(C) *The Peace Offering*

If men felt that they owed a duty to God their Creator and Lord, and offered Him the Burnt Offering in token of homage; if they tried to make reparation for their neglect of Him and manifold shortcomings, in the hope that He might be propitiated, they also longed for real communion, that they and God might be at one. In ordinary life the test of friendship is the meal eaten in common. The man who will not feed with you cannot be your friend. This idea was even more emphasised among Orientals. They have always thought that those who ate together of the same food were in some sense made one. What then could be more natural than the ritual of the Peace Offerings, Thank Offerings and Free Will Offerings.

Lev. iii.

In all of these the victim was dedicated to God and slain; and its blood was sprinkled as in other sacrifices. It was then divided into three parts—one was burnt on the altar, one belonged to the priests, and one was returned to the worshipper that he might feast on it with his household and his friends. The priests' portion was heaved and waved before the Lord, and the whole offering belonged to God. It was therefore God's feast, and in S. Paul's phrase " they which eat of the sacrifices were partakers of the altar." The worshipper was to be hospitable and not frugal in his entertainment, so it was ordained that nothing was to remain until the third day, or all that was over was to be consumed by fire.

Lev. vii. 31-33.

Lev. vii. 34.

1 Cor. x. 18.

Lev. vii. 15-17.
Lev. xix. 5-7.

The Passover was the great Thank Offering, commemorating the deliverance from Egypt, and had a ritual proper for the occasion. It also found its con-

Ex. xii. xiii.
Lev. xxiii.

summation in a Communion feast, where the youngest
asked the reason, and the eldest told the story which _{Ex. xii 26,} Ex. xii 26,
27.
occasioned the Commemoration.   It was during the Ex. xiii. 8.
Passover Feast that Our Lord suffered.   His was the
great deliverance, and His broken body and poured
out blood was for the sustenance of all His Church.
As S. Paul says, " Christ, our Passover, is sacrificed
for us : therefore let us keep the Feast."   1 Cor. v. 7, 8.

IX. MAN'S APPROACH TO GOD IN SACRIFICE

(D) *The Day of Atonement*

Men had not only a duty which they owed to God,
and a reparation to offer God for their neglect of Him ;
they likewise desired communion with God, and a place
where that communion might be held.   The individual
was not merely concerned with his own virtues and
vices, he was a social being, he belonged to a nation and
he believed that nation to be the chosen people of God.
But the world was lying in wickedness, and he could
only meet with God in a Holy Place.   A central 1 S. John v.
19.
sanctuary had to be set apart if the unity of the nation
and its worship was to be preserved.   Not only the Deut. xii.
5–14.
place, but the people also as a people needed consecra-
tion.   They were to be the people of God and in consequence separated from all the nations on the earth.
We must understand these ideas if we would enter into
the Ritual of the Day of Atonement.

This day of national Atonement was a day of fasting
and prayer and no work was permitted to be done.   It
began with the customary burnt offerings ; and then
the High Priest clad in linen garments confessed his Lev. xvi. 8.
own sins over a bullock, slew it himself, and carried the

K

Lev. xvi. 12. blood under a cloud of incense into the Holy of Holies Lev. xvi. 8. and sprinkled it towards the mercy seat. Having Lev. xvi. 9. made an atonement for himself, he returned to cast lots on two goats. The chosen one was then sacri- Lev. xvi. 15. ficed; and the High Priest again visited the Holy of Holies, in order to make atonement for the people. The Holy Place, the golden altar of incense, the brazen altar without, and the court of the temple were then Lev. xvi. 18-20. sanctified with blood; the ordinary parts of the victim were burnt as in the sin offering at the altar, and the rest burnt without the camp. Then the priest con- fessed the national sins over the live goat, which was Lev. xvi. 21. sent away into the wilderness for Azazel. Lastly, the High Priest arrayed himself in his gorgeous garments, Lev. xvi. 24. and offered peace offerings. Leviticus sums up the objects of the ritual, saying of the High Priest, " He shall make an atonement for the holy sanctuary, and he shall make an atonement for the tabernacle of the congregation, and for the altar, and he shall make an atonement for the priests, and for all the people of Lev. xvi. 33. the congregation."

No full rationale of the ceremonies need be given. It is sufficient to point out, (1) that it was a local sanctuary and a peculiar people which were conse- crated : (2) that the ritual had to be repeated every year, and that therefore the Covenant with God was of a temporary character : (3) that the High Priest was himself a sinner and could only act after making a public confession, and offering a sin offering for him- self : (4) and that the sins symbolically transferred to the scapegoat were put away but not destroyed— they were symbolically driven out of the Temple that it might be ritually clean.

It was only through Our Lord's Atonement that

the whole world was reconsecrated for God's worship, so that in every place men might worship the Father. ^{S. John iv. 21-23.} Salvation indeed was of the Jews, and Our Lord came as the Son of David; but as the great High Priest, after the Order of Melchizedek, He offered His sacrifice for the sins of the whole world. He needed to ^{Heb. vii. 26-28.} make no confession for Himself, and He passed into no earthly sanctuary, but into Heaven itself with the Blood of the New Covenant to intercede on our behalf. ^{Heb. ix. 11, 12.} There was no need that His sacrifice should ever be repeated. It was offered once for all. Sins were no ^{Heb. x. 11, 12.} longer merely to be put out of sight, but were to be forgiven. He died that the power of sin and sinfulness might be destroyed.

X. The Mystery of Blood

If we regard sin as a debt, the whole burnt offering was at least an acknowledgment of something due to God. If we think of the dishonour done to God by sin, the sin offering expressed men's willingness to make reparation. If, in spite of sin, men still yearned for communion with God, the peace and thankofferings provided the means of approach. But in all these sacrifices it is necessary to note the importance of blood. It consecrated, expiated, cleansed and propitiated; and so we read in the Epistle to the Hebrews, " according to the Law, I may almost say, all things are cleansed with blood, and apart from shedding of blood there is no remission."   ^{Heb. ix. 22.}

Volumes have been written on this subject, and the study of comparative religions has multiplied the evidence and been productive of new theories, but the mystery of blood remains a mystery which cannot be rationalised. The Israelites indeed were taught in Leviticus, "the life of all flesh is the blood, and I have given it upon the altar to make atonement for your souls, for the blood maketh atonement by reason Lev. xvii. 11. of the life." The sacrifices were therefore regarded as of God's appointment, and were not human devices to excite His favour; and so we may argue that the application of blood was sacramental—an outward sign ordained by God as a means of grace—and rationalising on the subject is inappropriate. Men may indeed ask us to give a reason for what we do; but it is a sufficient answer to say that God commands it. A man is not irrational who obeys a superior when he does not understand the reason of the command. Secondly, we may conclude that the sacrifice was regarded essentially as offering a life. The life was in the blood; and, by slaying the victim, the life was set free, in order that it might be applied on behalf of those who offered it. Thirdly, the original meaning of *Kipper* or atonement was a covering; and so the thought arose, that the living worshipper, in his unworthiness, approached the holy God, covered as with a veil by the life of another; *i.e.*, by the blood of the innocent animal. This interpretation provides a clue to what the author of the Epistle to the Hebrews meant when he spoke of "entering into the Holy Place by the blood of Jesus, by the way which He dedicated for us, a new and living way, through the Heb. x. 19, veil, that is to say, His flesh." It is Our Lord's life 20. which has become our way, and it is by the offering of His life and the shedding of the blood that we are united with Him. His blood atones for us, and is a S. Matt. xxii. veil like the marriage garment in the parable—the 11–13. gift of the king to adorn and cover the guest, who comes in rags to his entertainment.

XI. The Efficacy of Levitical Sacrifices

The sacrificial systems of other religions need not be considered, for they exercised no influence on the development of Christian theology. The Levitical code is, on the other hand, important, because the writers of the New Testament, when they began to interpret the death of Our Lord, naturally derived their metaphors and analogies from the sacrificial system with which they were familiar. How far were these sacrifices in themselves efficacious, for it is impossible to think of them merely as types pointing to an event, which those who offered them did not anticipate?

It is obvious that God was not enriched by men's gifts, for " the Lord of heaven and earth dwelleth not in temples made with hands; neither is worshipped with men's hands as though he needed any thing." Acts xvii. 24, 25. He can say, " Every beast of the forest is mine, and the cattle upon a thousand hills." It is equally Ps. l. 10. obvious that of themselves " the blood of bulls and goats cannot take away sins "; while the answer is Heb. x. 4. also obvious when God asks, " Thinkest thou that I will eat bulls' flesh, and drink the blood of goats? " Ps. l. 13. What then are we to conclude? Had the sacrifices no objective value, and did they merely symbolise the devout aspirations of the worshippers?

Our answer to this question depends on whether we believe that the sacrifices were man's device, or due to the command of God, just as our belief in the value of Christian sacraments depends on whether we regard them as symbols of man's faith, or as conveying God's grace in His own appointed way. We have seen that the teaching of Leviticus is clear on this point, and must therefore regard the sacrifices as outward and

visible signs of inward and spiritual grace, given to
the Jews by the ordinance of God; and we may add
that though sins were not done away, there was a
real " passing over of the sins done aforetime, in the
forbearance of God." He Who prescribed the gifts,
accepted the offerings. He Who demanded the sin
offering really cleansed those who pleaded it. He
who made the feast for His people, in a spiritual sense
shared it. The sacrifices were indeed imperfect.
The gifts, like those of a little child to his mother, were
only valuable because of the spirit in which they were
offered. Men came, saying, like David, " All things
come of Thee, and of Thine own have we given Thee."
There was no sin offering for presumptuous sins—
only a hope in the uncovenanted mercies of God,
" that a broken and a contrite heart He would not
despise." There was a real communion with God,
but it was not free because of sin which deserved
punishment. Men aspired to know God, but being in
His presence, cried like Isaiah, " Woe is me ! for I
am undone, because I am a man of unclean lips, and
I dwell in the midst of a people of unclean lips."

The sacrifices then were efficacious but imperfect.
God was training mankind, and providing for their
needs as they arose. God gave the Law, God sent
His Son, God indwells His Church. He is the One
God Who changes not, and down through the centuries
we may trace the correspondences, which reveal one
purpose and the consistency of one mind, amid all
the diversities of human life and its conditions.

Rom. iii. 25.

1 Chron.
xxix. 14.

Ps. li. 17.

Isa. vi. 5.

XII. The Prophetic Standpoint

Social life and united worship alike necessitate
ceremonies and external acts of religious devotion.
So the laws of true worship were preserved and illustrated in the sacrificial system of the Jews. Through
the eye and ear, by act and by gesture, men were
taught, and the great drama of God and humanity
was rehearsed and revealed. But all external worship
has its dangers. Custom dulls perception, and forms
cease to represent realities; Superstition intervenes,
careful about forms and careless of their significance;
while Magic is ever lurking in the way, to steal the
treasures of religion and satisfy her base desires.
Religion is destroyed when ritual is divorced from life.

It was natural for men to bring God gifts, conscious
of their debt to Him, and anxious to testify their
obedience. But the customary gift became a form,
men cared only that it was made in the prescribed
way, and began to delude themselves that the God
Who accepted their offering had no other claim on
their obedience. They had to be reminded that " To
obey is better than sacrifice, and to hearken than the
fat of rams." It was natural for men to make sin 1 Sam. xv.
offerings, which entailed self-denial and confession; 22.
but the man, who conceived that it was a transaction
to avert God's punishment, had to be adjured to
wash and be clean, to cease from evil and do well. Isa. i. 16.
It was natural to elaborate feasts to commemorate
God's mercies, but, as with our own Christmastide
festivities, it was possible to celebrate the feast and
forget God, so that Isaiah represents God as saying,
" Your new moons and your appointed feasts my
soul hateth." It was natural to reverence Holy Isa. i. 14.

Places and adorn them; but great churches may only be expressions of national pride, and there is an awful irony in Hosea's words—" Israel hath forgotten his Maker, and buildeth Temples."

Hos. viii. 14.

Throughout the Prophets and the Psalms there are frequent denunciations of the formal worship of those who served God in unrighteousness. The Prophets were full of ethical enthusiasm and zealous for national purity; they longed for a day when " judgment should run down as waters, and righteousness as a mighty stream." When the priesthood was corrupt, and the ritual without life, it was natural that Reformers were not " ecclesiastically minded "; but the opposition between Priest and Prophet has been very much exaggerated. Even a Psalm like the fiftieth, which seems to be contemptuous of sacrifices, has the verse—" Offer unto God thanksgiving; and pay thy vows unto the Most High." Even the fifty-first Psalm, with its insistence on " truth in the inward parts," on repentance and the value of a contrite heart, ends with the words—" Then shalt thou be pleased with the sacrifices of righteousness, with burnt offering and whole burnt offering : then shall they offer bullocks upon Thine altar." No prophet is more unsparing than Isaiah, who asks " to what purpose is the multitude of your sacrifices? " who calls the oblation " vain," the incense " an abomination," and the feasts " hateful "; but it should be noted, he equally condemns the sabbaths and the prayers which he says God will not hear. It is obvious that it is not the cult which is condemned, but the men whose sins were as scarlet, who without repentance dared to offer worship unto God. Amos, the herdman of Tekoa, is equally emphatic when face to face with the schis-

Amos v. 24.

Ps. l. 14.

Ps. li. 6.

Ps. li. 19.

Isa. i. 11.

Isa. i. 13.

Isa. i. 18.

matic worship at Dan and Bethel; but there is no word against sacrificial worship. Jeremiah insists on the priority of the Decalogue, and finds in it, and not in sacrifice, the real covenant with God. This represents one side of the truth, but we must not forget that when Jeremiah tells of the restoration, he says, " Neither shall the priests the Levites want a man before Me to offer burnt offerings, and to kindle meat offerings, and to do sacrifice continually." Lastly, in Deuteronomy we find the Priestly and Prophetic teaching reconciled; and in Ezekiel, who was priest and prophet, we find an ardent ritualist, who insists on inward righteousness, and goes beyond all others in determining individual responsibility.

But it was during the Captivity that the prophetic soul of the second Isaiah was inspired with the vision of the perfect sacrifice, which the Servant of Jehovah should offer on behalf of His people. It was to be a sacrifice of God's appointment, for " the Lord was to lay on Him the iniquities of us all." But the Victim was to be a willing one, who would not open his mouth to complain, who would suffer until the end, and " pour out His soul unto death." He was to be perfectly innocent, " One who had done no violence, neither was any deceit in His mouth." He was to be " led as a Lamb to the slaughter," " to be numbered with the transgressors," to bear their sins, " to suffer for their iniquities," and to intercede on their behalf. Through this sacrifice many were to be justified, and by his stripes men were to be healed. Lastly, although to onlookers He would seem " stricken, smitten of God and afflicted," He would after being " cut off from the land of the living," none the less " see His seed, and prolong His days." His work

Amos iii. 14.
Amos iv. 45.
Amos v. 4-6.
Jer. vii. 21-23.
Cp. vi. 20.

Jer. xxxiii. 18.
Deut.
Ezek. xl.
xlviii.

Esp. Ezek. xviii.

Isa. liii.

would not be fruitless, for " He would see of the travail of His soul and be satisfied."

Isaiah, pondering on the nature of sacrifice, had grasped what sin involved, what a sin offering should be, and interpreted the old ritual in the terms of personality.

XIII. THE SYSTEM OF WORSHIP IN OUR LORD'S DAY

It may be thought that when Our Lord came into the world it was less ready to receive Him than in the days when the second Isaiah wrote his " Golden Passional." But this would be a mistake. Isaiah was an inspired genius; and, as such, belonged to no age and certainly did not reflect the mind of his contemporaries. When we survey the history of thought concerning sin and sacrifice, his prophecy stands forth as a shining peak in the far distance, but Our Lord came in the fullness of time, when the sacrifice was most needed and could be best understood.

Multitudes of the Jews were dispersed in many lands, who had never or rarely seen the ritual, which could only be celebrated at Jerusalem. Men, born at Tarsus or Alexandria, had grown up with a knowledge of the Levitical code long before they saw it in operation. They were accustomed to the use of sacrificial language and had thought out its implications, and found it, in consequence, much easier to apply the ideas to Our Lord's death than if they had gained their first impressions from the material altar and the smoking holocausts.

But the old religion was very visible in the splendid Temple built by the pagan Herod, rather to his own glory than to God's. Never was the ritual more punctually performed, or the services of the Temple more efficiently organised, or the accessories of worship more gorgeous and complete. Antiquaries and lawyers settled the minutest points with meticulous precision. The Temple was the focus of Judaism, the sacrifices witnessed to the proud traditions of a long descended race, the priesthood formed a well endowed aristocracy with conservative views and an almost cynical worldliness. The ancestral ceremonies celebrated with such pomp redounded to their credit, but the God of Holiness was well-nigh forgotten. The God Who was worshipped was the Deity Who had chosen Israel as His peculiar people and granted to them privileges in which no other nation shared, so long as they kept the Law.

The Law indeed was spiritual, but those who administered it were not. The sacrifices had once expressed the worship and religious needs of the people, they had come to require for their elucidation the researches of antiquaries. The sacrifices were ceasing to be sacrifices in any real sense, and were becoming spectacles. Life had died out of the old forms and needed to be renewed; but it was impossible to pour new wine into the old bottles. A new sacrifice was needed as the basis of a new covenant, for that which existed had waxen old, and was ready to vanish away. Heb. viii. 13.

If worship was conducted by the Sadducee, instruction was assumed by the Pharisee, who at least insisted on conduct and the performance of good works. But his very insistence on personal righteousness made him forget that he needed a Saviour. He became self-centred and devoted to self-culture. He ended by being self-satisfied and contented with his own merit. He came before God to pray; and thanked Him that he was not as other men were, extortioners, unjust, adulterers, or even as this Publican. For morality apart from religion at best produces prigs, and often leads to hypocrisy.

S. Luke xviii. 10–14.

Both Ritualists and Moralists were dominated by the Law, and their spiritual life was strangled in the bonds of many obligations. God had given the Law, but the Lawgiver was forgotten. The Law was regarded as impersonal; and an impersonal Law can only be interpreted according to its letter. So what had once been done in loyalty to God ended in being a routine, supposed to be admirable in itself. What had been designed for social life and corporate worship ended in differentiating men, so that the Pharisee said, "This people which knoweth not the Law is cursed." Ordinances intended to express man's dependence on God, or his repentance for rebelling against Him, ended in a ceremonial celebrated by those who congratulated themselves on their ritual propriety.

S. John vii. 49.

Conduct is not nine-tenths of religion, it should be the fruit of faith. Religion has to do with persons, with the relation between God and men. Religion dies when rules of ritual or rules of conduct are substituted for the communion of Spirit with Spirit. The second Isaiah, we have seen, had reinterpreted sacrifice in the terms of Personality. It remained for a Person to come and offer Himself as a Sacrifice. The Son came and offered Himself to the Father on behalf of those whom He called His brethren.

XIV. Our Lord's Life and Death of Sacrifice

(A) *His Utter Obedience*

The author of the Epistle to the Hebrews quotes the fortieth psalm and applies it to Our Lord :— Sacrifice and offering Thou wouldest not, but a body didst Thou prepare for Me; in whole burnt Offerings and sacrifices for sin Thou hadst no pleasure : Then said I, Lo, I am come (in the volume of the book it is written of Me) to do Thy will, O God. Ps. xl. 6, 7.
Heb. x. 8, 9.

We pray, " Thy will be done in earth, as it is in heaven "; and the Son of God, become incarnate, S. Matt. vi.
10. not only revealed the nature of that will, but revealed in His own Person all that it might entail. He had come on earth that as a man, and in the terms of manhood, He might teach us the nature of Love. God is Love and is known to us as the Unity of Three Persons—Father, Son and Holy Ghost—a unity so absolute that it transcends our imagination. So when God the Son became incarnate, and limited Himself by the conditions of manhood, He showed by obedience, submission and self-surrender a perfect Filial relationship—the relationship of One who could say, " I and the Father are One." S. John x.
30.

But He took our nature, being Love, in order that He might be One with us, and that we might be One in Him; so with us and for us He offers to the Father what is His due, what all mankind owed and had not paid, what the whole burnt offering had originally symbolised—obedience, submission and self-surrender.

In consequence, while we accept the necessary distinction between the two Natures of the One

Christ, we have not to think of a divided personality in His human Life. He was at one and the same time and by the same acts manifesting, as far as man could understand it, the character of God; and offering as man, and on man's behalf, a perfect oblation of Himself. For man was made after God's likeness, man was made to love; and love expresses itself in sacrifice and self-surrender. In Palestine, during three and thirty years, Our Lord revealed in manhood Who the Divine Logos is; and, as a man, He offered to the Father in Time what as Son He offers eternally —a complete conformity of Will.

There was nothing servile about Our Lord's obedience; and it was no grudging service rendered from a dull sense of duty, nor was it due merely to an intelligent concurrence with what had been commanded. He had no eye to His own advantage; He did not strive to merit His own approval, nor to preserve His own self-respect. His was a perfect loyalty; He obeyed because He loved, and was eager to respond to every claim which could be made on His devotion.

Men may be respectable, honest and industrious, men may even pursue noble ends, and yet be all the time concentrated on their own interests, desiring to justify themselves and eager for fame and glory. Such men are without any sense of vocation, and have no idea that they belong to God and came into the world to do God's will. They usually obtain just what they want, and are discontented. Our Lord, on the other hand, lived a life of self-denial. He

Rom. xv. 3. pleased not himself. " The Son of Man," He says,
S. Matt. xx. 28. " came not to be ministered unto, but to minister,
S. Mark x. 45. and to give His life a ransom for many." He came

to serve men, He came to serve His Father, and He
knew that in this joint service His life must culminate
in sacrifice, that " the Good Shepherd must lay down
His life for the sheep." S. John x. 11, 15.

He loved men, and therefore went about doing
good; but, because He loved men, He respected their Acts x. 38.
rights. Having made Himself of no reputation and
taken the form of a servant, He was no rebel, and Phil. ii. 7.
could not be, for He represented the God of Order.
So as the submissive boy, we are told, " He went
down with Mary and Joseph, and came to Nazareth,
and was subject unto them." He had come, not S. Luke ii. 51.
only to reconsecrate home life, but to confirm the
authority of parents. In after days, He disappointed
the revolutionary populace by telling them to
" render unto Cæsar the things that are Cæsar's," for S. Matt. xxii. 21.
" the powers that be are ordained of God," and so S. Mark xii. 17.
Our Lord acknowledged the authority of the State. S. Luke xx. 25.
He told the Leper, whom He had cleansed, to go and Rom. xiii. 1.
show himself to the Priest, and make the offerings
which Moses had commanded, and so recognised the S. Matt. viii. 4.
authority of the Church. He assured His Disciples :—
" Think not that I am come to destroy the Law, or
the Prophets : I am not come to destroy, but to
fulfil." He claimed no exemptions for Himself, and St. Matt. v. 17.
when S. John the Baptist protested that He had no
need of baptism, He answered, " Suffer it to be so now :
for thus it becometh us to fulfil all righteousness." S. Matt. iii. 15.
Even when the Scribes and Pharisees were avowedly
His enemies, He reminded the people that they sat
in Moses' seat : " All things therefore whatsoever
they bid you, these do and observe : but do not ye
after their works, for they say and do not." When S. Matt. xxiii. 2, 3.
at His trial there was no real evidence against Him,

He recognised the right of Caiaphas to put Him on His oath, and gave without faltering the answer which was certain to ensure His condemnation.

But if Our Lord came to serve men, and as a man accepted the conditions of human society, still more truly He came to serve God, and as man to render God all that was His due. From early boyhood He showed His sense of vocation, saying, " Wist ye not that I must be about My Father's business ? " As a man He exclaimed, " I have a baptism to be baptised with, and how am I straitened till it be accomplished." He said again, " Man shall not live by bread alone, but by every word that proceedeth out of the mouth of God," and " My meat is to do the will of Him that sent Me, and to accomplish His work." He took no credit to Himself, but all was ascribed to the Father. Though He spoke as one having authority, He said, " As the Father hath taught Me, I speak these things. The words that I speak unto you I speak not of Myself." Though He did many wonderful works He said, " The Son can do nothing of Himself, but what He seeth the Father doing." He ever lived, as man, in loving correspondence with that Father ; and rejoiced for the sake of others, because the Father heard and answered His prayers.

But, as we saw in the last chapter, He was aware that this life of obedience was to end in death. Even in the pleasant Spring time of the Galilean Mission, when all were happy as at a Bridal feast, He knew that the Bridegroom would be taken away, and that His disciples would fast in those days. He asked of His ambitious disciples, " Are ye able to drink of the cup that I drink ? or to be baptised with the baptism that I am baptised with ? " He had just

S. Matt. xxvi. 63, 64.

S. Luke ii. 49.

S. Luke xii. 50.

S. Matt. iv. 4.
S. Luke iv. 4.
Deut. viii. 3.

S. John iv. 34.

S. Matt. vii. 29.
S. Mark i. 22.
S. John viii. 28.
Cp. vii. 16;
viii. 38; xii. 49.

S. John v. 19.

S. John xi. 41, 42.

S. Matt. ix. 14, 15.

S. Matt. xx. 22.
S. Mark x. 38.

spoken explicitly of His death, and He warned His disciples that for them as for Himself there can be no crown without the Cross. But as the time drew near His manhood felt the strain which comes of anticipation. So He cried in the Temple, " Now is My soul troubled : and what shall I say? Father, save Me from this hour; but for this cause came I unto this hour : Father, glorify Thy Name." Could loyalty be more perfectly expressed? S. John xii. 27, 28.

We have seen that coming into an evil world and placing Himself at human mercy, it was inevitable that Our Lord should be put to death; but Our Lord's mind dwelt upon His conviction that, in dying, He was fulfilling God's will. That is the thought which lies behind the agonised prayer in Gethsemane—" Let this cup pass from Me; nevertheless not My will, but Thine be done." The same S. Matt. xxvi. 39. thought is even more clearly expressed at the time S. Mark xiv. 36. of His arrest—" The cup which the Father hath given S. Luke xxii. 42. Me, shall I not drink it? " S. John xviii. 11.

His obedience was to be tested to the uttermost. The martyr who dies for a cause or an opinion, however unpopular at the moment, is at least sustained by the thought of the importance of the Truth for which He makes a good confession. The Lord Jesus Christ died because men accounted Him a sinner. He Who had gone about doing good was adjudged a felon; He Who had lived in holy conversation with His Father was denounced as a blasphemer; He Who had respected all men's rights was condemned and executed as a rebel. No circumstance of shame was omitted. He was made an object for derision, stripped of His clothes, nailed to a cross, and hung naked between two thieves.

L

His physical sufferings must have been terrible; and His very perfection made Him most sensitive to pain. Through the long night He was bullied by the Priests and baited by their serving men. He was scourged by the soldiers, so that His bleeding body could not bear the Cross. The sharp infliction of the nails was followed by the lifting of the Cross, when the weight of His body swung forward on the nails : and before He died He knew the maddening horror which comes of thirst.

He was " obedient unto death, even the death of the Cross." His obedience was to know no reserves, His surrender of Himself was to be complete. His very loyalty to the Father was tested when He felt Himself deprived of His presence, and cried, " My God, My God, why hast Thou forsaken Me ? " And yet at the end He could say, " It is finished." He had accomplished the work which His Father had given Him to do.

From the world's point of view the finish was a failure. The Kingdom of Heaven had not come, His foes had triumphed over Him, His disciples had forsaken Him and fled. From God's point of view, the Life of perfect obedience was ended, the perfect offering had been made, and the salvation of the world had been made possible. " For as through one man's disobedience many were made sinners, even so through the obedience of the One shall many be made righteous."

Phil. ii. 8.

S. Matt. xxvii. 46.
S. Mark xv. 34.

Rom. v. 19.

XV. Our Lord's Life and Death of Sacrifice

(B) *The Reparation which He Offered to His Father*

Our Lord came not only to offer His Father a perfect homage and to do His will on earth as it is done in heaven; but He came also to hallow His Holy Name, by making a perfect reparation for our sins, and to be our sin-offering. We must not, however, forget that it was " God sending His Own Son in the likeness of sinful flesh, and as an offering for sin, condemned sin in the flesh," for the sin offering under the New as well ^{Rom. viii. 3.} as under the Old Covenant was of God's appointment and not of man's device. The Cross is at once the Father's condemnation of sin and the Son's reparation for sin. The fruit of sin was the slaying of the Lord of Life and Lord of Glory; and the fruit of holiness was the Life set free and the glory manifested of Him Who allowed Himself to be slain in order that He might save.

To put the matter in this way may suggest the thought that we are describing a transaction between two persons whose interests are not the same. But of any such thought, or even of such suspicion, we must beware. Let us keep in mind that the Cross provided the stage for the greatest Drama of Love in all the universe, that we are called to meditate on the wonderful correspondence of Love in Father and in Son; and that all attempts to interpret it in the terms of reason, or explain it on intellectual grounds, must needs be inadequate. The act is one and complete in itself, but we can only apprehend it by thinking of it first from one side and then from the other.

Man was created in the image of God to love and to ^{Gen. i. 27.}

be loved. So Our Lord as perfect man loved His Father, and loved men. In His great High Priestly prayer on the night before He suffered, He affirmed again and again His oneness with the Father, and prayed that a like unity might exist in His Church. His prayer is grounded on two fundamental convictions :—" I have known Thee " and " Thou hast loved Me." We know a person just in so far as we can talk to him and tell him everything. So Our Lord knew God, and His life was a continual prayer. Again and again the Evangelist tells us of His retreats so that He might be alone with God. After His first success at Capernaum " in the morning, a great while before day, He rose up and went out, and departed into a desert place and there prayed." So after His first missionary tour, " He withdrew Himself in the deserts, and prayed." Before choosing His twelve Apostles " He went out into a mountain to pray, and continued all night in prayer." When His disciples returned elated from the success of their first commission, He took them apart; and after He had fed the five thousand, He departed into the mountain to pray. It was while He was praying that He was transfigured; and it was through watching Him in prayer that His disciples desired to be taught His method. At the end of His Life we are told, " in the day time He was teaching in the Temple, and at night He went out and abode in the Mount that is called the Mount of Olives." So He prayed for His disciples on the road to Gethsemane, and prayed for Himself among the olive trees in the garden; and He was ever assured that His prayer was heard. When His disciples asked why they could not cure the lunatic boy, He replied, " This kind can come forth by nothing but by prayer."

S. John xvii. 25, 23.

S. Mark i. 35. *Cp.* S. Luke iv. 42.

S. Luke v. 16.

S. Luke vi. 12.

S. Matt. xiv. 13. S. Luke ix. 10. S. Mark vi. 31, 32. S. John vi. 15. S. Luke ix. 38. S. Mark ix. 1. S. Matt. xvii. 1. S. Luke xi. 1. S. Luke xxi. 37. *Cp.* S. John viii. 2. S. John xvii. S. Luke xxii. 42. S. John xi. 42.

S. Mark ix. 29.

When before the tomb of Lazarus He prayed aloud, He acknowledged that He knew the Father heard Him always. S. John xi. 42.

Three times we are told of the voice from Heaven. At His baptism, while He was praying, a voice came out of Heaven, " This is My beloved Son, in whom I am well pleased." At His Transfiguration there S. Matt. iii. 17. came a voice out of the cloud, " This is My beloved Son; . . . hear ye Him." After the Greeks had come S. Matt. xvii. 5. to Him in Holy Week, He said, " Now is my soul S. Mark ix. 7. troubled; and what shall I say? Father, save Me S. Luke ix. 35. from this hour. But for this cause came I unto this hour. Father, glorify Thy Name. There came therefore a voice out of heaven, saying, I have both glorified it, and will glorify it again." It was His Father's S. John xii. 27, 28. Name which was to be hallowed and glorified by His death upon the Cross.

If we consider Our Lord's knowledge of the Father, His communion with the Father and His love for the Father, we may in some degree understand His zeal for His Father's honour. We know that it impelled Him on more than one occasion to cleanse the Temple S. John ii. 14–17.
S. Matt. xxi. 12, 13. of a huckstering crowd.

A man hears of a stranger being wantonly insulted and expresses his disapproval, but his equanimity is not disturbed; but if the same man hears that his wife or child has been insulted, his indignation is like a flame, and his brain throbs with the thought of it so that he cannot sleep. Now, it was just because Our Lord in His human consciousness knew God and loved Him as no one else has ever done, that He felt as no one else how sin is a dishonour to God's Name and an outrage upon His perfection. He knew how good God was, how loving and how wise, and He saw God's

Laws flouted by those whom they were designed to protect from ill. He saw God's creation which was meant to reflect the eternal Beauty marred, abused and sometimes desolated by man's caprice, man's idleness, his vice and his greed. He saw God's truth turned into a lie, and men using their God-given faculties to prove that evil was their good. He turned on the teachers, Scribes and Pharisees who perverted what they pretended to expound. He saw man formed to love and to be loved, and only happy when loving and being loved, losing all the joy of existence through selfishness, and disturbing the order of the world through hate. He saw all the pain, disease, misery and ugliness which results from sin, and heard men blasphemously ascribe it all to God, questioning His goodness, truth, and beauty. Cannot we dimly understand how awful to Our Lord was the vision of sin, how he bowed beneath the burden of such knowledge, and how sorrow like an overflowing flood drowned His spirit, for He loved God?

S. Matt. xxiii.

Secondly, cannot we understand Our Lord's shame, for He shared our humanity, although He did not share our sin? His shame was all the more intensely realised because He was innocent, for the sinner is always more or less a pervert, who persuades himself that his sin was natural, and therefore to be condoned. It is the good mother who sits sobbing beneath the criminal in the dock who feels the shame, more than the judge who pronounces sentence, or the criminal who is thinking of his punishment. She bore him, she loved him, and she cannot dissociate herself from him, stained as he is with crime. He may be reckless and defiant in his sin, but she longs to make some reparation to the person he has injured. Supposing the

person injured to be her friend or her benefactor, how
abject she will feel in his presence and how desirous to
make amends.   So we pass from Our Lord's vicarious
shame for humanity to the reparation which He offered
to His Father.   It was an offering for our sins.   Our
sins deserved punishment, the consequences of sin
were suffering.   He entered into our sufferings, bore
them on our behalf and condemned sin in the flesh.

Sin culminated in the Crucifixion of Jesus, and
through the Crucifixion of Jesus the one offering for
sin was made.   Men had aimed at independence, He
was bound with cords and nailed to a cross.   Men had
aimed at sovereignty, and He was crowned with thorns.
Men had been covetous of wealth, and He was stripped
naked.   Men had given themselves over to the lusts
of the flesh and His back was torn with stripes; men
had been intemperate, and He knew the raging thirst
of those who die in pain.   Men had sought ease and
comfort, He was tortured.   Men had been angry and
passionate, He endured with patience.   Men had
courted popularity, and He heard the execrations of
the multitude.   Men had been selfish, but His heart
was pierced with a spear and His blood poured out for
the remission of other people's sins.   For men and on
their behalf was the offering made by the perfect Man
to the God Who had been dishonoured by Men.   It was
the Just One offering for the unjust, the Sinless One   1 S. Pet. iii.
                                                        18.
for sinners, and when we consider who He was, the
dignity of His Life and its inestimable value; when we
consider the wonder of His love and His willingness to
suffer for His murderers; and when we consider how
great those sufferings were, mental and physical, we
begin to understand that here indeed is a sin offering
sufficient for the sins of the whole world.

XVI. Our Lord's Life and Death of Sacrifice

(C) *The Expiation which He Offered for Our Sins*

We have not yet done with the sin offering. Our Lord loved His Father and for the Father's honour He made reparation; but Our Lord also loved men; and though they rejected Him, He went on loving. When they slew Him, He died for them; and when creation staggered at their crime, in silence He offered a sacrifice of expiation on their behalf. That and His act of reparation were in fact one, for loving God He loved all things in God, and no reparation to God would have been perfect that did not also restore to His communion those whom God had made for Himself.

To understand this, let us first remember that He compared Himself with the physician; and said that He had come to seek and save those that were lost. He had gone to the very worst and been known as the friend of the publicans and sinners. It was a personal relationship which He established and only through personal influence would he work. But this necessitated His identifying Himself with men, sharing their lot and enduring the consequences of their acts, and submitting to the penalties which those acts occasioned. Sin has its consequences, and the consequence of sin was the Cross. Sin deserves punishment; and, though the Sinless One could not be punished, He could suffer with sinners, and win one of the thieves by sharing in his pain. S. Peter tells us " His own self bare our sins in His own Body upon the Tree," and S. Paul says that " God made Him Who knew no sin to be sin on our behalf." Every one who would convert a sinner must be a sin bearer, for

it is only through the love with which the sinless
embraces the sinner that sin can be atoned for.

Every priest under the Old Covenant was reminded
of this when he ate of the sin offering. Every priest
of the New Covenant as he listens to confessions and
intercedes for penitents knows this also.

The Cross was not merely the pulpit from which Our
Lord preached His doctrine of self-sacrificing love; it
was also the altar at which He interceded, and His
intercession is still availing for those who come to
Him.

Believing this, let us try to understand how horrible
sin must have been to One who knew God and loved
goodness. Even bad men revolt from those sins to
which they are not themselves addicted. The respectable worldling, selfish and smug, feels physically
sick if he is by chance introduced to some den of vice
and profanity; and the defiant sinner will loathe the
hypocrite who treads so circumspectly in his own ways.
The hard man of business, cruel and avaricious, is
morally indignant when he meets with loafers whom
he would like to kick : and the shirker who calls himself a Labour man and is full of envy, none the less
really hates the rich for the ostentatious way in which
they waste their money. We all hate sins which are
not our own. On the other hand, men are so accustomed to sin and have lived so long in a sinful atmosphere that they have ceased to notice it in their own
environment. They are like the sick man in the stuffy
room, quite unaware of the bad air which is so offensive
to one who enters from outside. Again, those who
have never known God as He is, or the joy which only
the innocent can feel, do not miss Him very much,
and distract themselves with the excitement of low

pleasures. It is not the man who was born in a slum who finds it intolerable, but the man who has seen better days and been accustomed to the comforts and amenities of life. These illustrations help us to understand what sin meant to the Sinless One, of how He could not be other than the Man of Sorrows and Isa. liii. 3. acquainted with grief. And yet He willed to endure all; and, as He came to save, so He came to suffer all the results of our misdoings. From the very start of His ministry this was so, and, to S. John the Baptist's S. Luke iii. 10, 12, 14. S. Matt. iii. 14, 15. surprise, He associated Himself with rude soldiers and rapacious publicans by being like them baptised.

But when the sinners among whom He lived turned against Him, when He Himself became the object of their sin, when they hounded Him up the way of sorrows, and declared that He was not fit to live, when they attributed to Him their own baseness, their own rebelliousness, their own blasphemy, their own disregard for the God-given Law, they were confessing that such sins deserved punishment, and heaping the penalties on the devoted head of One Who was innocent and willing to endure. He accepted it all without expostulation. He had made Himself one with them that He might receive and expiate their sinfulness.

The first three words from the Cross were spoken shortly after it was lifted up and the last four words were spoken just before Our Lord died. For nearly three hours He was silent : and in darkness and alone He passed the night of His soul.

We have been taught to believe that He felt the weight of the whole world's sin. We know that He was silent, and can feel in the silence of that sympathy something too intimate for expression. He put

Himself in the sinner's place, and He knew the sinner's desolation. When He spoke again it was to cry— "My God, My God, Why hast Thou forsaken Me?" S. Matt. xxvii. 46. S. Mark xv. 34.

It is sometimes argued that as Our Lord drew near to death His powers of apprehension waned and so His human mind was no longer conscious of His Father's presence. Many a man has died murmuring, "Where is So-and-so; why has she gone away?" and all the time the object of his attachment has been bending over the bed. But no such explanation will here suffice, for Our Lord spoke with a loud voice.

Others have suggested that, as the words are a quotation from the twenty-second Psalm, they only Ps. xxii. 1. imply that Our Lord was meditating on that wonderful forecast of His Passion; but the awful cry which startled the onlookers cannot be reconciled with a devotional exercise. It is true, however, that in moments of intense feeling the mind is incapable of expressing itself otherwise than through quotations or by some well-remembered phrase.

Before His Passion, Our Lord had told His disciples—"Behold, the hour cometh, yea, is now come, that ye shall be scattered, every man to his own, and shall leave Me alone : and yet I am not alone, because the Father is with Me." Was this faith falsified? S. John xvi. 32. That we cannot believe. It was only that, through the consciousness of God's presence being clouded, Our Lord could experience the sense of dereliction. He had identified Himself with sinners. He not only bore their sins, but felt the guilt which is man's curse, and knew what the terror must be of their ultimate experience. His Faith did not fail even then. He still called, "My God." He still longed for communion with God in the very darkness of His overwhelming sorrow.

Many martyrs have died rejoicing in the divine consolations. They have suffered well-nigh incredible pain because sustained by superhuman grace. They have testified to their sense of God's presence in the torture chamber and at the stake. It was not so with Our Lord. He willed not to die what has been called the death of the righteous, but to taste death for every man. He died as a sinner dies, for He was the sinner's Friend.

But how was this possible? Sin separates, so that the sinful and righteous cannot be at one. Is no atonement possible? We answered that question in the preceding chapter when we pointed out why man was a fit object for the Divine compassion. The worst of men was not all bad, and the love of Christ could find some soul of goodness in those who looked most evil. He sought for that goodness and clung to it. It was to be rescued for the God of all goodness. In union with Himself the sin was to be purified; and on the Cross He purged our sins, His action was not merely retrospective. We too are sinners, and may be joined with Him, and in Him be cleansed.

Heb. i. 3.

2 S. Pet. i. 9.

Purification by suffering is not only an idea found in most religions, it is also a fact of experience; while cleansing by blood is an idea found everywhere, which defies those who seek for its rational explanation. Our Lord made His soul an offering for sin, and speaks of His blood as being shed for the remission of sins; but we have need to remember that nothing of a magical nature is intended. We are forgiven through Christ and His intercession : we are redeemed by Christ as a consequence of His Victory; and the Atonement is for us a reality, when we are in Christ Who is the Sin Bearer and the Sin Offering.

Isa. liii. 10.

S. Matt. xxvi. 28.

XVII. Our Lord as the Peacemaker

(A) *Peace and Communion with God*

Atonement leads to communion, just as the Sin Offering preceded the Peace Offering and Thank Offering. In the Sacrifice of the Cross all types found their fulfilment.

Before Our Lord died, He said to His disciples, " Peace I leave with you : My peace I give unto you "; but it was peace within, the peace of a reconciled spirit, for He said again, " In Me ye may have peace. In the world ye have tribulation." So after His resurrection, He came to His disciples, saying, " Peace be unto you; " and that peace was to be guaranteed by His abiding presence, " Lo ! I am with you alway, even unto the end of the world." S. John xiv. 27.
S. John xvi. 33.
S. John xx. 19.
S. Matt. xxviii. 20.

S. Peter went to the House of Cornelius, proclaiming, " the good tidings of peace by Jesus Christ, Who is Lord of all " ; and S. Paul taught his Ephesian converts that the peace was won upon the Cross. It was through the victory over sin, the world and the Devil that peace became possible; for though peace is the end proposed in every war, it can only, in a sinful world, be won at the price of blood and tears. Acts x. 36.
Eph. ii. 14–17.

The peace which we are at present contemplating was the peace between God and man. It was a peace man needed and God longed for, but which could only be attained if the barriers between God and man were broken down. Where debts have been incurred they must be faced and acknowledged, or no one will pay them and no one can forgive them. Where rebellion has taken place, the rebels must make a real submission, if order is to be restored. No peace

ensues by ignoring the facts, no peace can be maintained by each going his own way—that is not peace,
but acquiescence in anarchy. You cannot have
peace by assuming conditions which do not exist. No
peace can be based on a lie. Where rebellion is of
long standing with widespread ruin, the suppression
will cause suffering to the conqueror as well as to the
conquered; but the magnanimous conqueror only asks
for submission; He will not unduly press his claims
for compensation. The world was full of hatred, and
Love came. Love suffered but conquered by suffering. As men make their submission, true order is
restored. Men have what their souls need and that is
peace, and God's longing for reconciliation is satisfied.

The Peacemaker is a person who represents both
sides—the Man Christ Jesus, Who is God the Son. In
Him Godhead and Manhood meet and are reconciled.
It is by our being joined to Him, living in Him, and
receiving His nature that we are reconciled with
God. It is all the result of personal relationships, and
not of transactions mechanically conceived.

But as in the Old Testament, the reconciliation must
be celebrated by a feast. There must be a real communion or the peace becomes a frigid compact for the
cessation of hostilities. We go on therefore to think
of the sacrifice upon the Cross as providing the means
for Our Eucharist—our sacrifice of praise and thanksgiving.

" The Lord Jesus the same night in which He was
betrayed took bread : and when He had given thanks,
He brake it, and said, Take, eat : This is My Body
which is broken for you : this do in remembrance of
Me. After the same manner also He took the cup,
when He had supped, saying, This cup is the New

Testament in My Blood : This do ye, as oft as ye
drink it, in remembrance of Me." 1 Cor. xi.
23–25.

This command was given at the Feast of the Passover when the Jews celebrated their national deliverance. On the next day, when the lambs were being
slaughtered in the Temple, the True Lamb of God was
sacrificed on the Altar of the Cross. The greater
deliverance had come, and the greater feast was prepared. But there can be no communion with God
apart from Calvary, and so S. Paul reminds us, " As
often as ye eat this Bread and drink this Cup, ye do
show the Lord's death till He come." 1 Cor. xi. 26.

XVIII. Our Lord as the Peacemaker

(B) *Peace on Earth to Men of Good Will*

While we think of the reconciliation between God
and man, we must not forget that the Angels pro- S. Luke ii.
14.
mised " peace on earth to men of good will." The
peace offering was God's feast, but the worshipper
did not feed alone. The peace offering brought
men together and the social side of the service was
insisted on.

But it will be remembered that on the Day of Atonement the blood was used to consecrate a local
sanctuary and to sanctify a peculiar people. Our
Lord did not die in any closed court, but outside the
Gate, for He came to consecrate the world. The Heb. xiii. 12.
soldiers of the world empire were the ministers of His
sacrifice, for He came to sanctify no peculiar people,
but that all men might be saved and come to the
knowledge of the truth.

When the woman of Samaria had wished to argue

about her local sanctuary, Our Lord had replied, "The hour cometh when neither in this mountain, nor in Jerusalem, shall ye worship the Father." The hour came, His blood was shed on the earth, but it was to be presented in heaven, and heaven is as near to one place as another, and so the whole earth was consecrated to His service. "For," says S. Paul, "it was the good pleasure of the Father that in Him should all the fullness dwell; and through Him to reconcile all things unto Himself, having made peace through the blood of His Cross; through Him, I say, whether things upon the earth or things in the heavens." The wider aspects of the Atonement are beyond our ken; and about them we cannot profitably speculate, but we infer that the redemptive power is present in nature apart from humanity, and that, in consequence, old distinctions between what is clean and what is unclean are done away.

More clearly we understand how the old barriers between the commonwealth of Israel and the Gentiles were broken down; and the enmity which had existed between races was to be abolished. Our Lord came to reconcile all things to Himself; and from the high Cross He preaches peace to them that are afar off, and to them that are nigh. In Christ there should be neither Jew nor Greek, barbarian, Scythian, bond nor free. All are the objects of His proffered Mercy, for all He made Atonement; and He wished all to share in the same communion, eating of the one bread and drinking out of the same cup.

S. John iv. 21.

Col. i. 19, 20.

Eph. ii. 14.

Col. iii. 11.
Gal. iii. 28.

XIX. Why is Our Lord's Sacrifice Availing

So far we have striven to expound how Christ died for our sins according to the Scriptures, and opened for us a new way of life and communion with God. But all the time a critic has been lurking in ambush with his well-known questions, " How can Our Lord's death of self-sacrificing love be more than an example? Can the sufferings which men inflicted on Him really be for men's salvation? Is not a doctrine whereby the innocent is punished for the guilty clearly unjust and immoral? Why did a good God permit His Son to suffer? Can a good God be propitiated by the pain of one who is innocent? or accept the death of the innocent one as an atonement for those who are guilty? "

I hope it will be admitted that these questions do not fairly arise out of anything which has been taught in this book. They are due to bitter controversies in the past, to misunderstandings, to the extravagant language of men eager to stress their particular views, and to imperfectly stated premises being pressed to logical conclusions. At the same time, when such questions are asked, they deserve an answer, for it is clearly impossible for any thinking man to believe in the Atonement so long as he imagines that it contradicts the fundamental postulates of justice.

Vicarious suffering need not detain us. It is a fact of experience. A man pays the debts of a friend, a mother gives her life for her child, a soldier dies that his country may be free. There is no moral problem in consequence raised when we say that Our Lord died to be the Saviour of the world, for vicarious suffering like a golden thread runs through the dingy tapestry which illustrates the history of man.

M

Neither can we question the propriety of human salvation depending on someone not ourselves. Humanity is one, and we are all linked together. We derive our civilisation from those who went before us; and most of the comforts which we enjoy are due to the labours of others. The same law runs through the spiritual world. It is by the act of another that we have been redeemed, made children of God, and heirs of heaven.

It is true that to-day we are still inclined to talk overmuch of tendencies and world movements, and to minimise the personal factor, because we are still obsessed by the way in which the doctrine of physical evolution was taught in the last century. But the fact remains that we owe little to popular movements, a good deal to institutions and the educative force of law, and most of all to the individuals who founded the institutions or proposed the Laws. The history of progress is the history of great men who did not reflect the popular opinion of their age. God, it seems, has elected special nations and individuals, not for their own sake, or even because of their merits, in order that, through them, His purpose for the world might be accomplished. The ideas of representation and mediatorial relationships are by no means confined to the religious sphere.

Great men are sometimes examples, but the world has not so much advanced by marking their examples as by receiving gifts at their hands. What they were is the secret behind their actions, but it is what they did which makes us what we are. You would not suggest that Moses, Socrates, Luther and Napoleon were examples for an old maid living in a back street, but the civilisation which she inherits and her outlook upon life are largely conditioned by what these men did, although she knows but little about them. So there is nothing necessarily irrational in our faith when we say Jesus Christ died that He might atone for sins; and unless He did so His labours were in vain; and if His life was a failure He is not even an example to be followed.

But the Objector still asks, " Can the sufferings which men inflicted on Him really be for men's salvation ? " and the answer of course is *No*. It is not, however, a question of what men merited by crucifying Our Lord, but what Our Lord merited by being willing to suffer. He at least prayed, " Father, forgive them, for they know not what they do," and no one has yet S. Luke xxiii. 34. challenged the morality of that prayer. It has been noted that the plea was just; and are we prepared to question the morality of God, if the plea be allowed and the request granted ?

The Objector, however, is scandalised because the Innocent One was punished for the guilty. That, he says, is clearly immoral, but that also is what the Catholic Church does not teach. God did not punish the Innocent One : Caiaphas and Pilate punished Him and their punishment was unjust. On the other hand, Our Lord did suffer the consequences of our sins and died because we were sinners. That is a fact of history from which no one can escape. There is the further fact of experience, that in this world the innocent very often do suffer for the guilty. So there is nothing exceptional about Our Lord's sufferings; but they do shed a ray of light upon what is otherwise a very dark subject. We cannot pretend to fathom the mystery of God's moral government of the world; and when, like Job, we feel inclined to arraign the justice of the universe, we remember Calvary, and the uncomplaining eyes of the Saviour. In the midst of our eloquence we are answered by His silence on the Tree. If God in this world allows the innocent to suffer for the guilty, let us remember that God, when He became man, was prepared to suffer for the guilty. If by His undeserved sufferings the world was redeemed, we too may be encouraged to look beyond the present. He, "for the joy that was set before Him, endured the Cross, despising the shame, and is set down at the right hand of the throne of God."

Heb. xii. 2.

But while we must not speak of Our Lord being punished for our sins, there is a sense in which we may say that His sufferings had a penal character, though they were not penal to Him. We have just distinguished between punishment and consequences, but we must not forget that the said consequences of sin are in accordance with the law of God. We call them consequences to avoid any suspicion that they are of an arbitrary or capricious character. What we call Nature is our understanding of the way in which God acts; and for those who believe in the personal distinctions within the Blessed Trinity, the laws of all creation must ultimately be regarded as having a personal sanction, and being manifestations of Will. So we may go on and argue that the God Who hateth iniquity has from all eternity assigned penalties for the breaking of His law; and that, when God became man, He did not flinch from the eternal decree, but, being in a sinful world, accepted the consequences, which, we repeat, had no penal reference to Himself.

But the Objector is not yet satisfied. " Granted,"

he may say, "that you can safeguard the morality
of your doctrine, you have yet to deal with the
intellectual difficulty. How could the sufferings of
Our Lord help others, for it is not a matter of general
experience that the sufferings of the innocent lead to
the reformation of the guilty ? " A complete answer
to that question is at present beyond our powers,
but we must be careful to distinguish between the
salvation of a Society menaced by ruin and the
forgiveness of the individuals who compose it.
Remembering this, the best reply may be through
a parable. Let us imagine two men who are set to
mind a complicated machine. One is careful and
industrious, the other idle and incompetent; one
keeps an eye on his work, while the other is often
reading the betting news. Suddenly the good man
sees that his fellow has omitted to do something, and
that a disaster must immediately occur which will
wreck the machine and kill his fellow in the place
where he stands. Without thinking of his own safety,
he springs to the spot and does what is necessary.
He has averted an accident, and saved his friend's
life. Nothing can alter that fact, but the betterment
of the friend is problematical. All we can say is
that he has another chance. But let us suppose
that the man's heart is touched by gratitude, and
that he wishes in future to do better. He will attach
himself to the man who has saved him, and the man
who has saved him will help and encourage him.
Gradually he may cease to be incompetent and learn
to recognise himself as a responsible being. This
story may help us to understand what we mean
when we say that Our Lord saved the world from
destruction, though it cost Him His own life. He

gave to all a new chance; and He is ready to stand by us still and help us to be like Himself.

We may say that Our Lord died because of our sinfulness—that is so obvious that it needs no proof. We may say that Our Lord died on behalf of us sinners, and for that we have His own teaching. Can we go on and say Our Lord died instead of us and as our Substitute?

The theory of substitution has at times been taught in a way that cannot be reconciled with morality, and could only be justified by a belief in the arbitrary decree of a tyrant God. At the present day, in consequence, the theory of Representation is more popular, and that also has been pressed to an extreme until Our Lord becomes Humanity; and the theorists seem to rob us of the Jesus Whom we love, and give us an abstraction in His place. Considering the theological history of the word " substitution " (and words are more bound by their history than by their etymology) it would be well to abandon its use, but we must be careful not to lose what is true in those who maintained substitutionary theories. The atonement is not due to anything that we do, but is of God's sovereign will. What we could not do for ourselves God has done for us through the Son Who was sacrificed on the Cross. The grace which flows from the Cross is God's free gift, and does not imply any merit in the recipients, though they, as we shall see hereafter, have to co-operate with grace, and may resist it. On the other hand, the word " representative " is not as yet bound up with any exaggerated view of the recapitulation theory. We can still call Our Lord our Representative, meaning that He became one of us, acted for us, died on

Gal. ii. 16.
Gal. iii. 11, 22.

our behalf, and pleads our cause in Heaven. We
can go further, and say just in so far as we endorse
His acts they become our very own. But does not
S. Paul go further still when he says, " One died
for all, and therefore all died " ?   I think if we read $_{2\ \text{Cor. v. 14.}}$
the whole passage of how the love of Christ constrains
us, we shall find that it teaches, not substitution, but
incorporation. Those who have been joined to Christ
have already passed through a mystical death to the
world, and belong even now to the eternal order. It
is therefore incumbent on them " no longer to live
unto themselves, but unto Him, Who for their sakes
died and rose again." Our Lord, for S. Paul, is $_{2\ \text{Cor. v. 15.}}$
always the New Adam, not merely the Representative
of the race, but its Head.

$_{\text{Rom. v.}}$
$_{\text{12–14.}}$
$_{\text{1 Cor. xv. 22,}}$
$_{\text{45.}}$

XX. Why did God Permit Our Lord's Sacrifice

The Objector is not yet satisfied. He asks, " Why
did God send His Son into the World, and why did
He permit the agony of the Cross? How can He be
said to be satisfied and propitiated?   What is meant
by the expiation of sins, and in what sense can the
Atonement be spoken of as the reconciliation of God's
justice with His love ? "

The answer to most of these questions is implicit
in much that has been said, but when surveying any
object from a new angle of vision, previous impressions need confirmation, and fresh details have to be
related to those already seen.

All theologians are agreed that " God so loved the
world, that He sent His only begotten Son, that
whosoever believeth in Him should not perish, but

S. John iii. 16. have everlasting life "; but theologians are not agreed on whether the Incarnation was merely a remedy for the Fall, or was part of God's eternal purpose quite apart from man's sin. Some argue that God, when creating, intended to perfect His work, and that His work could only attain perfection when it was perfectly united with, and perfectly expressed by, the Uncreated Word. This involved more than the immanence of God in nature, for as men were persons, the Word had to enter into a personal relationship in order to unite Himself with them, and this began to be realised when " the Word became flesh and S. John i. 14. dwelt among us." The Incarnation therefore is due to the absolute Will of God, but the manner in which it took place, and the Cross to which it led, may be assigned to His contingent Will, for it was determined by the sin of man. Other theologians think that had there been no sin and no need of redemption there would have been no Incarnation, but man would have attained to the Beatific Vision in some other way. In consequence, for them the Atonement is the central fact in Christian theology, and the Incarnation is the means which made it possible.

Both theories are speculative and concerned with what might have happened had the conditions been other than they were; but they are of importance because of the cleavage they have caused. Everything depends on the point from which you start to think, and we may trace the results in the following series of propositions. (1) God willed to reveal Himself from all Eternity : He did reveal Himself in Jesus Christ : Men being sinners rejected the revelation and nailed Our Lord to a Cross. Hence the

Cross is primarily the proof of man's sin, and we believe that those who repent of that rejection become at-one with the God Who is revealed. (2) God loved sinners and willed to save them : He sent His Son as a Saviour, Who offered Himself on the Cross as a Sacrifice for Sin. The Cross is then the proof of God's love, and we become at-one with Him because of what He has done. Following one line of thought, the Atonement is naturally conceived of as having a subjective effect, following the other as having an objective result. The position maintained in this book is that it has both. For both lines of thought are true, though you cannot think of them at once, any more than you can see both sides of a shield at the same time. The second sequence is, it will be seen, more important when considering sin and salvation, and it has more authority in Holy Scripture, where we are taught "God commendeth His love towards us, in that, while we were yet sinners, Christ died for us." Rom. v. 8.

We reply, therefore, to the first question—God sent His Son into the world that He might reveal the Divine Nature; and also God sent His Son into the world that He might save men. If God could be revealed, or men saved, in some other way, it is open to the objector to disclose it.

We may gain perhaps a clue to answering the second question by thinking how the two theories we have been discussing find their point of reconciliation in the eternity of God. We think naturally of Creation, the Fall and Redemption as a sequence, for they happened in time; and we, being in time, arrange them in order. But God is outside the time process, and so what we think of as a contingency which afterwards arose, was for Him coeval with His original purpose. The dispute therefore is not ultimately concerned with the direction of God's will, but about the order of man's thought. We cannot see things from the eternal standpoint, but can only trace a process from point to point. It is therefore necessary for us to maintain the distinction between the absolute and contingent will of God, for we need some concept of what that Will is in Itself, if we would not be confused when we study isolated instances of how It has been exercised. Hence we are justified in saying absolutely that God has always willed man's good; but we should not be justified in saying that God would have willed Our Lord to die on the Cross if man had not sinned. We are justified in saying absolutely that Sin is abhorrent to God, and we cannot modify that conviction because God is very long-suffering with sinners, giving them time for repentance. When we see something wrong, we are justified in saying it is contrary to God's will; but when we ask the further question, " Why does God permit it ? " we are not competent to give the answer, because we do not know the end.

Does this give rise to a fresh difficulty ? If so, we have a clue to its solution in the Story of the Cross. God has given man freedom to will, and permits him within certain limits to use that freedom, though he sometimes uses it wrongly and causes much misery. Are we in consequence doubtful about the goodness of God's gift? Secondly, we learn that God sent His only begotten Son into the world and yet did not restrict man's freedom, though men took His Son and nailed Him to a Cross. Are we still more doubtful about God's goodness, and do we say, " He

is without excuse, for He knew what would happen? "
S. Peter was even bolder when he said that God
" by His determinate counsel and foreknowledge "
delivered Our Lord to men; and that men " with
wicked hands crucified and slew Him." Where then _{Acts ii. 23.}
is God's goodness? Thirdly, we learn that the death
of the Lord was the salvation of the world. If this
be true, cannot we take courage and believe that out
of evil God still produces good?

How then do we conclude? It was God's will to
save men and for that purpose He sent the Son
Whom He loved. The Son Who loved the Father
and was one with Him came willingly, and both
Father and Son knew the consequences of the advent.
Such was the reciprocal love of Father and Son and
so great was their love for men. Men had permission
to do as they would, and men crucified the Son.
But the will of the Son to save was more powerful
than the will of men to destroy. Men failed for they
could only kill the body; and, when they had done
that, the Son in the body rose from the dead. The
Son triumphed, and because He rose in the body,
men were convinced and His message of salvation
went throughout the world.

If we look at the event in this way we have surely
not to ask ourselves the question, " Why did God
permit Our Lord to suffer? " but let us remember
that we dare not impute any responsibility to God
for those sufferings, except in so far as He had given
men free will, and, having given it, refused to deprive
them of the gift.

Men may further ask, " But has the salvation
purchased at so great a cost been really effective? "
That is a question which will have to be discussed

in a future chapter; and here it is only necessary to remember that we are still within the time process. The end is not yet, and those who have Faith in the Cross look forward confidently to the great Assize, and the final justification of God's dealing with the world.

XXI. SATISFACTION

Passing from this attempt " to justify the ways of God to men," it is necessary to think of how the ways of men were justified to God by the sacrifice of Our Lord and what we mean by satisfaction and propitiation.

The idea of satisfaction arises through thinking of sin as a debt which has to be paid. It has been argued, " God created men to do His will and men have not done it; Our Lord, however, as man by offering to God a life of perfect obedience has satisfied God's claims as regards Himself. But men were still liable to suffer forfeiture, and the wages of sin is Rom. vi. 23. death. Our Lord by dying paid the forfeiture on our behalf. A creditor is not concerned with the source of the money paid for the liquidation of his debt, so our debts could be cancelled in the heavenly ledger when Our Lord paid the price of our redemption."

This theory, so simple at first sight, is not so easy to justify, for the moral equivalents of the metaphors are not obvious. The theory as a whole awakes no response in the heart; and to this money-making, money-grubbing age, the idea of interpreting our relations with God in the terms of trade is altogether repugnant.

No one objects to the parallel between the earthly and the heavenly kingdoms, for politics are conducted on a grand scale. No one objects to metaphors from landowning, for landowning is dignified. We speak of " the Son of God going forth to war " and revel in military metaphors, but there is romance in the soldiers' profession. The doctrine of the Atonement has again and again been stated in the terms of jurisprudence, but in the Law we venerate the shrine of our highest learning, wisdom and morals. It is when we come to the shop that men are offended, and yet honesty and plain dealing are not unrelated to the Divine justice, so that metaphors derived from buying and selling should not be ruled out as unworthy of consideration.

If Our Lord told parables about the conduct of kings and landowners, judges and stewards, He spoke also of the romance of merchandise in the man seeking goodly pearls. He repeatedly alluded to the making up of accounts. He told also the parables of the talents and the pounds.

S. Matt. xiii. 45,46.
S. Matt. xviii. 23.
S. Matt. xxv. 19.
S. Luke xvi. 2, etc.

There are certain developments of this " commercial theory " which can be at once ruled out. Men have spoken of Our Lord's suffering as more than an equivalent for the punishment deserved by man's sin; but we cannot assess moral obligations in terms of arithmetic, and the attempt to do so comes of treating metaphors as facts. Secondly, it is impossible even to think of God being satisfied with suffering, it is only gods like Moloch that delight in pain. Thirdly, we must rid ourselves of the unscriptural doctrine of imputed righteousness. A man may pay another's debts, a man may perform another's duty, but the virtue of a good man cannot be credited to

S. Matt. xxv. 14–30.
S. Luke xix. 12–27.

a bad one; and, if it could, the transaction would be immoral.

How then are we to think of God's satisfaction? Let us remember that God is Love and that Love is very exacting. It is never satisfied until it has established a complete correspondence with the beloved. Man had been created by the Love of God. The two commands to man were that he Deut. v. 5. S. Matt. xxii. should love God and should love his neighbour, and 37. man had flouted both. God's thwarted love for man is sometimes spoken of as His wrath. It was very stern, very uncompromising, for love cannot tolerate indifference, or be outraged, and say it does not matter. Man seemed to have failed, but there can be no ultimate failure for God. Then came the Son of Man and offered, as man, the life of perfect obedience, perfect loyalty, responding to every claim which love could make. God is Love, and in Christ Jesus Love at length was satisfied; there was no debt which He had not paid.

Our Lord's life and death, then, is a complete satisfaction for the humanity which He represented, but how is it a satisfaction for the humanity which we have abused, or for the penalties which we ought to pay? We have a clue to the answer in the fact that He became man and loved men. We can imagine a life of perfect obedience and loyalty in congenial surroundings. In heaven with the elect angels such a life redounded to His exceeding glory; among men it brought Him to death. But He chose to live among men. He wished to save men, sinners as they were. He became man and shared man's lot. He was ready to go all lengths to achieve His object. He prayed for men even on the Cross. Was such a life of sacrifice to go without its recompense? He claimed men for His own. He said of His disciples " they are Mine "; and the Father was satisfied that ^{S. John xvii.} the claim had been made good. Those whom He had laboured for, and died for, were His. They would form the Church of God, which " He purchased with His own blood "; and in that Church He would ^{Acts xx. 28.} wipe out the long score which was against those who were joined to Him—" Blotting out the handwriting of ordinances which was against them." S. Paul, it ^{Col. ii. 14.} will be noted, did not disdain " commercial " metaphors.

XXII. PROPITIATION

When we go on to think of what we mean by propitiation three questions arise. 1. " In what sense is God the Father pleased by His Son's sufferings? " 2. " Why were these sufferings necessary, if God already loved men? " 3. " How can God be pleased with us because the Son suffered? "

1. Imagine a master of a large business who has discovered that a young clerk is dishonest, and none the less forgives him out of respect for his heartbroken mother. How surprised that kind-hearted master would be to hear it stated that he had forgiven his clerk because he was so delighted with the sight of a good woman in trouble! And yet men have dared to think that the God of Love was so pleased with the sight of His Son's sufferings that He forgave those who inflicted them. Rather let us think of the Divine Compassion, and we may even dare to think that in the sufferings of the Son on Calvary the Heavenly Father was suffering with Him, for when we speak of the God-

head as impassible, we do not mean that God is incapable of emotion. The Father did not send the Son because He wished Him to suffer, any more than a fond mother sent her son to the late war wishing him to die. The cause was worthy of the sacrifice—so thought mother and son—and she thinks so still and is proud of him to-day, as she plants flowers for remembrance above his grave in France. For his sake, what would she not do? She only lives to fulfil the requests in his last letter. But the Heavenly Father loved His Son more than any mother can. He values His Son's sacrifice more than she does. Will He not listen to the Son's last prayer that men may be forgiven?

2. The first question is therefore easily answered. We can understand in what sense God was well pleased in the death of His Son. The second question is due to confusion of thought. It is quite possible to love intensely those who displease and disappoint us. God loves men and has always loved them, but God was displeased with men because of their sin and rebellion —in evil he could take no delight. God's love in consequence could only be shown in wrath—in that righteous wrath which proves that God cares not only about the evil deed that has been done but also about the sinner that did it.

A righteous being cannot be indifferent either to sin or sinners, but the nature of His wrath against sinners depends upon the reality of His love. A man hears of a boy's misdoings and condemns them, but they make little impression on his mind, and he is not angry, for the boy is a stranger whom he does not love. But should the same man hear the same story about his son, he is disturbed, very angry, and cannot forget the fact. And why? Because he loves the son, has such a high standard for the son's conduct, and has cherished such hopes for his future. But however angry he is, he still loves the boy and longs for the time when he can think well of him again. Does not this help us to understand the love of God, His holy wrath and His longing to be propitiated? So S. John writes: "Herein is love, not that we loved God, but that He loved us and sent His Son to be the propitiation for our sins." _{1 S. John iv. 10.}

3. This brings us to the third question. "Why should God be pleased with us because His Son suffered on the Cross?" But to ask such a question shows a misconception of why God is propitious to us now. Our Lord became man for our sakes, and as man He triumphed over evil. Humanity which had seemed a failure in Him was justified. At last among men was one in Whom the Father could delight. But this perfect Man came to help us, died to save us, and His work has not failed. It is not only that we are pardoned for His sake, but also that in Him, and as members of His body, we become pleasing to God.

We have indeed still to confess our sins, be cleansed from our sins, and helped to lead a new life. We have, moreover, to be clad in the garments of salvation _{Is.lxi.10.} belonging to the great Elder Brother. Even then, knowing our unworthiness, we dare not without Our Lord approach the Father's presence; but in Him we find that "we have an Advocate with the Father . . . . who is the propitiation for our sins." _{1 S. John ii. 1, 2.}

N

XXIII. Expiation

Satisfaction, propitiation and expiation are often confused, and it is well to illustrate how distinct they are.

A boy, the son of a neighbour, throws a stone, which he has been forbidden to do, breaks my window, and denies that he did it. His father, however, saw him throw the stone and heard the crash. He comes at once to apologise, and sends a glazier with a new pane of glass. I am satisfied. He canes the boy, who takes his punishment as a just recompense for his thoughtless disobedience, and the father is satisfied. But the boy avoids me, until he summons sufficient resolution to come and, with stammering lips, confess his lie. I am at once propitiated, and the boy leaves me with the feeling that he has recovered his self-respect and expiated his sin.

Expiation must not be confused with forgiveness. We are sorry when we have wronged another and want to be forgiven; we are ashamed when we are conscious of some moral lapse and want to expiate it. But it would seem from the above illustration that expiation cannot be vicarious. The father satisfied me, but the boy had to expiate his own sin. In what sense, therefore, can we believe that Our Lord by His death was an expiation for the sin of the world?

First, man is a social being and the world is lying in wickedness. The better a man is the more keenly he feels the wickedness of his children, the selfishness of his class, or the overwhelming nature of a national disgrace. He feels this, not merely because he loves his children, is proud of his class, and a patriotic citizen; he feels it also because he is identified with, and therefore involved in, the evil of his surroundings. Let us suppose that he devotes his life to the reformation of society, that he suffers and sympathises with those who are the victims of their own sins, that he is persecuted and insulted by those whom he tries to help, that he accomplishes very little before his death. Afterwards, he is acclaimed a Saint, but only a few dwell on the fact that his whole life was one long vicarious expiation for the sins of others. Most are content to praise efforts which have had splendid results, and forget that he was provoked to activity by his concern for the world's sin.

This reminds us that good actions have their consequences as well as bad. They are in fact more lasting, and the Crucifixion to-day is of more importance than any enormity of Herod or Nero. The good cancels the evil, and when the good deed is done by someone conscious of the evil, it may be said to be expiatory in its nature. Now almost every moral advance is due to some individual, and the many benefit by what one endured in labour, suffering and pain. So we may regard Our Lord's life and death as offered in expiation for the sin of the world; and the consequences of evil are counteracted by the enduring fruits of His Passion. We may also understand how when we suffer without complaining from the sins of others, we may, in S. Paul's phrase, " fill up that which is lacking in the sufferings of Christ." Col. i. 24.

It is easier to explain how Our Lord's death was an expiation for the sins which have been done than how it can be an expiation for anyone's sinfulness; but do not let us misconceive the problem. A man denouncing vicarious expiation asks, " Because a good man provides for the necessities of a deserted wife, does

he in any way decrease the guilt of the husband ? "
Of course not, and he did not intend to do so.   No act
is expiatory apart from its motive.   No one either
maintains that the expiatory sacrifice on the Cross
is efficacious in any magical or mechanical fashion.
Nobody's sins can be expiated apart from his concurrence, just as nobody can be forgiven apart from
his consent.   The subject can only be discussed on the
plane of morality and moral issues are alone involved.
The ultimate question is, " Can sin be abolished, can
men who have been forgiven become free ? " and it is
on experience rather than on logic that we must rely
for our answer.

The more penitent a man is, the less is he willing
that his sins should be passed over as of no importance.
He has a pathetic desire to do something or to suffer
something to atone for his past.   The rash, careless
man, indeed, notwithstanding his repeated falls,
continues to assure himself and his neighbour that he
will yet " make good "; but the penitent man has
tried and failed, has set himself penances without
establishing his own righteousness; and then the
modern moralist tells him that vicarious expiation is
impossible, or could only be possible if God were
immoral.   How then is the penitent's deep-seated
craving to be satisfied ?   Is the moralist right, or is
there a " Lamb of God, who taketh away the sin of the
S. John i. 29. world ? "

The answer is that we can trace the fact of expiation
in the lives of the Saints, and that their testimony is
very uniform from S. Paul to men now alive.   First,
there is the attempt to " make good " by themselves,
and it fails.   Then there is the whole-hearted submission to Our Lord, and it succeeds.   Men learn to
trust in His merits rather than their own, in what He

did for them and not in what they do for themselves.
They are united with Him; and, in Him, His sacrifice
becomes their sacrifice, and they know that it is
availing.   They are conscious, not only that they have
been forgiven, but also that their sins are expiated.
And therefore they are free from them.

None of the explanations offered by the Saints of
their experience may be true, and they are certainly
very different, but the facts remain.   There is an
analogy between the man with a sick soul and the man
with a sick body.   They both wish to get well and
cannot help themselves.   The man with a sick body
sends for a physician, submits to his treatment, and is
cured.   He knows nothing about the drugs administered and would probably give an absurd account of
what they did for him.   He is a bad authority on
the means of his cure, but an excellent authority when
he declares that he is well, and that the disease has
been driven out of him.

We know what an understanding sympathy will do
for one who has a mind diseased; and we believe that
Our Lord offers to the penitent a complete sympathy,
nay, has translated that sympathy into action by
dying on behalf of men.   If, then, we were right in
explaining how Our Lord's life and death was an
expiation for deeds that have been done, cannot we
believe that, when sympathy is established between
us and Him, our sinfulness is expiated also.

Anyhow face to face with the testimony on which we
rely, we are ready to affirm with S. Paul that " the
redemption which is in Christ Jesus, God hath set
forth to be an $\iota\lambda\alpha\sigma\tau\eta\varrho\iota o\nu$."   And we should like Rom. iii. 24,
25.
to translate that word as " a means of expiation."
The means work when we have " faith in His
Blood."

XXIV. How Love and Justice are Reconciled

If we accept the views of expiation stated above, must we go on and argue—" It is evident that the Law of Righteousness demanded the punishment of sin, but God in His love yearned to save the sinner. Somehow He had to reconcile His Love with His Righteousness; and, as He could not abrogate His Law, He paid the penalty which His Law decreed in the person of His Son."

This argument seems in every way objectionable. It suggests a conflict in the Divine Mind between love and justice; and it treats Our Lord's death as an expedient, so that neither love nor justice might be compromised. We men know how we are torn asunder by conflicting desires, or perplexed by the claims of rival duties, but in " the peace of God which passeth all understanding," nothing can disturb His mind, and His will is at one with itself. God is not merely loving, He is Love : God is not merely righteous, He is Righteousness : His love and His law are not at variance, for perfect law is the expression of love. Living in an imperfect world where love is often fond and blind, where righteousness is sometimes hard and literal, we have to distinguish between them, and only find the two perfectly at one in the revelation of God made upon the Cross. There " Mercy and Truth are met together : Righteousness and Peace have kissed each other. Truth springeth out of the earth, and Righteousness hath looked down from heaven. The Lord hath shown His lovingkindness . . . and Righteousness shall go before Him."

Ps. lxxxv.
10–13.

CHAPTER V

I. APPLICATION OF THE ATONEMENT. FORGIVENESS AND SOME DISTINCTIONS

CONTEMPLATING the story of Our Lord's life and death, we have striven to understand what He did for us and why He did it. We have thought of how He came with God's offer of reconciliation; we have thought of the Victory won on our behalf over sin, the world, and the devil; and we have thought of the offering which He made to His Father on behalf of the human race. We have yet to think how we, responding to God's appeal, receive forgiveness; how we share in the fruits of Our Lord's victory, entering into "the glorious liberty of the sons of God"; Rom. viii. 21. and how we may make His sacrifice our own, and attain through that at-one-ment to the Beatific Vision.

In this chapter we shall consider the nature and manner of forgiveness, and it is necessary at the start to remember some obvious distinctions.

I. We must not confuse forgiveness with salvation, for forgiveness has to do with the past, while salvation has to be worked out in the future. Forgiveness is an act which may be many times repeated, while salvation is the result of a process. We can say—" I have been forgiven, but I am only being saved."

183

Every time we are forgiven we have the opportunity of making a fresh start, forgiveness is a beginning and salvation an end.

II. By forgiveness we are freed from the imputation of guilt; and God restores us to communion with Himself in spite of our past sin and present imperfection. It is God's free gift and is made without conditions, but from its very nature it can only be given when it is desired. A mother cannot forgive her little son who stamps in the corner and shouts, " I won't be good." He writhes himself free from the hand that would caress him; and the mother, in her solicitude so forgiving, has to wait until he is forgivable. Presently, he comes, a woe-begone little creature, with dirty hands and a smudged face, to say that he is sorry; and at once she can take him into her lap, and though he sobs with penitence he feels the thrill of reconciliation.

III. It is one thing to forgive and another to condone an offence. The indifferent will readily condone, but only those who love can forgive. A man who does not care whether or no I am friendly with him, will lightly pass over my enmity and feel that he has nothing to forgive. If he does not much care whether I do right or wrong, he will readily condone such offences of mine as do not concern himself. On the other hand, the man who loves me, whom I have wronged, cannot lightly pass over the offence, and if he hates my sin, he can only forgive me when I have dissociated myself from it.

IV. We must distinguish between forgiveness and pardon, although the words are often used as if they were synonymous. By pardon we mean the remission of a penalty, and by forgiveness the restoration of friendly relations. You may pardon a nation and not exact reparations; but you can only forgive individuals. You may pardon and not forgive, you may also forgive and not pardon, for you may be convinced that the person whom you freely forgive ought to pay the penalty. By pardon sins are blotted out of remembrance, but it is only by forgiveness that guilt can be done away.

V. This leads us to distinguish between the sins that we have done and the guilt which has been incurred. We are responsible for our sins, although their consequences develop apart from our volition. If we desire pardon, we must be willing as far as possible to make amends, but the most complete satisfaction would not of itself entitle us to forgiveness, for by sinning we have ourselves been corrupted. Sin is a disease of the soul; and we need not only the pardon of a judge, but the skill of a physician, of one who can heal, restore and renew. Forgiveness is the remedy, and forgiveness is a personal act. If we want it we shall seek for One who can say: "Come unto Me, all ye that are weary and heavy laden, and I will give you rest." S. Matt. xi. 28.

VI. Next we must distinguish between guilt which is the effect of sin and guilt which is a cause of sin and comes from sinfulness of disposition. This latter S. Paul calls τὸ φρόνημα τῆς σαρκός, and our Article Rom. viii. 6 ff. says that it has the nature (*ratio*) of sin; but it is not, as the Council of Trent reminds us, really and properly sin. It is evidence of our imperfection, it reveals our need of grace, but there is no culpability attaching to it.

VII. We must distinguish between things which are forbidden because they are wrong and things which are only wrong because they are forbidden. We admit this at once when we distinguish between moral and ritual offences, but we are not always mindful of it in other spheres of life. Yet a schoolboy will boast in the holidays of how he was caught out-of-bounds and caned; but he will be silent about the fact that he was convicted of telling a lie, though he was not punished for it. It is difficult to pardon one who breaks a rule, but it is quite easy to forgive him. It is often wise to pardon a liar, for the lie was told out of fear, but it is not easy to forgive him. We know that he has tried to deceive us and we cannot be sure of his penitence.

VIII. A similar distinction exists between sin and crime. Only such sins as obviously infringe the rights of others, or are contrary to State policy, are calendared as crimes; and some crimes, because they are only concerned with positive law, will not rank high in the list of sins. All States retain the prerogative of mercy : they pardon but do not forgive. The criminal who has served his time has satisfied the claims of justice, but if he needs forgiveness he must seek it elsewhere in a different way, for forgiveness comes from a person and is an outpouring of love, of that charity which covers a multitude of sins.

II. Difficulties

(A) *In Forgiving*

For many writers to-day the story of the Prodigal
S. Luke xv. Son is the whole Gospel, and in consequence they can see no special significance in Our Lord's passion and death. They forget that before telling this story,

Our Lord told others of the lost sheep and of the lost coin. It is true that the Prodigal, when he came to himself, returned to his father's house of his own accord; but it is also true that the lost sheep had to be sought for, while ninety and nine others were left in the wilderness; the lost coin was only found when the woman had swept diligently—a great deal of dust and dirt had first to be removed. It is right that we should love the most beautiful story in the world, but we should read it all, and not forget the elder brother's attitude, or the fact that the father made clear to the elder brother—" All that I have is thine." The Parable of the Prodigal Son brings out quite clearly not only the wonder of forgiveness, but the difficulties which forgiveness entails, and the distinction between forgiveness and complete restoration.

Some of these difficulties in the way of forgiveness we are bound to examine, and probably we shall understand them best by a series of illustrations.

I. We have already thought of the mother and her little son. His offence was against her, and when he wanted once more to be restored to her loving arms, he knew that it was only his own naughtiness which separated him from her. The conditions were quite simple, and the moment he repented he could be forgiven, for no one else was involved in his sin.

II. But let us think of another mother, who, hearing loud cries, rushes to the nursery. Her eldest son has been bullying her youngest and a sister has been expostulating freely on her little brother's behalf. What is the mother to do? There is the small boy shouting, " He hit me "; there is the sister, round-eyed with indignation, demanding that justice should be vindicated; and there is the elder boy, who says sullenly, "He upset my soldiers three times : I did not mean to hurt him : but he is such a baby."

You will say, "As the elder boy is obviously unrepentant, he cannot be forgiven"; but you must not forget that the elder boy is speaking the truth and does not see that he needs any forgiveness. For the moment forgiveness may be ruled out, and the mother's position is that of judge. She knows how irritating a little brother may be, but she has to see that he is not knocked about unmercifully. The elder boy must learn to control his temper, and must be taught to understand what pain is like. Let us now suppose that she is about to whip the elder boy, when the little one begins to plead on his behalf, and owns that after all it was his fault. Will not his interference awake a spirit of penitence in the elder brother's heart? Not to be outdone in generosity, will he not own up to his temper and be sorry that he hurt his brother? Will not the mother be able both to pardon and forgive her elder son, *for his little brother's sake*; and by so doing will she not reconcile all three children?

III. Let us think of a weak and self-confident young man, who is tired of living with a widowed mother in a provincial town, and tired of his work in an office, where his guardians have placed him because it was such an excellent opening. He has a small capital of his own and in London he finds many to encourage him in speculation. He has golden visions of getting rich rapidly, and awakes one morning to find himself ruined. He tries in vain to retrieve his fortunes, and then takes refuge in drink. He changes his lodgings and ceases to write to his mother. He frequents low haunts and worse company. He is utterly ashamed of himself, bitter with the sense of his failure, and incapable of escaping from his surroundings. All the time he knows that the mother in the country would receive him, but he cannot go home. He is afraid of his evil associates and cannot break away from them; he is afraid also of his mother and feels he could not endure the sight of her sorrow at his downfall. Then let us suppose an elder brother comes back from the East where he has made a fortune. He seeks for the lost brother and finds him, pays his debts and lends him his own clothes. He scares away his bad companions, and with his countenance, the younger brother re-enters the society in which he was born. It is some time before he can conquer his evil habits, and the elder brother has to bear with more than one relapse. It is a long time before he can be persuaded to go home, but when he does so the love of his mother completes his penitence, and he becomes forgivable.

IV. Let us imagine a husband who has been convicted of fraud and sent to prison. His reputation is gone, his home is broken up, he has no hope for the future. But he has a good wife and she stands by him. She feels the disgrace horribly, she has to endure the pity of some and the unkindness of others. But she goes forward steadfastly to make a new home for him when he is released, and to plan a new life with very humble beginnings in a place where they are unknown. It is possible that her love may save him, may bring him to repentance. Not until he is penitent is he forgivable, but love seeks his welfare while he is yet a sinner.

V. Let us imagine a farmer's son who has made

his native village too hot to hold him. He has cheated a neighbour over a horse and seduced the daughter of the schoolmaster. He is supposed to be in league with a gang of poachers out of the town; he has assaulted when drunk the respectable church-warden; and his blasphemous talk has been reported only too faithfully to the vicar's wife. He has a long score against him at the local public house, and a longer one at the hotel in the market town, where he has been expelled the farmers' club for not paying his card debts. Is it any wonder that his father has turned him out of the house and washed his hands of him? Six months later, he creeps home, very ill and very penitent, having experienced conversion at a Church Army meeting. His father receives him and believes in his repentance, but the neighbours do not, and spiteful remarks are made about the whole family. The Squire declares that the yearly agree-ment for the farm will not be renewed if that young blackguard is about the place. The churchwarden's daughters will no longer know his sisters. The farmer, once more responsible for his son, has to impoverish his family by satisfying the creditors. Forgiveness is given freely, but it is also given at great cost.

Pondering these instances, the reader may under-stand in part the relation of forgiveness to what we have tried to teach about Our Lord's work and Our Lord's sacrifice.

III. DIFFICULTIES

(B) *In Being Forgiven*

It is hard sometimes, with the best will in the world, to forgive; but it is often equally hard for those who desire forgiveness to accept it. We can leave out of account the unrepentant who do not want it; the proud who want it but will not stoop for it; and the frivolous who run away from their consciences, and hope that God will be like themselves and forget their sins.

There are morbid souls who dwell continually on their past, and live their sins over again in their perverted imaginations. They analyse their sins and magnify them; they profess to hate them, but will not let them go. They stimulate their own self-pity by proclaiming that they have no sense of forgiveness : and they have none because they really want none. They are interested in their own wickedness, and enjoy the tragedy of their own desolation. They are egoists, too concerned with themselves to think of God : He calls, but they do not hear. How can they be forgiven?

Then there are the diffident folk who rejoice in the Gospel message, but cannot believe that it is for them. They are depressed with a sense of their own unworthiness, and doubt the depth of their own peni- tence. They often live blameless lives, but for long, like Christian in *Pilgrim's Progress*, they carry their burden upon their backs because they will not lay it down at the foot of the Cross. We need not believe that such people are not pardoned, for pardon is God's act, and independent of our power of perceiving it. So S. John would comfort these humble doubters, saying :—" If our heart condemn us, God is greater than our heart, and knoweth all things." Pardon is 1 S. John iii. already theirs, forgiveness is intended for them. They 20. are under no condemnation.

There are also the high-minded people with so lofty

a conception of the law of righteousness that forgiveness seems derogatory to God. They look round about them and proclaim that they find everywhere a reign of law. They declare that Nature never forgives, and then they argue from analogy that forgiveness is impossible. Professed students of Nature so often leave man and human experience out of account.

Men of similar mind but a different outlook sometimes argue in this way: " God is revealed to me through my conscience as well as through Holy Scripture, and the more I enquire of that conscience the more I am convinced of the absolute holiness of God and the necessity of His divine law. Secondly, the further I examine myself, the more I am convinced of my own sin, and how completely it must shut me out from communion with such a God. Thirdly, while I acknowledge that my repentance is all that I have to offer, my repentance will not undo the past, or destroy the memory of my sin. My conscience declares that I ought to suffer for it, but it could not be expiated by any suffering which I am capable of enduring. Lastly, I cannot see how the sufferings of another can atone in any way for my sin, and therefore all talk of forgiveness by the Cross leaves me cold."

Those who have read the last three chapters should not be unduly impressed by this argument. Our opponent's view of God's holiness is too abstract, and his conception [1 S. John iv. 8.] of God's law too mechanical. God is Love : perfect love is pure and disinterested, and it is in this perfect love that His holiness consists. God's Law is Love, and when we speak of Law we do not mean something external to Himself, but the expression of His Will; and we cannot be wrong in supposing that a Good God wills our good. We acknowledge the exceeding

sinfulness of sin, and the impossibility of any man Rom. vii. 13.
saving himself; but it is just this which drives us into
believing that we must be saved through another, and
how this has been done has already been largely
explained.

But here one who defends the doctrine might
intervene, saying : " If a man does me a wrong, I
have a right to complain. The courts are open and
will respect my claim to compensation. If, however,
I endure the wrong without complaint, the whole
matter is at an end, passed over and covered up, and
that is the sense in which Atonement is used in the
Old Testament. Men have sinned against God and
have crucified God's Son. As we believe that He has
passed over that, is it not clear He will pass over anything, and should we not acclaim His sovereign
mercy ? " No ! Such an argument is fundamentally
immoral. It assumes that God does not think as
hardly of sin as we do, and that our moral sense is
superior to His. I am indeed at liberty to exact
damages for an injury or to forgo my right; but I
cannot condone sin without becoming accessory to
it. We do not want our sins to be merely passed over,
we want to be forgiven and we want our sins to be
done away.

A weak, good-natured man may pass over offences
because he does not feel their gravity, or because he has
not sufficient energy to resent them. Forgiveness, on
the other hand, is more difficult. It nearly always
entails some effort on the part of the person who forgives, and sometimes can only be bestowed at the cost
of sacrifice. It is also difficult to accept; for some are
so concerned with the wrong done that they forget the
person who has suffered from it; while others are so

o

sure that the wronged person ought not to forgive that they will not listen when he offers to do so. Again no theory of forgiveness can be expressed in forensic terms, or can be understood by those whose minds are dominated by legal considerations.

We have hitherto thought of the subject in our common experience, but we must go back to the Bible if we would really understand how the Law failed, and the Gospel made reconciliation with God a possibility, how the precious Blood shed upon the Cross cleanses from all sins.

IV. FAILURE OF THE LAW

The last error concerning forgiveness lies in remembering the law and forgetting the Law-giver. It was this error which S. Paul had to contend with when he wrote his Epistle to the Romans, and it is the same error that we find to-day in those who discuss the Atonement from a purely ethical standpoint.

Originally the fact that God was personal was the distinguishing characteristic of the Jewish religion. Abraham was the friend of God and so received the promises. When at a later date the Law was thundered out of Sinai, those who fell on their faces had no doubts about God's presence. Later again when the Prophets came proclaiming, " Thus saith Jehovah," they were convinced that their communications were immediately from Him. But as time went on, the Jews, out of a mistaken reverence, refused to pronounce the Divine Name, spoke of God by metaphors, and thought of Him under such symbols as the Shekinah. His awful transcendence was taught in such a way that it became almost impossible to think of man having any personal relationship with Him. The Law, however, remained—that had to be obeyed : but when permanent legal enactments of an unchangeable God took the place of personal intercourse, anything so personal as forgiveness became inconceivable. At most men could expect the pardon of a Judge.

" The Law indeed was holy, and the commandment holy, and righteous and good." It was not the Law Rom. vii. 12. which was wrong, but man's relation to it. God had educated His people as children are educated to-day, by means of external rules, which are necessary before principles can be grasped and applied. Some of them will always remain necessary if men are to live and worship together, for they uphold a common standard and their educational force is never exhausted. But we must not exaggerate their value. They have no power to make anyone better, for only personal influence can do that. They may decree the nature of punishment or the conditions of pardon, but they have nothing to say about forgiveness.

The Law was a witness to the fact of sin and condemned it, but the Law offered no remedy. The Law, moreover, was provocative of sin, for S. Paul says, " I had not known lust, except the Law had said, Thou shalt not covet." Many things also would not Rom. vii. 7. have been wrong unless the Law had forbidden them. This positive law had once been right, but it made provision for a social life which had passed away. Yet the Law remained, and hedged men in as long as they lived. It could not be altered, for it was supposed to have come entire and immediately from God. From it there could be no appeal.

So men conscious of their bondage to sin were confronted with the terrifying bondage of the Law. It had once been spiritual, for it was once the expression of a Person with Whom priests and prophets were in communion. There was no longer any open vision; the Law-giver was thought of as very far away, and the Law was thought of as something quite external to Him, an end in itself. In consequence, the Spirit of the Law was no longer considered and only its letter remained. It was left for S. Paul to explain how " the letter killeth, but the spirit giveth life."

2 Cor. iii. 6.

Written and engraven on stone it came only to serve the ministrations of death. No progress was possible under it; but as social conditions varied owing to outside pressure it had to be constantly interpreted afresh. Hence arose the Traditions of the Elders, which began by applying the Law to special cases, and ended by showing how it might be evaded, and the word of God made of none effect.

This process found support in the belief that all the five books of Moses had been literally and verbally inspired; and that therefore each jot and tittle of the Law had an equal value and importance. This worship of the letter in time led to a casuistry which was more ingenious than honest. The legally minded soon discovered that no two cases are ever exactly alike, and that no enactment in human language can be expressed with sufficient precision to baffle a lawyer who is intent on proving that his particular case is not covered by it.

As the interpretations multiplied it became more and more difficult for the simple to understand what the Law was, and specialists with the arrogance of specialists were sure that " this people which knoweth not the Law are cursed."

S. John vii. 49.

But even they were uncertain how men could be

justified by a code which had become so complicated. Some, indeed, argued that as every part of the Law was equally holy and important, and that every part was inter-related, so in keeping some part of it perfectly, such as the law of the Sabbath, or the law of Fringes, Ex. xx. 8, 11. Num. xv. 38. the whole might be thought of as obeyed. Others starting from the same premises maintained " that whosoever shall keep the whole Law and offend in one point, he is guilty of all." S. James ii. 10.

But many men did not argue, and it is strange how interested men will become in observing a system of intricate rules. Year in and year out, punctually to fulfil a difficult duty produces exactly the same satisfaction as establishing a record in some game of skill. Jews became proud of their proficiency, and went up, like the Pharisee, into the Temple to boast before God and advertise their own righteousness. The keeping of rules, excellent S. Luke xviii. 12. in itself, compelled them to concentrate their minds on their own conduct; and ultimately they became so full of their own righteousness that they had no eyes for the righteousness of God. Apart from Him they lost all sense of sin, and felt no need of a Saviour. They really believed that they were justified by the works of the law; and, for any lapses, they tried to atone by works of supererogation.

These Jews kept an account of their good works, as cricketers to-day keep their averages. Their good works were often in themselves entirely praiseworthy, but they were done for their own glory, and had in consequence no religious value, for religion has only to do with the relations between persons—it forges the links between God and man. There were sinners then, just as now, who wanted God, and were discontented and unhappy because they had not found Him. Yet these shrank from all approach to His Holy Presence, feeling themselves debarred by their sins. How could they be cleansed from them and forgiven. In old time God had sent many gracious promises by the mouth of His prophets, but before John the Baptist the prophetic order had long ceased. Had God ceased to be gracious and gone far away, leaving them to the terrors of a Law, whereby no flesh could be justified? S. Paul had tried to fulfil all the requirements of that Law, and found it a burden greater than he could bear, overlaid as it was by a multitude of interpretations, and developed as it had been by authoritative deductions. By keeping rules he found that he made no spiritual progress, and by breaking them he knew that he was self-condemned. He wanted God, and the Law seemed to keep him at a distance : he knew that he required forgiveness, and the Law offered him none.

For a soul afflicted with a sense of sin, forgiveness we have seen is a difficulty. The more a man was alive to the enormity of his offences, the more he was convinced that he could only be forgiven at great cost. An easily-accorded absolution could only wound and could not cure a sensitive conscience. A man hungering for righteousness could only receive forgiveness from one who regarded his sins as seriously as he did himself. He could only believe that forgiveness was valid if the Person who forgave had a complete knowledge of the offence.

God, and God alone, could satisfy man's needs; and man had first to know His willingness to forgive, and then whom He regarded as forgivable. Secondly, man wanted to know how the forgiveness was bestowed, and when, apart from his fluctuating emotions, he might be sure that he had received it.

So Our Lord, very God of very God, became incarnate that we might know Him and His love. He dwelt among sinners, experienced their temptations and understood the nature of their sins. He offered to all a free forgiveness, but He only did so at great cost to Himself. He taught men the necessity of faith and repentance, and provided in the sacraments of Baptism and Penance outward means for those who needed assurance in receiving His grace. Unlike the Mosaic Law, there was no limit in the range of His forgiveness, so that S. Paul was justified in proclaiming in Pisidian Antioch forgiveness of sins through Jesus and that " by Him everyone that believeth is justified from all things, from which ye could not be justified by the Law of Moses." Acts xiii. 39.

V. Our Lord's Dealing with Sinners

Considering how the Apostles preached forgiveness it is remarkable how little we hear about it in the Gospel Story. During Our Lord's earthly life, He seems to have been more engaged in curing bodily ailments than in healing diseases of the soul, for " first cometh that which is natural; and afterwards that which is spiritual." He spoke much more about 1 Cor. xv. 46. the rule of right conduct and the establishment of the new kingdom than about the nature of repentance and the wonder of forgiveness : and yet this also is right, if the ground of forgiveness was His death on the Cross. It was after His resurrection that He sent forth His disciples to preach the remission of sins in His Name. On the other hand, we must not forget that much of His teaching tells of a God Who will forgive, that there is the Parable of the Prodigal Son, and that there are the instances when He directly forgave sins.

Twice S. John the Baptist, pointing to Our Lord, said : " Behold the Lamb of God, which taketh away the sin of the world " : and in doing so prophesied of His death and redemption. The title used suggested at once a sacrificial victim, and one provided by God and not by man. Forgiveness was not to be merely a declaration from above ; but was to depend upon the removal of sin, and for that purpose Our Lord had to come in contact with sin and sinners.

Our Lord's first teaching was " Repent and believe S. Mark i. 15. the Gospel " ; so that from the first He did not leave men in doubt as to the ultimate meaning of His Mission; while by always speaking of God as the Father, He restored to men in the most intimate way that sense of direct personal relationship with God out of which alone any true conception of forgiveness can arise.

Very early in His ministry, Our Lord forgave the sins of the man stricken with palsy, and when the S. Mark ii. 12. Scribes thought that He blasphemed, He cured the man and so confounded them, for the Rabbis taught that disease was God's punishment for sin, and renewed health a sign of His forgiveness. But it is to be especially noted that He forgave sins as the Son of Man. It was His prerogative as incarnate, and it is in line with this teaching that we have been taught to believe in the forgiveness of sins through the offering of His Body and the shedding of His Blood.

S. John iv. 7 ff. We may pass over the instances of the Woman of S. John viii. 3–11. Samaria, the Woman taken in adultery, the Man at

the pool of Siloam, and the Man who was born blind; S. John v.
for though forgiveness is implied in all these stories, it 1–10.
S. John ix.
is not definitely stated in the text of the Gospel.   It 1–38.
should, however, be remembered that it was only to
the Woman of Samaria, sinful and a schismatic, and to S. John iv.
the Man who was born blind, an outcast from the 36.
S. John ix.
synagogue, that Our Lord definitely disclosed Him- 37.
self as the Messiah, and offered Himself as the object
of faith.   We should also note the story of Zacchæus,
the despised Publican.   When he made his act of
reparation, Our Lord said " To-day is salvation come
unto this house "; and His words imply more than
simple forgiveness.   S. Luke xix.
9.
   To the woman in the house of Simon the Pharisee,
Our Lord said, " Thy sins be forgiven thee," and added S. Luke vii.
48.
the information that she had been saved by her faith. S. Luke vii.
50.
From His previous conversation with Simon, we learn
that her sins had been many but that she had loved
much, whereas Simon, who was not conscious of many
sins, loved but little.   The punctuation and consequent
translation of the words are in dispute; but we shall
not be wrong if we learn that faith and repentance
spring from love, that faith and repentance are re-
warded by forgiveness, and that with the sense of
forgiveness love is intensified.
   Lastly, it was upon the Cross that Our Lord forgave
the Penitent Thief.   His words went beyond forgiveness, beyond even the remission of sins, for they were
an assurance of almost immediate salvation.   He who
shared His suffering on earth was to be united with
Him in the world beyond, receiving the promise :—
" To-day shalt thou be with Me in paradise."   S. Luke xxiii.
43.
   We can only conclude that during His earthly life
and in prospect of His death, Our Lord as Son of Man

forgave men's sins; and, secondly, that He had become the Son of Man in order to fulfil all the conditions
which would satisfy the consciences of men desiring
to be forgiven.

VI. Our Lord's Death the Ground of Forgiveness

While Our Lord was here on earth, His saving
power was for the most part restricted to those who
came in contact with Him.　It was not until His Life
had been set free by death that His forgiveness was
offered to all men everywhere.　That forgiveness He
Himself associated with His Passion, for at the Last
Supper He said, "This is My Blood of the Covenant
which is shed for many."　S. Matthew adds "for
the remission of sins."　These words may be a gloss,
but there is not the least doubt that they represent
the sense in which all New Testament writers understood Our Lord's words.　On Easter Day, the Risen
Saviour came to His disciples, saying, "Receive the
Holy Ghost : Whose soever sins ye forgive they are
forgiven, and whose soever sins ye retain they are
retained."　But the explanation of this power of
forgiving was to be found in His death and the proof
of its reality lay in His resurrection.　So He taught
them, "It behoved Christ to suffer, and to rise again
from the dead the third day; and that repentance and
remission of sins should be preached in His Name
among all nations, beginning at Jerusalem."
It was this mission that the Apostles, after Pentecost, began to fulfil.　In the face of the Sanhedrin
they maintained that the Crucified Jesus was "Prince
and Saviour," and could "give repentance to Israel
and forgiveness of sins."　So S. Paul taught : "We

S. Matt.
xxvi. 28.

S. John xx.
22, 23.

S. Luke xxiv.
46, 47.

Acts v. 31.

have redemption through His Blood, even the forgiveness of sins "; and S. John wrote in his Epistle Eph. i. 7.
" The Blood of Jesus Christ His Son cleanseth us from
all sin." S. Peter addresses " the elect . . . through 1 S. John i. 7.
the sprinkling of the Blood of Jesus "; while in the 1 S. Pet. i. 2.
Apocalypse adoration is offered " unto Him Who
loved us and washed us from our sins in His own
Blood."   Rev. i. 5.

There cannot then be the least doubt about what
the Church of the New Testament believed, and in
previous chapters the grounds have been given on
which this belief was founded. In Chapter II we
thought of God's willingness to forgive—of how He
sent His only begotten Son, not only to convince us of
sin, but also to demonstrate His desire for reconciliation. In Chapter III we thought of how the Son
came to be true man but new man, the second Adam,
so that men might be born again into His family, and
sharing His nature might share also in the fruits of
His victory over sin. In Chapter IV we thought of
Our Lord as Son of Man making reparation to the
Father for our sins, and offering satisfaction on our
behalf in order that we might be forgiven.

But the objector may here interpose, saying, " The
Prophets ages before Calvary and apart from Calvary
proclaimed God's willingness to forgive; and therefore
Our Lord can have done nothing more than seal their
testimony in His Blood. If this be so, it is clear that
His death made no change in God's attitude towards
us, and it is impossible to argue that the forgiveness of
sins is the fruit of His sacrifice. It is clear that S.
Paul and the other New Testament writers altogether
mistook the nature of the Gospel. Forgiveness is
and has always been the reward of man's repentance;

but man's repentance has been stimulated and deepened by the love of God as revealed in Jesus."

Now, I have already quoted the Prophets and have shown that the Life and Death of Our Lord did not change God's attitude towards us. But it is just because we believe God does not change that we are bound to regard the Cross as having an eternal significance, and to look on Our Lord as the Lamb Rev. xiii 8. that has been slain from the foundation of the world. If this be so, God in Eternity has ever been willing to forgive, and it is not illogical to argue that He has always had the same reason for forgiving. We may go on to suggest that the New Testament may be right after all in assuming that the only adequate reason is the sacrifice of His Son.

Secondly, we do not worship a Monad but a God in Three Persons, and, if God be immutable, their relations will always be the same, and if the Three Persons are a Unity we cannot separate their acts. This God we believe is Love. The love of the Father ever finds its perfect object in the Son, the Son ever makes a perfect response to the Father's love; and the love of both ever finds its complete expression in the Spirit of Love, God the Holy Ghost. Now a unity so transcendent must surely have the same attitude towards all the creatures, and when we say that God is Love we are sure that He loves men. But men have sinned, and sin is the negation of love, and yet God still loves, would save men from their sins and would win them to desire forgiveness. The objector whom I have imagined admits all this, and therefore he ought also to admit that all Three Persons must co-operate in this work. And the New Testament teaches us that the Father so loves men that while they are sinners He will give them His only beloved Son.   It teaches us that the Son so loves men that Rom. v. 8. He will associate Himself with them while they are sinners in order to make a perfect response to the Father's love on their behalf.   The Holy Spirit so loves men that He will convey to sinners the forgiveness of the Father which is due to the Son's response. The Atonement then is no arbitrary expedient, but the result of what God is and what God does.   It is the Father Who wills to forgive and does so because of the response of the Son Who dies that we may be forgiven.   We cannot, while believing in the Holy Trinity, exclude the death of the Incarnate Son from the process.

Thirdly, God is immutable, and the totality of things is eternally in the infinite Mind, but men change and are only in process of becoming, their minds are not infinite, and they can only know things in succession—they are bound by time and space.   In consequence, God has had to teach us here a little and there a little.   He has had to reveal Himself in space and time, and we may interpret His revelation in the terms of space and time, and are justified in saying that we are forgiven for the sake and in the Name of Jesus, Who suffered under Pontius Pilate.

It is because He did so suffer that we know God's attitude towards sin and His sympathy with sinners. Apart from that knowledge, we might desire pardon, but we should not desire forgiveness, and we have seen that forgiveness is impossible until it is desired. The prophets indeed announced God's willingness to forgive, but the response was made by few, for the revelation was not complete.   The sinful boy who has been expelled from school will not be comforted if his schoolmaster informs him that forgiveness follows on repentance. He only knows what forgiveness means when he mingles his tears with those of his mother, and knows in her presence that her love transcends the awful pain and disappointment which he has caused her : and it is through her sympathy that he may be enabled to start afresh.

Yet men in their pride are always trying to save themselves. " I will make good," so they say, " and thus merit forgiveness." At one time they thought that they could do this by the works of the law, now the same temptation assails them in a more subtle form, and they endeavour to do so by stimulating their emotions. They say that forgiveness is the reward of repentance; but repentance does not merit forgiveness, it is only a condition of its being received. Imagine that a man, who cannot swim, falls into a deep river and cries aloud for assistance; imagine also that a man with a weak heart hears him, plunges after him and dies exhausted as he gets him to the bank. Can you imagine the man who has been saved saying, " I was saved because I called out, and not because my friend here dived in to rescue me. All I have to learn from his death is to appreciate how great was my danger, while I was in the water " ?

We need to escape from modern theories, clear but shallow, to the deeper teaching of the New Testament which we cannot altogether fathom. We shall learn there that a man cannot save himself or merit forgiveness, and needs a Saviour rather than a theory. Contemplating the Cross as a fact which happened in time, we shall find through it the fact eternal in the

heavens, which is God.   Jesus alone reveals God and
so is the source of God's forgiveness.   Resting in no
one less and no one else, we shall say with S. Peter :
" There is none other Name under Heaven given
among men, whereby we must be saved "; and shall Acts iv. 12.
agree with S. Paul that " In Christ we have redemption through His blood, the forgiveness of sins,
according to the riches of His grace."   Eph. i. 7.
Cf. Rom. iii.
24, 25.
1 Cor. i. 30.

VII. Our Lord requires of us

(A) *Repentance*

That " Christ died for our sins according to the
Scriptures " was the doctrine which S. Paul preached 1 Cor. xv. 3.
and claimed that he had received from others.   He
appeals to it as the doctrine received by the Church.
We have striven to explain this doctrine, and to
show that it is more reasonable than modern theories
which are offered us as substitutes.   It is also true
that no one can be forgiven until he desires it, and
no one can desire forgiveness until he has some
sorrow for his sin and some faith in the person who
forgives.

We need not stop to consider whether faith or
repentance has priority, for they are the occasion of
one action—the turning from sin to God.   From
hatred of sin a man may turn to God, or from faith
in God he may turn away from sin.   There can be
no real hatred of sin without some knowledge of
God, and there can be no real knowledge of God
without some disgust with sin.   Yet faith and repentance must not be confused, and if we would understand the conditions of forgiveness we must think

first of one and then of the other. We will therefore
follow the order indicated in Our Lord's exhortation,
S. Mark i. 15. "Repent and believe the Gospel."

When a man repents of a sin, the sin is always
thought of as affecting someone else. A man may
be ashamed of himself, be filled with remorse, or
drowned in despair without being in the least penitent.
No degree of self-pity can be called repentance. It
is only when a man is sorry that he has offended
God or wronged his fellow man that he is repentant;
and that is why a true repentance never ends in
sorrow for sin, but always leads to confession of sin,
and its depth may be tested by the desire to render
some satisfaction.

Let us turn again to the New Testament and ponder
some examples of repentance and forgiveness.

S. Luke xv.
11–32.
When the Prodigal found himself ruined and
deserted by his friends, he at first accepted his
degradation and was no doubt full of self-pity. But
as he came to himself he contrasted his miserable
condition with the abundance in his father's house,
and from the memory of his home came the first
stirring of repentance. It no doubt cost him an
effort to leave the master he had served and give up
the husks which he had shared with the swine; but
in making that effort he was making an act of faith
in his father. From the far country to his home
was a long and toilsome way, but, as he went it, his
penitence deepened and he conned his pitiful confession, "I have sinned against heaven and before
thee and am no more worthy to be called thy son :
Make me as one of thy hired servants." He who
had been so intent to live his own life and so confident that he would prosper, was now ready to face

the humiliation of coming home as a beggar, barefoot and in rags, with no plea on his own behalf save his exceeding need. But the father was waiting for his son, watching the long white road, wondering, " Will he come to-day ? " When the son was yet a great way off, the father knew him, ran to meet him, and received him with a kiss. Before the son had completed his oft-recited confession, the father said, " Bring forth the best robe and put it on him, and put a ring on his hand and shoes on his feet; and bring hither the fatted calf and kill it, and let us eat and be merry. For this my son was dead and is alive again; was lost and is found."

Wonderful and immediate was the father's forgiveness : but terrible had been the son's experience, and long had been the way by which he came home. Our Lord, in telling the story, did not intend us to think lightly of sin or that repentance was easy.

Coming now to the Cross, S. Mark tells us : " They that were crucified with Him reviled Him "; but S. Luke, who certainly made use of a special source, adds the story of the one thief who was repentant at the end. He writes :—" One of the malefactors which were hanged railed on Him, saying, If Thou be Christ, save Thyself and us. But the other answering rebuked him, saying, Dost not thou fear God, seeing thou art in the same condemnation ? And we indeed justly; for we receive the due reward of our deeds : but this Man hath done nothing amiss. And he said unto Jesus, Lord, remember me when Thou comest into Thy kingdom. And Jesus said unto him, Verily, I say unto thee, To-day shalt thou be with Me in Paradise."

S. Mark xv. 32.

S. Luke xxiii. 39–43.

The malefactors probably belonged to the robber-

P

band of which Barabbas was chief, and the mob
who had rescued their leader no doubt sympathised
with them. When the one thief was convinced by
the dignity of Our Lord and won by His patience,
he went over resolutely to the unpopular side. His
repentance was sudden but complete. He acknowledged the justice of his own condemnation and did
not ask for pardon. All he wanted was forgiveness,
to be at one with this Jesus; but he dared only to
ask for remembrance, for some kindly thought hereafter. There was faith also inspiring his request, the
faith which found in itself the evidence of things not
seen as yet—the derided Jesus hanging on the Cross
would yet enter into His Kingdom. He was the
first to turn from sin to God, and to find in Christ
crucified the source of his salvation.

Now it is clear that neither the Prodigal nor the
Penitent Thief had any claims to be forgiven. The
Prodigal said, "I am not worthy to be called thy
son"; and the Thief submitted to "the due reward
of his deeds." Neither had been taught that repentance merited salvation. Forgiveness came to both
as a free gift. It was a personal act. The Prodigal
grounded such expectations as he had on his knowledge of the father and his home. The Penitent
Thief's only hope lay in his fellowship with the
Crucified.

Christ had been lifted up that He might draw all
men to Himself, and the penitent are forgiven as
they creep to the Cross.

Those who teach that forgiveness follows naturally
on repentance, in one sense state the truth and in
another state it wrongly. In disregarding the value
of the Cross, they obscure the personal element in

Marginal references:
Heb. xi. 1.
S. Luke xv. 21.
S. Luke xxiii. 41.
S. John xii. 32.

forgiveness. They are returning to the bondage of a law, in which because man does something, he can claim something. This, when applied to repentance, turns man's thoughts inwards to the state of his own feelings, instead of outward in desire for communion with God. It makes him seek for his own peace of mind, rather than to surrender himself into God's hands.

Secondly, repentance is usually a process, but forgiveness is an act. There is a great difference between a man with mere attrition and a man with a broken and a contrite heart. On the other hand, Ps. li. 17. you cannot think of a man as partly forgiven. A man is either forgiven or he is not. In consequence, it is impossible to regard repentance and forgiveness as if they were cause and effect.

It is said that a perfect penitence would merit forgiveness, but that is but cold comfort. It is really much more true to say that forgiveness quickens penitence, and that it is only those who have been forgiven and restored to communion with God who really entertain a horror for their sin. Some degree of penitence is necessary before forgiveness can be given; but forgiveness must be given before penitence can be perfected. We can learn of the great penitents S. Peter and S. Paul.

" The Lord turned and looked on Peter " after he S. Luke xxii. had thrice denied Him; and " Peter went out and 61. wept bitterly." On Easter Day, S. Paul tells us, xxvi. 75. Our Lord appeared to Cephas before He appeared to S. Mark xiv. all the Apostles; but the secret of that reconciliation 1 Cor. xv. 5. was too sacred ever to be told. We see, however, S. Peter as the true penitent on the shore of Galilee answering so humbly to the thrice-repeated question,

"Lovest thou Me?" There is no more blustering assertion; there are no more extravagant promises; the Penitent, grieved at the insistent questioning, only says :—"Lord, Thou knowest all things; Thou knowest that I love Thee."

S. John xxi. 17.

S. Paul at the moment of his conversion cries "Lord, what wilt Thou have me to do." As a Jew, bred in the Law, his first thought was how he could himself atone for his conduct. But three days later he obeyed the command to "arise and wash away his sins," and received the sacrament of baptism humbly from another. Years later he was to say, "I am not meet to be called an Apostle, because I persecuted the Church of God. But by the grace of God I am what I am." He was always amazed at the thought that he was forgiven, "that Christ Jesus came into the world to save sinners; of whom I am chief."

Acts ix. 6.

Acts xxii. 16.

1 Cor. xv. 10.

1 Tim. i. 15.

Our Lord is quick to forgive; He does not wait until penitence is perfected; or defer forgiveness lest we sin again. He Who told S. Peter to forgive his brother until seventy times seven has set no limit for Himself. He is ready to receive those who come to renew their broken promises, and to bewail their continual backsliding. But this graciousness on His part should not make sinning easy, for each time a man is absolved he is brought face to face with the Cross and made to realise what forgiveness cost.

S. Matt. xviii. 22.

Repentance is a condition, but not the cause of forgiveness. The cause of forgiveness is the love of God which was manifested on Calvary, and the revelation on Calvary is the ground of our faith.

VIII. Our Lord requires of us

(B) *Faith*

Faith also is a condition of forgiveness, but it is a faith in the Cross and not a faith in the validity of our own speculations. There was a time indeed when repentance was based on a theory that God was merciful, and faith sprang from a conviction that the order and beauty of the world were evidence for a God Whose government was directed by benevolence. But since God has revealed Himself in Jesus, and Jesus has died upon the Cross, our repentance wells up from a fact which we can contemplate, and our Faith has an object to embrace. Forgiveness is no longer a hope but an experience.

We note during Our Lord's ministry his insistence on faith, and how there were times when He could do no mighty works because of unbelief. Again and again, he tells men that their faith hath saved them. S. Mark vi. 5, 6. The Gospels prove that faith of some sort was necessary in order that His grace might operate. And what was true of bodily disorders was equally true about diseases of the soul. The woman in Simon's house was forgiven because of her faith. S. Luke vii. 50.

What then is the connection between faith and forgiveness? God in His love, as we have seen, seeks for reconciliation with men; but men can only respond to that invitation when they believe in it. Then considering Who God is and who man is, man surrenders himself to the Love of God, and God's act is an act of forgiveness.

Next, what is the relation of faith so defined to the death on the Cross? Abraham, we are told, was

Gen. xv. 6.
Rom. iv. 3. justified by faith, but he knew nothing of the Incarnation and Atonement. The woman in Simon's house had her sins forgiven because of her faith, but she did not anticipate the death on the Cross. Why then should faith in a particular event be necessary for Christians?

This question may still be asked by a man who is satisfied by the reasons given above for the Cross being the ground of God's forgiveness.

The answer must be sought for by trying to understand the progressive needs of men, and God treats us according to our knowledge and opportunities. As men advanced in knowledge of themselves and God, so they needed a fuller revelation of who God is, and because they received that revelation the demand upon their faith became more exact.

A heathen was scarcely conscious of sin, or at least did not for the most part regard his sins as affecting his relationship with his god. He was only anxious that his god should be propitious, and his faith was shown in his undeviating allegiance and devotion.

A Jew, on the other hand, numbered his sins, for he had a divine law. When he had transgressed a law, he atoned for it, if possible, by the appointed sin- or trespass-offering, which was in itself an act of faith. When this was impossible he could yet implore forgiveness and show his faith that God was merciful.

But as man's sense of his own personality developed, he was not so distressed by the evil deeds which he had done as with the evil nature from which they proceeded. He was no longer merely concerned with sins but with sin. He might compensate for a wrong, but he could not change himself; and if man was immortal so was his sinfulness. He could not justify himself to himself, still less could he justify himself in the sight of God. He had to be justified by God, for character can only change through personal influence. And what grounds had he for expecting that God would justify him? None, save in the coming of God's Son and the death of that Son upon the Cross. It is therefore through faith in the death of Christ that men who have reached to a conscious- ness of sin can be justified. Rom. iii. 24.

God's insistence on the necessity of faith is therefore not arbitrary. It arises naturally from man's know- ledge of his own condition. As he could not help himself he was driven to trust in someone else, and as he knew that he could not merit forgiveness he could only receive it as a free gift. Lastly, as he had no right to expect it, Our Lord died on the Cross to convince him of what God would do for sinners. Christ crucified is therefore the object of faith.

What then is the connection of forgiveness with justification? They are one and the same though viewed from a different angle of vision. When we think of forgiveness we think of a past which He Who forgives will no longer impute to us; when we think of justification we think of a present, the condition to which we attain the moment we are forgiven.

Justification means being accounted righteous, and enjoying the privileges belonging to the righteous. It must not be confused with sanctification, which is the imparting of righteousness, though as God by justifying puts us in the way of being righteous, we may say that with justification our sanctification has begun. Justification, like forgiveness, is an act, sanctification is a process, and our salvation is an end.

There are people who are offended at God treating anyone as righteous who is not really so, and they remain unsatisfied when told that God not only sees us as we are but as we are becoming.

Let us remember that we are for the moment thinking of sin rather than of sins, of persons and not acts. It is not a question of how the consequences of wrongdoing may be obviated but how a person may be forgiven. It is guilt which attaches to a person, and guilt needs not to be covered up but done away.

What is guilt? It is first of all the intention to do wrong. And how can it be forgiven? By the intention to do right. Directly a man forsakes his sin and has no intention of repeating it; when he hates himself in so far as he has committed it; he is on God's side and sees his sin and his past self with the eyes of God; and therefore is forgivable. And God, in accepting him, accepts him for what he is in intention and treats him once more as His son, although he may fall again and require another forgiveness. In just the same way an earthly father treats his son. He is convinced of his penitence, he listens to his protestations, "I will never do it again"; and he forgives at once, although he is not so sure as the boy is that the offence will not be repeated. Guilt, then, used in this first sense, has to do with the will, and when the will changes, the guilt can be forgiven on the same terms as any other evil act or passion which occurs in time. Man, we need to remember, is not in a static condition; neither is he merely the result of his past; his freedom may be very limited owing to his sin, but he retains the power to repent and turn to God.

Guilt, however, is often used for the result of sinning in the person of the sinner. His conscience convicts him, he cannot undo what he has done, and he cannot forget it. Remorse only inflames his misery, repentance does not compensate for the sin, and how can faith in the Lord Jesus help? " God (it is argued) may pardon the sin and remit the penalty so far as it is imposed from without; He may consent to treat the sinner as if the sin had not been committed, but can He cleanse the man's own conscience and free him from the sense of guilt? " Unless He does so, forgiveness and justification are words that have no moral value, and the Gospel is no better than the Law. To these questions, John the Baptist provided the answer when he pointed out Jesus and said, " Behold the Lamb of God, which taketh away the sin of the world." S. John i. 29.

In the Apocalypse we are told of " a great multitude, which no man could number . . . which came out of the great tribulation, and they washed their robes, and made them white in the blood of the Lamb." Rev. vii. 9, 14. But we have not to wait for heaven in order to verify this fact. Christian history provides many instances of men and women who have experienced the cleansing through the blood of Jesus, or, to use another metaphor, of sinners who have known that the cords which bound them to past sins have been loosened, and they have been separated from their burdens. " So I saw in my dream," writes Bunyan, " that just as Christian came up with the Cross, his burden loosed from off his shoulders, and fell from off his back and began to tumble, and so continued to do, till it came to the mouth of the sepulchre, where it fell in and I saw it no more."

The way in which the forgiven have accounted for their experience does not concern us, their theology was sometimes deplorable, but their witness is true. They found themselves forgiven, and believed themselves justified by faith. They were assured also of their pardon and that their sins had been done away. These latter points will concern us hereafter. Here we would emphasise the point that religious experience has to be taken into account by those who would deny that an expiation for sins was made upon the Cross, and that our forgiveness in some sense depends on the faith by which we lay hold on that fact.

IX. Our Lord requires of us

(C) *The Forgiveness of others*

The third condition for receiving God's forgiveness is our willingness to forgive others. Our Lord taught us to pray : " Forgive us our trespasses as we forgive them that trespass against us " ; and then commented on his petition, saying, " If ye forgive men their trespasses your heavenly Father will forgive you. But if ye forgive not men their trespasses neither will your heavenly Father forgive you." This after all is reasonable. It is the divine version of the *Lex Talionis* —Love for love, forgiveness to the forgiving.

S. Matt. vi. 12, 14, 15.

But it is more than this. God by forgiveness restores us to communion and intercourse with Himself. He receives us saying, " This my son " ; but if we are unwilling to live in harmony with our brethren we have no part or lot in that heavenly inheritance where all is harmony and love. The Prodigal probably found it difficult to live with his elder brother after

S. Luke xv. 24.

he returned home, and we know that the father went out to that elder brother to plead with him on the Prodigal's behalf. The unmerciful servant who had been so freely forgiven refused a like forgiveness to his fellow servant, and found in the king's wrath the revocation of his own pardon.

S. Luke xv. 32.

S. Matt. xviii. 23–35.

Thirdly, from the very nature of man it is doubtful if one who cannot forgive is capable of receiving forgiveness. He may receive pardon and desire pardon, but that is not the same thing. A man with no desire to be reconciled with his brother can have no real desire to be reconciled with God. So S. John says, " If a man say, I love God, and hateth his brother, he is a liar : for he that loveth not his brother whom he hath seen, how can he love God Whom he hath not seen ? "

1 S. John iv. 20.

" How oft shall my brother sin against me, and I forgive him? until seven times? " asked S. Peter. The Jews taught that three times was the limit, basing their teaching on Job xxxiii. 29. (R. V.) and the first chapters of Amos. S. Peter was therefore making provision for Our Lord's extended law of love. But Our Lord replied, " until seventy times seven," for the love of man, like the love of God, should know no limit. Forgiveness comes from the heart or not at all, and love does not calculate in bestowing benefits.

S. Matt. xviii. 21.

Job xxxiii. 29.
Amos i. 3, 6, 9, 11, 13.
Amos ii. 1, 4, 6.

S. Matt. xviii. 22.

Men, like God, must be always ready to forgive, but men, like God, may not always be able to do so. Our Lord could forgive S. Peter who went out and wept bitterly, and the Penitent Thief who, after a life of violence, turned to Him in the article of death; but He could not forgive Judas, whose very kiss was a betrayal, although even in the Garden He showed His goodwill by calling him Friend; and He could not

S. Matt. xxvi. 75.
S. Mark xiv. 72.
S. Luke xxiii. 43.

S. Matt. xxvi. 50.

forgive Pilate, who washed his hands to show that he did not admit any responsibility for his own unjust sentence.

S. Matt. xxvii. 24.

But our Lord teaches us that when we cannot forgive, we are yet to seek for reconciliation. " If thy brother sin against thee, go, show him his fault between thee and him alone. . . . But if he hear thee not, take with thee one or two more, that at the mouth of two witnesses or three every word may be established. And if he refuse to hear them, tell it unto the Church : and if he refuse to hear the Church also, let him be unto thee as the Gentile and the publican."

S. Matt. xviii. 15–17.

There comes a time when offers of reconciliation will only defeat their own object and confirm a man in his enmity; but Our Lord, Who prayed for His murderers, goes on to point out the power of inter-cession, especially where two or three are gathered together in His Name. When our enemies will receive nothing else from us, we can still pray for them, saying, like Samuel, " God forbid that I should sin against the Lord and cease to pray for you." By such prayers we unite ourselves with Him Who " con-tinually abideth to make intercession for us."

S. Luke xxiii. 34.

S. Matt. xviii. 20.

1 Sam. xii. 23.

While we share His work we shall partake of His spirit. We are ourselves forgivable and may yet win the forgiveness of others. It is for Christ's sake we are forgiven, and it is for Christ's sake that we pray for our enemies because He died for them.

S. Paul sums up the whole subject, saying, " Be ye kind one to another, tenderhearted, forgiving one another, even as God for Christ's sake hath forgiven you."

Eph. iv. 32.

X. God Forgives

(A) *In Baptism*

We have now thought of the ground of our forgiveness, and the conditions for our receiving it. We have yet to think of the means ordained by God whereby it is conveyed.

We have seen that God does not change, and that in Eternity all is present to Him. We have also remembered that we do change : we live in space and time, and apart from those categories cannot understand God's Being and Action, which are One. We have seen that in consequence " for us men and for our salvation " God has revealed Himself during a particular period of the world's history, in a definite form, in Galilee and at Jerusalem. It is only by an extension of God's condescension to human needs that we receive His forgiveness at a particular moment through appropriate matter with a special form. After contemplating the mystery of the Incarnation, we shall find no difficulty in affirming : " I believe in one baptism for the remission of sins."

Baptism is not a symbolic ceremony invented by men for their own edification; it is the means by which it has pleased God to confer grace. It is not in consequence affected by what men think about it; all we have to discover is what God does. Even then our explanations are incomplete; but God's grace is ever sufficient for His own purposes.

Forgiveness, though an act of God, can only be effectual for men in time. Men want to know *when* they are forgiven and God responds to that want. He does not leave us to be tortured with doubts, to seek assurance in our fluctuating emotions, or to wonder if our faith and repentance are sufficient. His forgiveness is a free gift, but the God of order grants it by a form authorised by Himself, so that we, who believe in the Truth as it is in Jesus, are satisfied with the pledge which He supplied.

It offends some to-day, but it is in accordance with God's economy that we should receive spiritual benefits by material objects. The beauty of a sunset, the vibrations which occasion sound, the glance of the eye, the touch of a lover, bitter and sweet taste, or the scent which recalls old memories, are all material means by which our spirits are touched—the sacraments of nature which we take for granted. Our Lord went further when He taught us the Laws of His Spiritual Kingdom by interpreting the common facts and experiences of life. He went further still when He took the commonest things we use—water, bread and wine—and made them the means of union with Himself. So we learn the great lesson that there is One God over all things material as well as spiritual, that there is One mind consistent with Itself from whence comes the Law valid in the realms of nature and grace, so that we may argue from the visible to the unseen, and receive invisible benefits through the things that do appear.

Water cleanses the body; and water with the Spirit cleanses the soul. So Our Lord said "Except a man be born of water and of the Spirit, he cannot enter into the Kingdom of God." But nothing that defileth can enter therein, and therefore in that entrance we must be cleansed. Forgiveness we have seen always means a fresh start, and at baptism we begin a new life by being incorporated into the body of Christ.

S. John iii. 5.

This has been the teaching of the Church from the beginning. When those who had been converted at Pentecost asked what they should do S. Peter's answer was quite clear : " Repent, and be baptized every one of you unto the remission of sins." Then, Acts ii. 38. we are told, three thousand who received his words were baptized. Acts ii. 41.

When S. Paul after his conversion lay blind and confounded at Damascus in the street which was called Straight, he prayed, and no doubt his prayer Acts ix. 11. was that he might be forgiven for all that he had done " ignorantly and in unbelief." God heard his 1 Tim. i. 13. prayers, and sent to him the devout but unwilling Ananias, who came saying : " Arise, and be baptized, and wash away thy sins." S. Paul obeyed and never Acts xxii. 16 doubted of the grace he then received.

It is unnecessary here to examine all the instances of baptism in the Acts, and all the references to baptism in the Epistles. It is, however, relevant here to note that as forgiveness is the fruit of the Cross, so baptism, which is a means of forgiveness, is likewise related to the death of Christ. " Are ye ignorant," asks S. Paul, " that all we who were baptized into Christ Jesus were baptized into His death ? We were buried therefore with Him through baptism into death : that like as Christ was raised from the dead through the glory of the Father, so we also might walk in newness of life." Rom. vi. 3, 4.

The objector may here again intervene and say, " Granting that the grace of God is a free and an unmerited gift, we cannot forget that the rite is administered by the ' Stewards of the Mysteries,' and 1 Cor. iv. 1. what happens if they give it to them who have neither faith nor repentance ? Can we believe that

God forgives merely because a ceremony is performed? If so, baptism has more to do with magic than morals."

This objection has its force from confusing forgiveness with pardon, and then thinking of pardon as if it were a judicial acquittal pronounced in defiance of the evidence. But the Atonement springs out of the relations of God the Father with God the Son; and forgiveness which comes from the Spirit, proceeding from both, can only be understood in the terms of Fatherhood and Sonship.

Forgiveness is not an article which can be handed over the counter : it is the loving welcome of a Father to a disobedient son. The son may refuse forgiveness and stay away : God will not compel him. The son may accept forgiveness and not prize it; it is his none the less. The value he sets on it will depend on his horror of his sin and his love for the Father. Baptism is not a charm by which one escapes from responsibility : it may be more truly regarded as a door. Those to whom the door opens are *ipso facto* forgiven and free of the Father's home.

Secondly, a Father's forgiveness is none the less real because the son's repentance is feigned. It is a fact of everyday experience that a child is forgiven because the parent in his fond love is deceived. But God cannot be deceived; and can we believe that He forgives when the profession of faith and repentance are unreal?

Forgiveness we have seen is never merited apart from the death of Christ, but is it possible to believe that God is so eager to welcome men that He does not nicely scrutinise the motives of those whom His servants collect from the highways and hedges, or from the streets and lanes of the city?

We have to remember that Our Lord, " Who knew what is in man," chose Judas as an Apostle and ordained him, that He gave him every chance of repenting and confessing his treason, and that He treated him as a friend within His most intimate circle up to the very moment of His betrayal. Was it with reference to Judas that S. Peter asked, " How oft shall my brother sin against me and I forgive him ? " If so, in thinking of Our Lord's answer, we may find a clue to the mystery of God's forbearance. *[S. John ii. 25. S. Mark iii. 14, 19. S. Matt. xxvi. 21-25. S. Matt. xviii. 21.]*

Faith and repentance have many degrees. There is a great difference between the man who makes a bare assent to the Creed and an equally bare acknowledgment of his sin, and the man who surrenders himself utterly at the feet of Our Lord and sobs out his penitence for past disobedience. But both are God's children : He knows them and will make the best of them. He longs to welcome them home; but in His house are many mansions. *[S. John xiv. 2.]*

We may conclude that God pours out His grace on all who are baptized, just as He sends His rain upon the just and the unjust. The farmer, however, who has prepared his soil and sown his seed receives the full benefit, but what does the farmer receive who has left his ground waste ? In the Epistle to the Hebrews we read of " the land which hath drunk the rain that cometh oft upon it . . . if it beareth thorns and thistles it is rejected and nigh unto a curse; whose end is to be burned." This reminds us also of Our Lord's Parable of the Sower. The good seed is scattered broadcast, but it falls on very different soil. So we may think of God's forgiveness in baptism as being ignored by the hard-hearted, quickly forgotten by the shallow-hearted, undervalued by the half- *[S. Matt. v. 45. Heb. vi. 7, 8. S. Matt. xiii. 3-8.]*

Q

hearted, and only finding a whole-hearted response from those who continue to grow in penitence and faith.

Let us remember that forgiveness is not salvation; and that baptism is only an entrance into the Kingdom of God. Forgiveness treats the past as dead, and Our Lord died that we might be forgiven : He rose again that we might lead a new life.

XI. GOD FORGIVES

(B) *By Absolution*

Baptism is therefore the means by which God confers forgiveness, and there is full forgiveness for those who are buried with Christ in baptism. But is there forgiveness for post-baptismal sin, and has God provided any means by which this forgiveness may be received and known ?

There is a terrible announcement in the Epistle to the Hebrews. " It is impossible for those who were once enlightened (baptized) . . . if they shall fall Heb. vi 4, 6. away to renew them again unto repentance," and the same author says again, " if we sin wilfully after we have received the knowledge of the truth, there Heb. x. 26. remaineth no more sacrifice for sins." And it will be seen that by the insertion of the word " wilfully " the author does limit his assertion to those who Heb. x. 29, deliberately do " despite to the Spirit of Grace."

But we must not isolate these sentences from their context. Those to whom the Epistle was written had not progressed as they should in the spiritual life. Some of them were in danger of apostasy and all of them were sinners. Yet the author, notwithstanding his warning, does not regard their condition as hopeless or he would not have written to them at all.

Secondly, it is true for all who have the cure of souls that there comes a time when they feel that they have delivered their message, and that there is no use for them " to lay again the foundations." Heb. vi. 1. They also know that they have failed completely with some individual sinner. But it is just at such a time that they betake themselves unto prayer. S. John indeed teaches us that " there is a sin unto death," just as Our Lord teaches us that blasphemy 1 S. John v. 16. against the Holy Ghost will not be forgiven. And S. Matt. xii. 31, 32. secular writers like Shakespeare have conceived of men to whom evil has become good, and for whom wickedness is the only satisfaction. But even about this sin unto death, S. John hesitates, saying, " I do not say that you should pray for it "; and we may be pretty confident that the Apostle of love, hoping all things, continued in prayer for the very worst.

Thirdly, it is quite true that baptism cannot be repeated, and no one can ever know again the wonder of his first conversion. As a man cannot enter a second time into his mother's womb and be born, so S. John iii. 4. his spiritual life can have but one beginning. But the Gospels are full of stories of how Our Lord healed the sick, and there are three stories of how He restored the dead to life. So we may argue from analogy that there is some remedy for sick souls, and that even souls seemingly dead may be revived by the God for Whom all things are possible.

It is not right that we should minimise the character of post-baptismal sin, for the Epistle to the Hebrews teaches us " we crucify unto ourselves the Son of God afresh, and put Him to an open shame." We Heb. vi. 6.

were forgiven in baptism because Christ died for us, and then we live as if the Crucifixion would have to be repeated. We acknowledge in baptism His victory over sin, and then so live as to bring disgrace upon Him. Men once called Him an impostor because He could not save Himself, and we encourage them to call His Gospel an imposture because it has not saved us. The sins of the baptized are more grievous than those of the heathen; for from those to whom much has been given, much will be required.

And yet, not even the saints live free from sin. " We all have sinned and come short of the glory of God "; and S. John writes to his converts, " If we say that we have no sin, we deceive ourselves, and the truth is not in us." Surely then we must believe that the Lord Who commanded S. Peter to forgive his brother until seventy times seven will likewise forgive those who have been baptized as often as they seek Him. Also as God has provided for His initial act an outward and visible sign, given through men, of His sovereign grace, so for subsequent forgiveness there should be an outward means of reconciliation with Himself and the brethren.

On the night before Our Lord suffered, we are told that He washed the feet of His disciples, and when S. Peter expostulated, said, " If I wash thee not, thou hast no part with Me." Afterwards He added, " If I then, your Lord and Master, have washed your feet, ye also ought to wash one another's feet. For I have given you an example that ye should do as I have done to you."

So after the Crucifixion when He had risen, He came to them saying, " As My Father hath sent Me, even so send I you. And when He had said

Rom. iii. 23.

1 S. John i. 8.

S. Matt. xviii. 22.

S. John xiii. 3-12.

S. John xiii. 8.

S. John xiii. 14, 15.

this, He breathed on them, and saith unto them, Receive the Holy Ghost : Whose soever sins ye forgive they are forgiven unto them; and whose soever sins ye retain they are retained." S. John xx. 21–23.

Our Lord had been sent to reconcile men with God, and He sent His Apostles on the same mission. Sent as He was, they in turn had the power of sending others, for men will always need to have their sins forgiven. The Apostles received at Pentecost the gift of the Holy Ghost, and the dispensation of the Spirit still continues. Our Lord had come into His Kingdom and willed to act through His ministers, in spite of Pharisaic murmurings—" Who can forgive sins, save God only ? " S. Mark i. 7.

At any rate all down the ages the Church has acted on Our Lord's command and repeated His words authoritatively to those who were ordained to be priests.

We have, however, little evidence in the New Testament about how the Church exercised its power, but we have the instance of S. Paul forgiving the excommunicate Corinthian " in the person of Christ " ; 2 Cor. ii. 10. and we have the exhortation of S. John assuring us that " if we confess (openly own to) our sins, He is faithful and just to forgive us our sins and to cleanse us from all unrighteousness." Nobody can, of course, 1 S. John i. 9. forgive a sin which he knows nothing about, so that confession is necessary before absolution can be pronounced. We learn from S. James that a sick man was to summon the presbyters of the Church in order that they might anoint him with oil in the name of the Lord. It was not only that the prayer of faith S. James v. 14. might restore the sick man, but that the sins which he had committed might be forgiven. That this S. James v. 15.

forgiveness implied previous confession is obvious
from the connection of thought in S. James's mind,
for he goes on to advocate for all a practice of mutual
confession, as an incentive to mutual intercession.

S. James v.
16.

XII. God Forgives

(C) *Immediately*

Does it follow from what has been said that apart
from sacraments there is no forgiveness? Certainly
not. When we know about God's ordinances we are
bound by them, but God is not bound. He has
ordained sacraments for our help; but they are only
means to an end, and not ends in themselves.

An earthly father might promise a cake to his
children when they asked for it politely; but he
would not penalise a deaf mute who did not hear his
condition and was incapable of saying " Please."
An earthly father often finds that his gifts are more
appreciated if his children have to do something to
obtain them; but he only wants them to have and
to prize his gifts, and would not withhold them
because of some unwitting omission. An earthly
father in an ordered home expects his children to
observe his rules, but these do not extend to a guest
ignorant of the domestic tradition.

Thousands have been misinformed about the nature
of baptism, but have found forgiveness in the contemplation of the Cross, and God has whispered to
them words of love. Thousands have been brought
up to be prejudiced against sacramental confession,
but God has assured them of forgiveness as they
recited their sins in secret and professed their faith
in the power of the precious blood.

1 S. Pet.
i. 19.

There are people, however, who seem to think that if they can reason themselves into a belief that God forgives, all is well with them. But they are not forgiven. Forgiveness is not the conclusion of an argument, but a fact of experience. It can only come from a person to a person, and the persons must be in some way linked together.

Those who hearkened to the old prophets were no doubt forgiven, for they believed that the prophets spoke in the name of the Lord, and had authority behind their proclamations. So far they were in the same position as those who receive absolution from the ordained ministers of God. But they could not know God as we may know Him, for the full revelation had not been made.

Lastly, however highly we may value sacramental confession and priestly absolution, we must not forget that Our Lord has opened the way for all of us to the throne of grace. With Him and in Him we have access to the Father; and the Father forgives us for His sake.

XIII. THE RELATION OF FORGIVENESS TO PUNISHMENT

We have now thought of the nature of God's forgiveness, the ground of our being forgiven, the conditions which render us forgivable, and the means by which the forgiveness is conveyed. We have yet to think of the effects of forgiveness and its relation to punishment, pardon and the final abolition of sin.

It is quite obvious that forgiveness does not always coincide with pardon. The Lord put away David's 2 Sam. xii. 13. sin, but the child none the less died. The Penitent 2 Sam. xii. 13.

S. Luke
xxiii. 43.
Thief was forgiven, but he had still to endure the
due reward of his deeds. S. Paul washed away his
sins, but because of his persecution he remained for
Acts ix. 26. long a suspected person. We do not, however, need
to go to Scripture for this teaching, for it is the law
of life. However penitent the vicious man may be,
he cannot restore his ruined constitution; however
penitent the criminal may be, he has yet to serve his
sentence. The wrong we have done our neighbour
will have its consequences, although our neighbour
freely forgives us what he has to suffer.

We noted in Chapter IV that we must not identify
evil consequences with God's punishments; and yet
this view is hotly contended for by some modern
theologians. They are as obsessed by the immutable
laws of nature as their predecessors the Scribes were
obsessed by the immutable Laws of Sinai. So when
they teach that so-called punishments are really only
consequences, they are losing touch with a personal
God, and forgetting that behind all punishment, yes,
and also behind all Law, there must be a Will.

The fallacy that any evil we experience is the
consequence of sin was sufficiently exploded in the
book of Job, though the problem of unmerited suffering is not elucidated. Similarly, Our Lord did not
encourage such reasoning when He was asked con-
S. John ix. 2.
S. Luke
xiii. 4. cerning the man who was born blind, or the men on
whom the tower in Siloam fell; but He spoke with
great reserve, for to understand we should have to
know more than we can at present—we should have
to see the end towards which all things are tending.

On the other hand, men are right in recognising
that the laws of nature are the will of God; and also
that God's laws are not arbitrary, but designed for

the general good. When, therefore, we deliberately break either the physical or the moral law, we are quite justified in calling the consequences our punishment, for we have set our wills against the will of God, and the consequences are to us His retribution.

It is quite clear that as long as we are unrepentant we can only regard such punishment as the exhibition of His wrath. So the God Who hates sin vindicates the order of the world. So the God Who loves sinners reminds us terribly that He is not indifferent to our acts.

When a man repents and is absolved, when he is happy in the consciousness of renewed communion with God, it is equally clear that he is not always pardoned; and the Church emphasises the distinction between forgiveness and pardon by hastening to absolve the sinner before his penance is performed. It is also true that the really penitent do not ask for pardon, they wish by suffering to offer such satisfaction as is within their power. But though the same consequences continue after forgiveness they are no longer in the strict sense of the word punishment. Punishment is transmuted into fatherly correction when we are once more at one with God. Our evil is purged away by suffering willingly endured, and the suffering will not be continued beyond the time when God's work is perfected in us. Whether this discipline may go on after this life is a matter of controversy; but reason as well as some texts of Scripture lead us to believe that, in the intermediate state, we progress through purgation and illumination to be made fit for the presence of God.

It may be that we ask, like S. Paul, again and again that we may be no longer baffled by some

2 Cor. xii. 7. thorn in the flesh. Happy are we if we can hear the answer given to him, " My grace is sufficient for 2 Cor. xii. 9. thee, for My strength is made perfect in weakness." Perhaps we cry, " My punishment is greater than I Gen. iv. 13. can bear "; and then we gaze upon the Crucifix and hear the Man of many sorrows saying :—" I suffered for you on the Cross : I am suffering with you and in you now, that you may be conformed into My likeness, and attain to the stature of My perfection."

XIV. THE RELATION OF FORGIVENESS TO PARDON

From what has been said, some argue that God is free to forgive but not free to pardon. Personal reconciliation they regard as possible, because physical science knows nothing of forgiveness ; but pardon they regard as interfering with the law of causation, which they have learnt from physical science to conceive of as mechanical. But if they could escape from dead matter and the laboratories into the living world of men, they might not be so sure about the validity of their reasoning. Men do pardon and remit penalties ; they show mercy and believe it is God-like to do so. If there be a personal God, He must be more free than men.

Let us begin by considering God's positive and personal commands as they appear in His revealed word. To a believer they have the same force and authority as the laws which are formulated from the observed uniformities in the physical world, for the God of Nature and the God of Grace are One.

However, the half-believer, not being able to explore this sphere, will readily acknowledge that the positive laws of God, like the positive laws of man, may be remitted and that pardon for such sins presents no difficulties; whereas it presents exactly the same difficulty if we believe in a God Who does not change.

Secondly, let us think of sins of omission. Among men, we know that they are more easily pardoned than forgiven. Human law finds great difficulty in establishing culpable negligence, and is lenient in inflicting penalties. In ordinary social relationships, we often find it very difficult to forgive one who has failed us when we trusted him; but it is often a case for which there is no redress, and often we would not ask for it if we could. But the Lord taught us the terrible importance of these sins of omission and the S. Matt. xxv.
3, 30, 45. strict account that God will hold with those who have shirked their responsibilities. But who shall say God cannot pardon such offences? Physical science, at any rate, is not able to provide analogies from which we could argue to the contrary. The most the scientist can say is that when the high task is declined certain beneficial consequences, which might have been, will not ensue.

Thirdly, in our everyday experience we know that the consequences of sins are not inevitable. We find in Nature a partial impunity and relief. A poison which would kill has its antidote, and remedies may be found for many evils. We are rescued from destruction by some unforeseen event, or saved from the consequence of our own folly by somebody's intervention. Experience therefore leads us to believe in the Divine Compassion, and to maintain that the God Who forgives can also abundantly pardon.

Fourthly, let us remember that when a scientist tells us that B will inevitably follow if A runs its course, there is always the proviso that C and the other letters of the alphabet do not interfere. The discoveries of the laboratory are made by studying phenomena in isolation, but in the actual world there are so many counteracting, compensating and remedial causes that we are hardly ever justified in concluding that anything is inevitable. The laws of nature do not change, but the more we know the more we can adapt and control them for our purposes, and therefore the more free we become. The God Who is the author of all laws and knows them all is also master of them all, and therefore it is not illogical to affirm that anything may be pardoned, and nothing can be truly described as inevitable except the ultimate performance of the Divine Will.

We conclude, therefore, that although forgiveness must always be distinguished from pardon, and that pardon does not always coincide with forgiveness, pardon is possible and pardon may be asked for, because we do not live in a world where a mechanically-conceived succession of consequences prevails, but in a world where the immutable laws are utilised and controlled for individual needs by the God from Whom they come.

Secondly, we maintain that forgiveness implies an ultimate pardon, however long delayed, for when a man has been cleansed from sin and united with Our Lord, his responsibilities for his past sins must be limited to their results. Now no act done in time, however bad it may be, needs an eternity for its expiation; so that even supposing no penalties were ever remitted it would be impossible to believe in a God Who punished for ever an act which could only have temporal consequences.

But we have said that after forgiveness, punishment is only disciplinary and remedial. If so, the idea of expiation no longer enters into it. Every wrong, it is true, must ultimately be righted, and God's justice must be vindicated to everyone. This involves expiation; but we turn once more from ourselves to the Cross to learn that He suffered on our behalf. We may not be able at present to explain the mystery altogether; for that we must await the Day of Judgment; but we believe that He died in order that sin might be done away, and therefore also the consequences of sin.

XV. THE RELATION OF FORGIVENESS TO THE ABOLITION OF SIN

Can sin be done away? That is the final question. It may be argued, "If forgiveness covers up the sinner's guilt, and pardon remits the penalty due to his sin, the sin and its consequences remain to affect the external world; and memory is still active in the forgiven person, who for all eternity must bear about him the indelible stain." Now if this were true we could not talk of being cleansed by the blood of Jesus, for there would be no real remission of sin, and the world beyond would be peopled by dispirited men full of dull regret and incapable of joy or union with the God of all purity.

We have seen that forgiveness must lead to ultimate pardon, and no pardon could be complete that did not abolish sin and the consciousness of sin, for the stricken conscience is the greatest of all penalties. Communion with God is vouchsafed to the penitent, but union with God, the real At-one-ment, is only possible for the pure in heart. How then do we answer the argument summarised above?

Sin, we saw as early as Chapter I, lies in the will and not in the deed. So the killing of a man may be murder or it may be the execution of a righteous judgment. But it will be said the sinful consequence of an act may have nothing to do with the will of the person who performs it, but it is experienced by the person who suffers from it, and passes on to others whom the original sinner did not know. How, then, can sin be abolished? We have seen that the sinner is not in a static condition; he may by faith and repentance turn to God and be forgiven. Forgiveness is not the covering up or passing over of guilt. The forgiveness of God takes the guilt away. $\mathring{\alpha}\phi\epsilon\sigma\iota\varsigma$ and not $\pi\mathring{\alpha}\rho\epsilon\sigma\iota\varsigma$ is the characteristic word of the New Testament.

ἄφεσις is used 16 times in the N. T. πάρεσις only once. Rom. iii. 25.

Secondly, we have seen that God may overrule the wickedness of men, and bring good out of what they did with an evil intention. So men with wicked hands crucified the Lord of Glory, but from the Crucifixion came the salvation of the world. The evil acts in consequence are swallowed up by the grace which they occasioned to abound.

S. Matt. v. 10–12.

Thirdly, with regard to those who have suffered, they will in time rejoice and earn the blessing of the eighth beatitude. So S. Paul teaches us "if so be that we suffer with Him, we may be also glorified together. For I reckon that the sufferings of this present time are not worthy to be compared with the glory which shall be revealed in us."

Rom. viii. 17, 18.

If these three points are true, we see how sin is really abolished in the man who sins, in the consequences which ensue, and also in the persons who suffer from it. But this is of faith and we await the confirmation of the second Advent. At present we know that " Christ has been once offered to bear the sins of many," and we look forward to when " He Heb. ix. 28. shall appear a second time, apart from sin, to them that wait for Him, unto salvation."

He will not then conduct us into a dreary penitentiary, but call on us to " enter into His joy." S. Matt. xxv. 21. We shall then only think of sin as occasioning the wonder of His Sacrifice, and the saved will not be depressed objects of Divine pity, but the glorious fruits of His Passion. The angels that hymn God's praise will declare Him not only splendid in creative power, but still more splendid in the radiance of redeeming love.

CHAPTER VI

SANCTIFICATION

I. The Fruits of the Passion

WE do not only need forgiveness for our past, but also grace that we may lead a new life; and we believe that Our Lord won His victory upon the Cross in order that He might send gifts to men. Calvary cannot be understood apart from Pentecost, for it is through the outpouring of the Spirit that we receive the fruits of the Passion. Pentecost cannot be understood apart from Calvary, for the dispensation of the Spirit was contingent on the death of Our Lord.

We are sanctified by the Holy Ghost, but before the Holy Ghost could begin His work, Our Lord had to suffer and be glorified. We are sanctified in the Church, but it is in the Church which Our Lord " purchased with His own Blood." From the Church we receive the Scriptures for our illumination, but they testify how it behoved Christ to suffer and rise again. We are " buried with Christ in baptism, that we may rise to newness of life." We are sustained by the Body which was given for us upon the Cross, and by the Blood which was there poured out. We are cheered on our way by communion with the saints, who " have come out of great tribulation, and washed their garments and made them white in the blood of the Lamb." Our work is to leaven the world, but

Acts xx. 28;
Cf. Eph. i.
14.

Rom. vi. 4.
Col. ii. 12.

Rev. vii. 14;

240

we can only do it if we are animated by Our Lord's spirit of sacrifice. He exhorts us to take up our crosses and follow after Him, up the steep and narrow way which leads by Calvary to glory. When He comes a second time, the wicked will look on Him Whom they have pierced, while the redeemed will raise the triumph song of heaven, "Worthy is the Lamb that was slain." S. Matt. xvi. 24. S. Mark viii. 34. S. Mark x. 21. S. Luke ix. 23.

Rev. v. 12.

II. THE HOLY SPIRIT IN RELATION TO THE
INCARNATION AND ATONEMENT

The Holy Spirit has ever worked in creation, bringing all the forms of order and beauty out of the primeval chaos. He has also worked through all human history, lightening every man that came into the world. He has been recognised by saints, prophets and poets, who knew nothing of distinctions within the Godhead. The Old Testament as well as the New is the result of His inspiration. He ordered the issue of events, preparing for the Incarnation.

In the fulness of time and with the consent of Mary, Our Lord became Incarnate through the over-shadowing of the Holy Ghost; and when Our Lord submitted to baptism, the Holy Ghost consecrated the Humanity for His Mission. By the Spirit Our Lord was driven into the wilderness, and "in the power of the Spirit He returned into Galilee." "The Spirit of the Lord is upon Me," He quoted in the Synagogue at Nazareth; and by the Spirit He claimed to cast out devils. On the Cross, "through the Eternal Spirit, He offered Himself without spot to God"; and S. Paul tells us that the Spirit raised up Jesus from the dead. Gal. iv. 4. S. Luke i. 35.

S. Mark i. 12.

S. Luke iv. 14.

S. Luke iv. 18.

S. Matt. xii. 28.

Heb. ix. 14.

Rom. viii. 11.

R

The relationship between Our Lord as Son of Man and the Eternal Spirit was perfect; and Our Lord promised that a similar relationship should be possible between the Eternal Spirit and His disciples. For that to be so, the Holy Spirit was to come from Him to them. Our Lord said, " He shall not speak of Himself. . . . He shall glorify Me . . . for He shall

S. John xvi. 13, 14.

receive of Mine, and shall shew it unto you." He proceeds through the Incarnate Son, and is for us the Spirit as He is in Jesus. We are not in consequence to think of Our Lord upon the Cross atoning for past sin, and then sending the Holy Ghost to take His place with a separate Mission; but we are to think of the Holy Ghost perfecting Our Lord's humanity upon the Cross, that it might be the medium for His own work.

This brings home to us that there is no separate action in the Blessed Trinity, and cannot be, if there be unity in the Godhead. The Atonement is the work of all Three Persons, and the Holy Spirit sanctifies us by uniting us with the Son, in order that we may be presented to the Father.

Further, we should note how Our Lord said, " It is expedient for you that I go away, for if I go not

S. John xv. 7.

away, the Comforter will not come unto you." So after His resurrection, when He commissioned His disciples, He told them that they could not start on their work until they had been baptized with the

S. Luke xxiv. 49. Acts i. 8.

Holy Ghost, and endued with power from on high. In consequence, it seems to follow that Our Lord's death on the Cross was the necessary prelude to the dispensation of the Spirit, while the Spirit had to be poured out before men could enjoy the fruits of the Passion.

But why was Our Lord's death expedient? Because He had become one of us in order that we might be one with Him. He had lived with His disciples and worked for His disciples, but He wished to communicate Himself wholly to them, that they might be in Him, and He in them. On the physical plane, this was clearly impossible, as the men at Capernaum saw when they murmured, "How can this man give us His flesh to eat?" His humanity had first to be made perfect through suffering. He had to surrender all that bound Him to earthly conditions; and then He rose again in the same body, but it was being transmuted into a spiritual substance. It is this body which can be communicated by the Holy Ghost, and by it our bodies are redeemed. [S. John vi. 52.] [Heb. ii. 10.]

And why had the Apostles to await the Holy Ghost? Because they could not conceive of a spiritual union with Our Lord. They had lived with Him, they had heard His words with their outward ears, they had seen Him with their eyes and their hands had handled Him. They naturally depended on His visible presence. When they saw the dearly-loved form nailed to the Cross, they were in despair; when He appeared alive on Easter evening, they shrank from Him as from a ghost; when they saw Him ascend from the earth, they gazed steadfastly up into heaven, expecting His immediate return. It was only at Pentecost, through the coming of the Holy Ghost, that they realised His abiding presence about them and within them. Then they understood the fulfilment of His promise, "Lo, I am with you alway, even to the end of the world." [1 S. John i. 1–3.] [S. Luke xxiv. 17.] [Acts i. 10, 11.] [S. Matt. xxviii. 20.]

III. The Holy Spirit Sanctifies us in the Church

Properly speaking, a kingdom is composed of men of one blood. They are governed by a king, and obey him because he is the head of their race and the representative of them all. Therefore when we think of Our Lord as King, we think of ourselves as united with Him in race, and we think of our fellow Christians as related to ourselves through Him. So, Our Lord prayed, " that they may all be one; . . . even as We are one "; and there can be no more complete unity than that. It follows that such a community must have one Spirit, if all are to co-operate to do the King's own work in the King's own way. It is the King's spirit which must pervade the whole Body; it is the King's work which has to be done : He is the fount of honour and the source of grace. He won the kingdom for Himself and by Himself alone. All the powers of evil were vanquished upon the Cross, and humanity was vindicated when the Son of Mary sat down upon the throne of Deity—a King indeed.

But this kingdom, established in heaven, had also to be proclaimed on the earth. After His resurrection Our Lord taught His Apostles " the things pertaining to the Kingdom of God." He said, " All power is given unto Me," and He promised His Apostles sufficient authority. They were to witness for Him, to discipline all nations, to punish and forgive transgressors in His Name, to be stewards of His household and dispensers of His gifts.

It was obvious that they could not do these things of themselves, and hence they were to wait for power

S. John
xvii. 21, 22.

Acts i.

S. Matt.
xxviii. 18.

from above. On the day of Pentecost it came, and they were all filled with the Holy Ghost. Then a band of timid men, who had dwelt behind barred doors, went forth to turn the world upside down; men who had marked, remembered and misunderstood Our Lord's hard sayings, were empowered to preach the whole Gospel of Redemption; men who had disputed about their claims to pre-eminence— each eager for himself and jealous of the others— found themselves a united body—in a moment twelve men had become one Church.

In his sermon S. Peter began by accounting for the spiritual phenomenon, quoting a prophecy of Joel. *Acts ii. 14–36. Joel ii. 28.* He went on to speak of Our Lord's miracles, which were then matters of common knowledge, and so disposed men to receive the greater news. He spoke of Our Lord's murder and immediately added that it was in accordance with the "predeterminate counsel of God." He announced the Resurrection and Ascension and claimed that he and his fellows were witnesses of these things. He concluded by proclaiming that the Jesus Whom the Jews had slain was Lord and Christ. That was the Gospel which was first preached, and it is reiterated again and again in the Acts of the Apostles. It is the *Acts iii. 12–26.* simple testimony of men to facts. They have been *Acts iv. 8–12.* summed up for us in the Apostles' Creed, and there *Acts v. 29–32.* is no other Gospel unto salvation. *Acts viii. 29–35.*

Men we are told were "pricked to the heart" by *Acts x. 34–43. Acts xii.* the preaching of S. Peter and came to him with the *16–43. 1 Cor. xv.* altogether sensible question, "What shall we do?" *3–8. Acts ii. 37.* And S. Peter answered, as the Catholic Church has ever answered since, by insisting on repentance and baptism. Then they would share in the Holy Ghost,

"For the promise," said he, "is unto you, and to your children, and to all that are afar off, even as Acts ii. 39. many as the Lord our God shall call." The coming of the Holy Ghost was not an episode, and His gifts were not merely for personal distinction. His coming was the creation of a new life and the beginning of a new age, and through Him the Church will be sanctified until the end of time.

We are told that those who "received his (S. Peter's) word were baptized, and there were added in that Acts ii. 41. day about three thousand souls." Added to whom or what? Our Versions answer the question by saying "unto them," the Apostles. So the Church on earth first of all existed in the Apostolic College, God normally working through selected men. But the Apostles had been endowed in order that they might endow others. They were "in Christ" and shared His life. They communicated that life, and though it may be received in other ways, it is guaranteed to us through the Apostolic succession.

S. Luke is careful to note with great particularity that men from every nation in the then known world Acts ii. 9–11. were present at the Feast of Pentecost. They may have all been Jews or Proselytes, but they represented the countries from which they came, and would return with the tidings of what they had seen and heard. In consequence, from the first day, the proclamation of the Gospel went out into all the world. The Church was to be Catholic and of no one place.

S. Luke also insists on the unity which characterised the Church from the start. Each member was full of the truth, and brimming with the new life, and the value of the individual soul became clear to the individual consciousness; but the Truth was one and the Life was one, so the individuals, like cells in a living organism, made up the one Body of Christ. No man was to live to himself alone, and the faith of each was to be expressed in conduct. A common faith had to be formulated, a common life necessitated order, and corporate action called for direction. So we read of those first Christians that "they continued steadfastly in the Apostles' doctrine and fellowship, and in breaking of bread, and in prayers." There was no doubt in the begin- Acts ii. 42. ning about the seat of authority in the Church, or the means whereby the life was to be maintained.

We can conclude from the record that the Holy Spirit came at Pentecost to teach men about their Saviour, to infuse the new life which flows from Him Who triumphed over death, and to strengthen and confirm men in an orderly society which should represent the Crucified.

IV. The Holy Spirit guides us into Truth

The Church founded at Pentecost is to endure for ever and to be "the pillar and ground of the Truth." 1 Tim. iii. 15. In it men are to be taught the Truth as it is in Jesus, and so be sanctified. Why this is necessary, we have now to consider.

Truth is correspondence with reality, and if the highest reality be God, Truth must ultimately be personal. If we believe this, Our Lord's claim to be the Truth will be intelligible, and as the Cross was the S. John xiv. 6. consummation of His life, it will be from the Cross that we shall have to learn the supreme lessons.

Before Pilate Our Lord claimed to be a King Who had come to bear witness to the Truth; and He was S. John xviii. 36-37.

not using a metaphor to describe a philosophy, but was announcing the principle of His personal rule. Bad government is much more often due to ignorance than to wickedness, and the worst government is that of the idealist who will not face the facts of human nature, or the limitations which circumstances impose. Our Lord came to reveal God's goodness, but He came knowing the evil and the stupidity which were in man. He faced the facts and accepted the consequences. He died for the Truth because there was no other way of convincing men. The Truth prevails when it is manifest; and it became manifest upon the Cross.

This is in line with Our Lord's previous teaching. He had told the Jews, " I am the light of the world : he that followeth Me shall not walk in the darkness, but shall have the light of life." He knew that they would not recognise this before His Crucifixion, but He prophesied, " when ye have lifted up the Son of Man, then shall ye know that I am He "; and again, " Ye shall know the Truth, and the Truth shall make you free." Men were walking in darkness, the victims of their confused senses and the devil's lies. Our Lord came as Light into the world, revealing the Eternal Father. Those who saw Him, saw the Father, and were at one with the Source of all things. We cannot say that we know the truth because we are in possession of any number of unrelated facts; we only know it when we share the mind of Him from whom the facts proceed.

The revelation of the Truth was to be preserved through the coming of the Holy Ghost, also a Person. Our Lord said : " He shall guide you into all Truth : He shall testify of Me : and He shall teach you all things, and bring all things to your remembrance, whatsoever I have said unto you."

S. John viii. 12.

S. John viii. 28.

S. John viii. 32.

S. John viii. 19.
S. John xiv. 9.

S. John xvi. 13.
S. John xv. 26.
S. John xiv. 26.

To describe how the Holy Spirit has done this would necessitate writing a history of the Church, defining the nature of inspiration, and determining the limits of ecclesiastical authority. That cannot be done in a book like this, and here it is only necessary to insist that, according to Our Lord, Truth is of the first importance if we would be sanctified. He died that we might have it, and certainly did not found a Church which could exist without a creed. We may indeed, without any knowledge of the Cross, be pardoned because of it; but we can only realise forgiveness when we know the Saviour. We must in some degree share the mind of God, and be indwelt by His Spirit, if we are to enjoy any at-one-ment with Him.

It is very important to insist on this to-day, for so many have been led to deny the validity of reasoning, and in consequence to deny the possibility of attaining Truth. Knowledge during the last century increased much faster than it could be assimilated, with the result that many have despaired of reason, and then pretended to despise it. Yet we have no other faculty to judge of anything, including the heterogeneous discoveries of modern science. This God-given faculty Our Lord intended us to use, and during His earthly life He was continually inciting men, who enquired of Him, to think for themselves. But to-day men complain that thought is futile, because, as no man can master all the facts, everyone can only guess like a blindfolded child playing at forfeits. It is not, however, necessary to know everything in order to reason securely. It is necessary to know the supreme fact or person from whom and to whom we may reason. That we might know this, the Truth became incarnate; and, in accepting Him, we find not only the redemption of the body, but also freedom Rom. viii. 23.

for the mind. It is indeed impossible to reason usefully so long as you do not believe in the possibility of arriving at truth, and about Truth many are to-day as sceptical as Pontius Pilate. Amid competing sects and conflicting philosophies, men are apt to take refuge in some specious phrase such as " all truth is relative," or they candidly avow that they accept as true what has proved useful to themselves. In consequence, politicians are opportunists, and commerce knows no morals, while the individual justifies to himself such conduct as his passions dictate. But if the world is to be saved from disaster, and society from dissolution, we must once again believe in truth and fixed principles. It is no good chattering about symbols, we want facts; and the facts will not help us until we have discovered the mind which gives them a meaning. That is what we mean by saying, Truth is ultimately personal.

S. John xviii. 38.

V. The Holy Spirit teaches us to interpret Life in the Light of the Cross

S. John xviii. 37.

" Everyone that is of the Truth heareth My voice," said Our Lord, and if we would be of the truth we shall mark His words. He also said, " He that hath seen Me hath seen the Father." It is in contemplating His Cross that we find the clue for the solution of our darkest problems.

S. John xiv. 9.

Our Lord by becoming incarnate proved that there was no contradiction between matter and spirit—a heresy which underlies much modern speculation. He revealed the unity of nature by interpreting the things of matter in a spiritual sense, until through the offering of His Body and Blood He made an atonement between God and men.

He was not only " born of the seed of David according to the flesh," the heir of an historic race, but His Rom. i. 3. Cross was the culmination of a long development, while the Church, which is His Body, has ever since been Eph. i. 23. entering on His inheritance. In Him we have the key to the understanding of human history. It is no mere flux of unrelated incidents. It can only properly be studied as revealing the purpose and the patience of God.

Nature seems so cruel, ravining with tooth and claw, that we doubt the goodness of the Creator, until we come to the foot of the Cross, and there behind the brutality of men, which we understand more fully than the savagery of beasts, we find that after all there is an overruling purpose of love. Society seems so unjust and we rebel against unmerited misfortune until we find Him, " Who for the joy that was set before Him endured the Cross, despising shame," Heb. xii. 2. Who " was made perfect by suffering." We doubt Heb. ii. 10. whether there be a purpose running through nature, and argue at length from instances of seeming waste and failure, but we pause to reconsider the evidence when we remember how utter was the failure of the Cross to immediate experience, and how it has proved to be the supreme triumph of human nature. Our Lord came to consecrate the uses of adversity, and proved by His death that while sin was evil, pain might be the way of recovery. The world had been too apt to think that pain was evil, and sin was natural. So, while Nature presents an awful spectacle of sacrifice, and we shudder at " the great world's altar stairs that slope in darkness up to God," above the stairs we see the Cross gleaming with its message that through sacrifice comes salvation.

It is by contemplating the Cross that we correct the hasty judgments formed from our incomplete experience. A satirist, longing to lash the vices of others, hears Our Saviour praying, " Father, forgive them; for they know not what they do." A superior person, after declaring that the case of some poor recidivist is hopeless, remembers how Our Lord promised the Penitent Thief, " To-day shalt thou be with Me in Paradise." A misanthrope, after condemning the whole world as evil, faces the Crucifix and seems to hear a Voice saying, " I so loved the world that I gave My life for its redemption." The easy-going optimist, after speaking lightly of sin, dares not look upon the same Crucifix with its moral, " This is what sin caused me to suffer." The busy man with a contempt for other-worldliness may learn from the Cross that this world is important because the pathway to another, and that he " who loses his life in this world shall save it unto life eternal." The Utopian dreamer who is quite sure that social reform can be effected by a few economic changes may discover in the story of the Cross that progress is the outcome of suffering and sacrifice. The Socialist, who exalts the claims of the State and would have all men to conform to one type, will find on the Cross One Who died for individual freedom, and to emphasise the value of the individual soul. The Individualist, who insists on the rights of self-determination as against society and its conventions, will find on the Cross One Who came into the world to serve, and Who laid down His life for His friends. The man worsted in life's battle and dying in despair may yet listen to a

Margin notes:

S. Luke xxiii. 34.

S. Luke xxiii. 43.

S. John xii. 25.
Cf. S. Matt. x. 39.
S. Matt. xvii. 25.
S. Mark viii. 35.
S. Luke ix. 24.

S. John xv. 13.

Voice whispering from the Cross, "I am the Resurrection and the Life." S. John xi. 25.

Our Lord, however, did not come into the world merely to correct our one-sidedness. He was not issuing an arbitrary command when He summed up the Law and the Prophets by saying, "Thou shalt love the Lord thy God, and thou shalt love thy neighbour as thyself." He was revealing man's S. Matt. xxii. 37, 38. nature and the reason for his existence.

Man is lovable and was created to love and to be loved. This is freely recognised by philosophers, on the one hand, and by the most perverted of erotic poets, on the other. It is recognised also by the plain man of temperate passions, for his happiness also depends on the people whom he cares for and who care for him. Self-evident propositions, however, are often ignored; and hence, instead of unity and happiness, we have discord and hate. Yet the whole world, irrespective of race or creed, acclaims the fruits of love when it is shown in loyalty to a leader under difficulties, or in self-sacrifice for the weak and helpless. Our Lord not only taught men : He was the Living Truth—Love itself. In perfect loyalty to the Father He made the One offering; and in perfect love for frail humanity He sacrificed Himself upon the Cross.

VI. The Holy Spirit unites us to Our Lord by Sacraments

The Holy Ghost is not only the Spirit of Truth, but also the Comforter—He Who makes strong. Strength S. John xiv. 16. is shown in life and liveliness, and the Holy Spirit is "the Lord and Giver of Life." All life comes from

Him, but since Pentecost He communicates the life of Our Lord to those who are His, in accordance with Our Lord's promise, Who, while speaking of the Spirit, said, " Because I live, ye shall live also."

S. John xiv. 19.

This life is normally communicated to us through sacraments, and we have already seen that there is nothing incongruous about our reception of spiritual benefits through material channels. The Incarnation is the greatest of all sacraments, for in it the eternal and infinite God limited Himself that we might know Him and behold His glory. But we believe also that Our Lord became incarnate in order that He might reconcile humanity with God. He first of all did this in His own Person, for he was perfect as God and Man; and no at-one-ment can be more complete than the union of the two natures in the One Christ. Furthermore, Our Lord sacrificed Himself for us, and gave Himself wholly to us, that we also might be at-one with the Father. His purpose of sanctifying us is summarised when He says, " I am in the Father, and ye in Me and I in you."

S. John xiv. 20.

The sacraments are not merely the extension of the Incarnation, but the means whereby we appropriate the life which was given for us; and the principle of self-limitation is continued in order that we finite creatures may have real communion with God.

God in Himself is infinite and everywhere, and Our Lord as God everywhere pleads before His Father the merits of His Passion. On the other hand, the humanity which Our Lord assumed of Mary the Virgin is neither infinite nor ubiquitous; and, therefore, however great its power of extension under spiritual conditions, it may or may not be in any particular place at any particular time. This is not derogatory to the sacred humanity, but a condition of that humanity being real, for the perfection of any created thing lies in its completeness and distinction, and its conservation depends on its maintaining this distinction. It was a real man Who gave Himself for us on Calvary under Pontius Pilate, and it is a real humanity which He offers to share with us. As there is a definite humanity so there must be definite means for its reception; and these means are of Our Lord's appointment.

About the necessity of this union with Himself, Our Lord is clear. " I am the Vine," He says, " ye are the branches : he that abideth in Me, and I in him, the same bringeth forth much fruit : for without Me ye can do nothing." Our life " in Christ " is _{S. John xv.} assured to us in baptism; and Christ's life in us is ^{5.} constantly renewed by participation in the Holy Communion. There is the visible Church, which is Christ's body, of which we became members and to which we belong, just as branches which have been grafted in belong to the vine. There is also the invisible spirit of Christ within us, strengthening and transforming us, which is like the sap issuing in the branches, that they may put forth leaves, and blossom, and finally in the vintage time yield their fruit.

This life " in Christ " is continuous with the life which we derive from our parents, for Our Lord does not come to destroy, but to redeem and transfigure. When the spiritual life begins at baptism, the physical and psychical life, called by S. Paul " the life of the flesh," remains. Until harmony has been established _{Gal. iv.} " the flesh lusteth against the Spirit, and the Spirit ^{23–31.} against the flesh." So S. Paul writes : " We our- _{Gal. v. 17.} selves also, which have the firstfruits of the Spirit, even we ourselves groan within ourselves, waiting Rom. viii. 23. for the adoption, to wit, the redemption of the body." Again he exhorts men to present their bodies " a Rom. xii. 1. living sacrifice, holy and acceptable unto God." The body, though indwelt by the Spirit, is only sanctified when there is a willingness to sacrifice it for spiritual ends. Then it is identified with Him Who offered His Body in sacrifice upon the Cross.

While we marvel at Our Lord's lovingkindness in bestowing His nature upon us in sacraments, we have yet to remember that " the Spirit bloweth where it S. John iii. 8. listeth," and we find evidence of His power where the Sacraments are through ignorance or prejudice repudiated. We are indeed bound by the revelation which we have received, but God is not bound. So, when we speak of sacraments as " generally necessary to salvation," the word " generally " must be interpreted in its logical sense. We dare not say that sacraments are " universally " necessary, and we dare not say that they are optional. They are necessary for those who are, or wish to be, within the Church of the Incarnate Redeemer and have had brought home to them the commands of Our Lord. We belong to the New Covenant and are bound by it, but we may well believe in uncovenanted mercies, for the God we worship is a God of Love.

Lastly, no sacrament is a charm : it is neither a mechanical contrivance to get us to heaven nor a magical instrument of salvation. It is a gift, and the nature of the gift is constituted by an act of God. It follows that a sacrament is what it is because God makes it so. No error of thought and no ignorance on our part can in any way affect its nature. On the other hand, a gift is something that we are free to accept or reject, to prize or disdain, to use or abuse, or even to cast away.

The heavenly Sower goes forth to sow. His seed is good, but it only takes root when it falls into the right soil. Even then there is a great difference in its productiveness. It may bring forth a hundredfold or only thirty. The parable was told of " the word of God " : it is equally true of the sacraments by which the Word of God Who became flesh tabernacles among us. *S. Matt. xiii. 3. S. Mark iv. 3. S. Luke viii. 5–8.* *S. John i. 14.*

VII. The Holy Communion

We are born again in baptism into Our Lord's family ; we are taught and trained by His Spirit ; we are endowed in Confirmation with the weapons of our spiritual warfare ; but we need also to be sustained by the food which comes from heaven if we are to share Our Lord's life and live for Him.

In providing this food, Our Lord adapts Himself to human experience, and satisfies natural instincts. Social intercourse all the world over has involved eating the same food at a common table ; and there is no great compliment in the lordliest feast unless the host be present. So Our Lord told the stories of the Great Supper and the Marriage of the King's Son. So we find that, in the Church, He has His own table, He provides the food, He is present Himself, and He bids all His servants to come. *S. Luke xiv. 10–24. S. Matt. xxii. 2–14.*

We know that our natural life is only sustained by food from without. We know that the food which is to nourish us must have life in it, but this life, whether it be animal or vegetable, has first of all to be sacrificed. Our spiritual life needs sustenance as well as our

s

bodies; and Our Lord sacrificed Himself upon the Cross that He might spiritually sustain the life of the world.

The vast power of extension in material things when possessed by spirit was shown when Our Lord fed five thousand with five loaves and a few small S. John vi. 9. fishes. This miracle, like the manna which fell in S. John vi. the wilderness, served a temporary purpose, but Our Lord used it as a parable for the food of immortality which He alone could give. So He said : " I am the bread of life. . . . I am the living bread which came down from heaven : if any man eat of this bread, He shall live for ever, and the bread that I will give is My flesh, which I will give for the life of the world. . . . My flesh is meat indeed, and My blood is drink indeed. He that eateth My flesh, and drinketh My blood, dwelleth in Me, and I in him. As the living Father hath sent me, and I live by the Father : so he that S. John vi. eateth Me, even he shall live by Me."
35–57.

We note in this passage that before men could receive this food Our Lord had to give His life for the world. Secondly, that the Oneness which He had as God with the nature of the Father was to correspond with the oneness which as man He should have with His own. Thirdly, His words were to be construed in terms of life and its communication.

His words offended the Jews. They did not understand Him when He said : " It is the spirit that quickeneth ; the flesh profiteth nothing : the words that I speak unto you, they are spirit, and they are S. John vi. life." Neither have Christians always understood these words, because they are always in danger of assuming that the phenomenal is real, and the spiritual is figurative. Our Lord's Body and Blood were once,

but are no longer, subject to physical laws; and He
offers to communicate that Body and Blood as they
now are to us, not that we may change Him, Who
cannot change, into ourselves; but that we may be
so united to Him as to say with S. Paul, "I live, yet
not I, but Christ liveth in me."   We cannot, indeed, Gal. ii. 20.
explain how the Body and Blood which Our Lord
took of Mary can be communicated to us under the
forms of bread and wine; but we believe that He took
a Body and offered it in sacrifice that our bodies might
be redeemed.   It is because we believe in the redemption of both body and soul that we feel our need of
participating in the perfected humanity of the
Redeemer.

On the night before He suffered, He instituted His
feast; and when He said, "Do this in remembrance 1 Cor. xi. 24.
of Me," His words had all the force which we associate S. Luke xxii. 19.
with a dying command.   He was the Paschal Lamb
without blemish and without spot, and His sacrifice
was the occasion of a world-wide deliverance from
bondage.   So S. Paul says, "Christ, our Passover,
is sacrificed for us : therefore let us keep the feast." 1 Cor. v. 7, 8.
Our Lord said, "This is My Body which is given for
you," and "This is My Blood which is shed for you
and for many"; and so it is impossible to separate 1 Cor. xi. 24–25.
the Holy Communion from the offering made on S. Matt. xxvi. 26–28.
Calvary, or think of that offering otherwise than as a S. Mark xiv. 22–24.
sacrifice.   We conclude that when He said, "Take, S. Luke xxii. 19, 20.
eat, and drink ye all of it," a sacrificial meal was
intended wherein the communion of God with man
was restored and provided for.

Lastly, as we all share in the same food, so we are
all united together.   All the Sacraments have a social
significance, besides conveying benefits to individuals.

S. Paul writes : "The cup of blessing which we bless, is it not the communion of (or joint participation in) the Blood of Christ? The bread which we break, is it not the communion of (or joint participation in) the Body of Christ? For we being many are one bread, and one body : for we are all partakers of that one bread." The Holy Communion then not only unites us with Our Lord, but is the sacrament of unity among ourselves. Having one Lord, one Faith, one Baptism, we frequent a common table, where we eat of the same food and drink out of the same cup, pledging ourselves to mutual service, and rejoicing in the communion which we have with the saints.

1 Cor. x. 16, 17.

Eph. iv. 5.

VIII. The Communion of Saints

The Holy Spirit guides us into Truth and unites us by sacraments to the living Lord; but He sanctifies us in a Church for "we are all members one of another" and cannot say to any of our fellows, "I have no need of thee."

1 Cor. xii. 21.

We are all "called to be Saints," to be "a royal priesthood, a holy nation, a peculiar people," but in this sphere of mutual obligation, some give much more than they receive. They have been sanctified and show in their lives the saving power of Christ's death, and so have an influence which does not die.

1 Cor. i. 2.

1 S. Pet. ii. 9.

This is all in line with God's normal method of working. Knowledge, civilisation, morality and holiness are principally due to gifted individuals, who by their energy, inventiveness, thought, aspiration and sacrifice have conferred benefits on all mankind. "There are diversities of gifts, but the same Spirit,"

1 Cor. xii. 4.

and the " Spirit divides to every man severally as He
will." 1 Cor. xii. 11.

An invention, a work of art, a good book or a good
law are things which we can receive apart from their
authors, but holiness can only be communicated
personally, and hence the need of communion with the
saints, that is with those who have been endowed with
special grace, and have an experience of God vouchsafed only to a few. Such people on earth inspire us
by their examples and encourage us by their sympathy,
but they are not always near and the wicked are more
apparent. We need in consequence communion with
the saints in heaven, but is this possible?

We are ready enough to acknowledge what the world
owes to the glorious company of the Apostles, the
goodly fellowship of the Prophets and the white-robed
army of the Martyrs. We pray that we may learn
from them to love Our Lord; and we hope some day to
join with them in the harmony of heaven. But this
is not enough.

We remember that Our Lord rose as " the firstfruits of the dead " and ascended into heaven to 1 Cor. xv. 20.
bridge the gulf between this world and the next; so
that the saints departed are still alive—" the Church
of the firstborn in the heavenly Zion." These Heb. xii. 23.
triumphant beings are not separated from Our Lord,
but share His interests, and " His delights are still
with the sons of men." They then, in the higher Prov. viii.
31.
world of greater opportunities and wider vision, will
not forget their past or be unmindful of those they
left behind. It is at any rate more reasonable to
suppose that those who while on earth ministered to
the sick, the suffering and the sinner still " condescend
to men of low estate." Moreover, Our Lord tells us Rom. xi. 16.

S. Luke xv. 7.
"that there is joy in heaven over one sinner that repenteth"; so we may not only expect their aid, but may also contribute to their happiness.

The author of the Epistle to the Hebrews imagines Heb. xii. 1. us "encompassed by a great cloud of witnesses," who are like spectators in an amphitheatre watching our struggles as we press on "looking unto Jesus, Heb. xii. 2. the Author and Finisher of our faith." They are spectators who can sympathise, for they were once themselves in the dust and the turmoil, and we enter into communion with them when we believe in their encouragement and support. The Seer of Patmos, far from his churches in Asia, felt very lonely and Rev. iv. 1. deserted, but a door was opened for him in heaven and he found himself in the presence of "multitudes Rev. vii. 9. that no man could number": he was not an unrelated unit, but even then had his part in the vast drama of judgment and redemption.

Believing in the sympathy of the saints, we may surely be certain of their prayers. We are told that "the effectual fervent prayer of a righteous man S. James v. 16. availeth much," and his prayers will be none the less availing because he is nearer to the throne of God. If we ask our friends on earth to intercede for us, there can be nothing wrong in asking God for the prayers of the saints in heaven.

But we should not merely seek communion with the saints for what we may obtain from them; we shall think first of the honour we receive in their society. The recognition of their presence with Our Lord has also its bearing on our belief in His atonement, for they are the proof of its success. When troubles overwhelm us, we know not why, are we not tempted to ask, "Does He indeed save?"

S. John was haunted perhaps by the same fear until he saw the vision of those " who had come out of great tribulation." When penitent, but afraid that Rev. vii. 14. we shall sin again, we are tempted to despair of attaining to purity, but we take fresh heart in remembering those " who have washed their robes white in the Blood of the Lamb." When conscious of our weakness and incapacity we shrink from some responsibility, we do well to remember those who " out of weakness were made strong." The Church in the Heb. xi. 34. beginning was built up of very unpromising material, and it is in communion with the triumphant saints that we find courage to follow the Captain of Our Salvation, not trusting in ourselves, but relying, as they did, on His assurance, " My grace is sufficient for you." 2 Cor. xii. 9.

IX. The Holy Spirit's Witness to the World

The Church besides ministering to her own members has a missionary work to do for those who are beyond her borders. She has to maintain the standard of the Cross in face of a hostile and unbelieving world. No terms can be made with the foe, but many of them may be won and induced to transfer their allegiance. So Our Lord foretold that when the Holy Spirit came to guide and inform the Church, He would " reprove (convince or convict) the world of sin, and of righteousness, and of judgment : of sin, because they believed not on Me ; of righteousness, because I go to My Father, and ye see Me no more ; of judgment, because the Prince of this world is judged." S. John xvi. 8–11.

Three translations of ἐλέγξει are here offered, for all are admissible, and each adds something to the understanding of the passage. The Holy Spirit is the Moralist Who *reproves* the world, not only for its sin, but also for its assumption of righteousness and judgment. He is the Logician Who *convinces* the world that it is sinful, needs righteousness and deserves judgment. He is the Judge Who *convicts* the world of sinning while it knows what righteousness is, and pronounces judgment. These three interpretations are not inconsistent but complementary.

It was on the night before Our Lord suffered that He spoke these words, and we are surely right to connect them with His death. Already in Chapter II we have seen how the sin which separates man from God found its ultimate expression in the Crucifixion. In Chapter III we have seen how the sinner is in bondage and cannot be righteous apart from the deliverance effected on the Cross. In Chapter IV we have seen in what sense the Cross was God's judgment on sin and also the way to man's forgiveness. But Our Lord, in telling of the Spirit's advent, looks still further. Sin He connects with unbelief in Himself, which conversely suggests the doctrine of justification by faith as explained in Chapter V: Righteousness He connects with His Ascension and therefore with His mediatorial kingdom which is the subject of the present chapter: Judgment He connects with the prince of this world, already judged, in part despoiled, whose power will be utterly destroyed. This last subject properly belongs to the chapter which follows and concludes the argument.

Our Lord spoke of the Holy Spirit bringing home to men the nature of sin and declared that their sin

would be manifest because they believed not on Him.
Face to face with His perfect goodness, the Jews
desired that He should be slain. Face to face with Acts xiii. 28.
the same facts, men still refuse to acknowledge or
even consider His claims. This failure to recognise
goodness, this will not-to-believe, reveals the awful
separation between sin and goodness, the alienation
of man from God. But the Holy Spirit through the
Church maintains His witness in the hope of convincing and at last convicting the most hardened
sinner.

Nobody wishes to be convicted of sin. All men
like to think well of themselves, and so long as they
only compare themselves with their neighbours they
retain their self-complacence, and are contented,
although blind to the truth. It is only when they
contemplate Our Lord that they are convicted of sin
and become contemptible in their own sight. Pricked
to the heart, they may then ask, " What shall we do
to be saved ? " and receive the old answer, " Believe
on the Lord Jesus Christ." Acts xvi. 30, 31.

Secondly, Our Lord spoke of the Holy Spirit
bringing home to men the nature of righteousness,
which is not of this world, but of Him Who goes to
the Father. The righteousness of this world consists
of doing what is expedient, and condemning one man
to die for the nation. It consists in conformity with
the world's customs and adaptation to its shifting
standards in manners and morals. True righteousness, on the other hand, consists in doing the will of
God ; and His will is the Law which ultimately
governs nature and therefore human life. The meaning of this Law was revealed by Our Lord once and
for all. He could then return to the Father, for

God's righteousness belongs to the eternal order, and does not change with the fluctuations of fashion.

It is to this righteousness that the Holy Spirit witnesses when He convicts men of sin. He forces men to recognise the contrast between their way and God's way; and they are convinced or convicted, as they respond to or react from the vision of Christ crucified. But the Holy Spirit has a further object in setting forth Our Lord's righteousness. By going to the Father and being at-one with the Father, He can impart His righteousness to us, so that we may speak of Him as " The Lord, our Righteousness." His charity will cover the multitude of our sins, and is like the wedding garment which the man in the parable neglected to put on. There are people who refuse help, resent influence and isolate themselves in order to maintain their independence. Such people will reap what they have sown, they will be speechless and unable to respond to One Who calls them " Friend "; they will go out into the darkness and know what it means to be alone.

Thirdly, Our Lord spoke of the Holy Spirit coming to convince men of judgment, and able to do so because " the Prince of this world is judged." In order to understand Our Lord's words, we should note the judgment of history upon His Crucifixion. Living in a world organised apart from God, men had to rely for justice upon public opinion, law, and an administrator supported by the necessary force. *Public opinion* was stirred up to denounce Our Lord as a blasphemer; the cry went up " By our *law* he ought to die "; and a *judge,* inclined to mercy, none the less bowed to the great voice of the people, and thought to wash his hands of any responsibility.

Jer. xxiii. 6.

1 Pet. iv. 8.

S. Matt. xxii. 12, 13.

S. John xix. 7.

S. Matt. xxvii. 24.

Granting that behind these forces, he, whom Our Lord called " the Prince of this world," was working, we may conclude that a unanimous vote, a holy law, and a judge supported by armed soldiers cannot ensure justice. The world, irrespective of religious belief, denounces the Crucifixion as a crime, and in so doing not only condemns the Prince of this world but also the secularised state. That is the judgment of history, but we also demand a judgment which shall right all wrongs.

X. How the World is Leavened

Throughout the centuries, the Holy Spirit has by means of the Church maintained His witness to sin, righteousness and judgment. Multitudes have in consequence been converted and found salvation through the Cross; but the work of the Holy Spirit has not been restricted to those who definitely accepted the Gospel. The whole world has to some extent been leavened by the Holy Spirit, and the work is still in process, for the end is not yet.

<small>S. Matt. xiii. 33.
S. Luke xiii. 21.</small>

It is almost impossible for us to think ourselves back into the old Pagan world. In trying to do so we are so apt to be misled by the occasional dicta of exceptional philosophers, or by the intuitions of inspired poets. There has been no change in man's mental capacity, the change is in character and outlook, and the cause of the change is the revelation of Jesus Christ. If we want to know what a world without Him is like, we can go to Turkey, Arabia or China, and among races of different cultures note the morals and manners which are tolerated.

Much might be said of the changes which have taken place since Christianity began to leaven the world. We might dwell on the new position accorded to women, the reverence felt for children, and the ordered freedom of the Christian home. We might note how slowly slavery was first mitigated and then abolished among the white races. How it was introduced again in order to exploit negro labour, and how the Christian conscience finally insisted on the emancipation of all slaves. Down through the Christian ages we note a widening charity and care for the poor, a multiplication of hospitals for the sick and demented and a zeal for the education of the young. With this care for the unfortunate and immature, public opinion has become more and more sensitive about cruelty either to men or animals; indecency has become repulsive, and public opinion at least condemns intemperance and lust. Thought has exercised itself more and more with the mysteries of personality, a higher value has been assigned to the individual and there is a new insistence on individual responsibility. The world has come to appreciate the virtues of humility, purity, truthfulness and self-sacrifice, which did not rank very highly in the Pagan world.

So the leaven is working among men, who often do not profess to be religious, and will not recognise what they owe to Christianity and the example of Our Lord. We are often told that selected agnostics compare very favourably with ordinary Christians; and it is true that many retain Christian virtues when they have lost the Christian faith. But these sad people—few of them are really happy—were born into a Christian world and have lived all their lives in a Christian atmosphere, heirs of a Christian tradition. The redemptive power of Christ extends far

beyond those who are His disciples. He died that
the whole world might be better.

We have to-day many, eager for social reform,
who are anti-Christian or, at any rate, anti-clerical.
Their hatred of the Church is due partly to the fact
that the Church cannot always endorse their denunciations, and partly because the Church does not
always believe that their projects will lead to the
Utopia they desire. But all that is good in their
aims to alleviate suffering and poverty is really due
to the leaven of that Christian spirit which, in their
ignorance, they deride.

Far beyond Christendom also the leaven is working.
The attempts of Hindoos to purify their faith and
moralise the worship of Krishna are due to contact
with Christianity. Among agnostics in Japan and in
Confucian China, there is a growing veneration for
the person of Christ. Some benefits of His Sacred
Passion reach even to those who are ignorant of His
claims, and the Cross, however imperfectly understood, is becoming more and more a force in the
world.

The Arts have been baptized and largely become
Christian, and the spirit of religion has been slowly
permeating the whole field of human endeavour.
Poets, musicians, painters and architects have produced a definite and distinctive Christian culture. It
is shown in a sense of mystery and reverence, it is
constant in its effort to divine what is spiritual under
natural forms, it is ever aspiring, pressing hopefully
forward, seeking and at times attaining to some
glimpse of the uncreated loveliness of God.

Lastly, even in our sports and games the leaven is
working. The ancients understood as well as we do

the necessity of training, and the value of self-discipline and self-control. It is the spirit which is altogether different. No one to-day would regard the wily Ulysses as a good sportsman, but he was an ideal of the ancient world. The ideal has changed with the coming of Christ, the mirror of fair play, for He was the truth and was prepared to suffer for the truth, and to suffer without complaints and without ill-temper.

But it will be said, If the Church has leavened the world, the world has also corrupted the Church. This is true, but it is not much for the world to boast of. Our Lord saw what would happen, but He still willed to work through human agents, and still refuses to compel men to be good. The Church, in consequence, has been a Mother of Saints, and also prolific in bringing forth children who, in spite of her solicitude, have become sinners. At times the sinners have seemed to prevail, and have even mono-polised the chief places in the Church, yet there has ever been a witness to the truth, and always a fount of renewal. Sinners within the Church retard her work and give occasion for the sinners without to blaspheme; they also provide opportunities for the saints to suffer and triumph. The work of leavening the world goes on, and will do so. Much has been done and much remains to do; and those who work hardest have to emulate the patience of God, and " remember the years of the right hand of the Most Ps. lxxvii. High."
10.

Looking back over the past centuries we note that the Church has won her greatest victories by suffering like her Master, and has declined in influence and spiritual power when she forgot her commission to

proclaim the mystery of the Cross. She is always
assailed by the temptation to win the world by
conforming to its fashions, but the world knows what
the Cross stands for, and only despises a Church
which would keep it out of sight.

XI. The Holy Spirit shows us things to come

The leavening of the world makes for its betterment
and a wider distribution of human happiness. The
edification of the Church is more permanent, and it
will only be complete in the eternal order. Here we
are constantly trying to purify her from defilement,
but in heaven she will attain to the purity of perfection; and what is perfect needs no change.

Hope is the inspiration of our present life. We
are at present being saved; and not until heaven is
reached can the full results of the Atonement made
on Calvary be known. At present, we rest, like
S. Paul, in the assurance, " He that spared not His
own Son, but delivered Him up for us all, how shall
He not also with Him freely give us all things." Rom. viii.
32.

We have been thinking about the gifts sent from
heaven to signalise His victory, but grace of itself is
not sufficient. As our sanctification is a process it
must have an end in view, and so Our Lord promised
that His Holy Spirit should " declare unto us the
things that are to come." And the Holy Spirit ever S. John xvi.
since, in the light of Calvary, has been teaching us 13.
about death and judgment, heaven and hell.

Death in the ancient world was something not to
be mentioned, or was only referred to by some
euphemism. Wisdom consisted in concentrating on
the moment, and *carpe diem* was the motto for life.

But Our Lord came into the world and died that He might conquer death. When, in the body, He rose again on the third day, life was found to have a new meaning and *carpe diem* a new significance—a man dare not waste his time. No one believing in the Resurrection can conceive of life as merely a succession of moments in which he experiences pleasure and pain. His life is one, thanks to his memory, and has a purpose. He is moving on not to annihilation, but to the living God, to Whom all that he has done is known.

But if death has been robbed of its sting by the resurrection of Our Lord, the responsibilities of living have been increased by Our Lord's teaching on the imminence of judgment. However, every man craves for a judgment on his work, and most men would rather be condemned than overlooked. Many also clamour for justice, and they will never be content until they have the verdict of a Judge Who cannot be gainsaid, Who knows all and has taken all things into account.

Standing before Caiaphas to be judged, Our Lord told him " Ye shall see the Son of Man sitting on the right hand of power, and coming in the clouds of heaven." S. Paul told the Athenians, " God hath appointed a day, in which He will judge the world in righteousness by that Man Whom He hath ordained; whereof He hath given assurance unto all men, in that He hath raised Him from the dead." He will judge all, heathen and Christians alike. He will judge those who never knew Him, by the kindness which they showed to their fellows; and He will judge His servants by the use which they made of the talents with which He entrusted them. All wrongs

S. Mark xiv. 62.

Acts xvii. 31.

S. Matt. xxv. 31–46.

S. Matt. xxv. 14–30.

will then be righted, all misunderstandings will be
cleared up; and the Judge is One Who has shared our
lot, and done everything possible that all men might
be saved.

His coming as Man to judge the world will be the
final proof of the victory which He won on the Cross.
Here on the earth where He was condemned He will
vindicate His cause and triumph. Here He will
receive the fruits of His agony; and here His mediatorial kingdom will have an end. So S. Paul writes,
" Then cometh the end, when He shall have delivered
up the kingdom to God, even the Father; when He
shall have put down all rule and all authority and
power. For He must reign till He hath put all enemies
under His feet. The last enemy that shall be destroyed is death." ^{1 Cor. xv. 24-26.}

An end! Some people find it hard to believe that
there can ever be an end, although Science is quite
clear that this earth on which we live must become
desolate. All men work for ends, except those who
are relegated to some mental asylum. It is only in
the sphere of the infinite, outside time and space,
that we can think of a changeless condition. When
God limited Himself in creation, worlds came into
existence which had a beginning and will have an end.
When God further limited Himself to become Man,
He entered into a finite world with a definite purpose,
and being God that purpose must be accomplished.
In one sense the work He came to do was finished upon
the Cross, in another the consequences which flow
from the Cross must some day be complete; and His
judgment upon all will be final and irreversible.

Every end is, however, also a new beginning; and
the end, we are told, will be accompanied with the

T

Rev. xxi. 5. announcement "Behold, I make all things new." In the new Order man will have his place, assigned to him at the Great Assize, in heaven or in hell. Then those who have been redeemed will be so at-one with God as to be able to enjoy the Beatific Vision, while those who have turned their backs on God will Rev. xx. 6, 14. Cp. ii. 11, xxi. 8. know the meaning of that final separation which S. John speaks of as "the second death."

Heaven and eternal life will be dealt with in the next chapter, but here we must recognise the difficulties so many feel in regard to Hell.

First, many argue that no deed, however evil, done in time can merit an eternity of punishment. This is true, but men will not be punished for what they have done, but for what they are. We know in this life how characters are formed, harden and tend to become permanent. As long as men are alive we may hope for their conversion, we may speculate on a conversion in the world beyond, although we have no Scripture to rely on; but sooner or later an end must be reached, and beyond that there can be no change. Should a man ultimately prefer evil to good, heaven would offer him no happiness, and heaven would cease to be heaven if he were there.

Secondly, many maintain that the existence of hell is inconsistent with a God Who is Love. Yet we know that men created to love and to be loved may be perverted until they are possessed by a devilish hate, and only find their satisfaction in its indulgence. It is also true that lust and impurity find their ultimate expression in cruelty—in tormenting and being tormented. In consequence, it is possible to suppose that hell may be the only gift which a God of Love can offer to thoroughly perverted souls.

Of this indeed we may be sure. No one will ever go to hell but by his own deliberate choice. He will go because he will feel more at home there than in heaven. This is in accord with Our Lord's teaching. He will welcome the Blessed into the kingdom prepared for them from the beginning of the world; ^{S. Matt. xxv. 34.} but He will dismiss the damned into the everlasting fire, prepared—not for them—but for the devil and his angels. ^{S. Matt. xxv. 41.}

Lastly, many would argue that if any go into hell, the Sacrifice on Calvary will be so far a failure. That is an admission we dare not make, but neither can we, with our present knowledge, give an explanation. We know that in this life Our Lord failed to win Judas and was rejected by the people. We know that He was willing to suffer all things on men's behalf, but would not compel them to be good. He is the same Jesus to-day, and will be the same on the Day of Judgment. Then all will have to acknowledge Him and bow before Him. In that sense His triumph will be complete. But we are not taught that all will be compelled to love Him; and those who prefer the outer darkness to His presence will apparently have their desire.

The subject is mysterious and we may not dogmatise upon it; but we should be unwise to neglect the plain warnings of the Holy Spirit which we find in Scripture. We may not minimise or explain them away. We ought to offer up our prayers for more faith in God and greater love of His Holiness. Then, whatever our perplexities may be, we shall have our assurance that the Judge of all the earth will do right. ^{Gen. xviii. 25.}

CHAPTER VII

MAN'S RESPONSE TO GOD

I. The Atonement and our Responsibility

WE have thought of sin, its nature and its consequences; and we have thought of Our Lord and His sacrifice on man's behalf. As a result of that sacrifice we have seen how man's sin is forgiven, and how grace is imparted by the Holy Spirit. Dare we in consequence say—"Jesus has done all for me, and there is nothing for me to do: I have only to accept His salvation?" No! The writers of the New Testament insist on the practical consequences of the Atonement. A new life has been made possible for men, but there are moral responsibilities for those who enter upon it. S. Paul sums up his own experience and conduct when he writes, "By the grace of God I am what I am: and His grace which was bestowed on me was not in vain; but I laboured more abundantly than they all: yet not I, but the grace of 1 Cor. xv. 10. God which was in me."

Our Lord died upon the Cross that we might know what God would do for sinners; and when His love is brought home to us our first thought must be, "What can I do for Him?" We are not content to be passive recipients of His bounty, for He loves us and His love is our inspiration: we would in consequence be at one with Him and share in His work. We can rejoice that He does not treat us as pets to be fondled, but calls on us to be labourers together with Himself. He, the divine Lover, craves for a response, and our at-one-ment with Him becomes a reality when we reciprocate His love.

I. We have thought of sin as a debt due to God, and seen how Our Lord paid it by His life and death of filial obedience. But when Our Lord had finished ^{S. John xvii. 4.} the work which His Father had given Him to do, He did not abrogate the duty which we owed to God. He only revealed it in a new light. It is no longer to be regarded as a debt owed to a hard master, but as the homage of a son to a royal Father. Disobedience is therefore not a less but a more heinous offence, for we can more easily excuse a slave who rebels against a master's whip than a son who outrages a Father's love.

II. We have seen that sin is a dishonour done to God and obscures His goodness. Also how Our Lord, jealous for the Father's honour, and identified with humanity, offered upon the Cross a reparation for the sins of the whole world. But in so doing He did not encourage us to think lightly of sin; still less did He license us to live as we liked, if we trusted in His merits. If we would be one with Him and at one ^{Rom. vi.} with the Father, we must see life as He saw it, our sense of sin must be deepened and our zeal for God's honour inflamed. We can indeed do little by way of reparation and cannot atone for our own past. But at least we should be ready " to fill up that which is behind of the afflictions of Christ . . . for His Body's sake, which is the Church." We cannot sever our- ^{Col. i. 24.} selves from the evil in the world and say, " It is no concern of ours."

III. We have seen that sin deserves punishment,

but from the Cross we learn how God offers to forgive. Our Lord died for our salvation, and as we read the history of the sinful world, we find that progress has only been made through men being willing to sacrifice themselves for others and to pay the price in blood and tears. Our Lord did not promise that His disciples should escape the common lot. He told them to take up their cross and follow after Him. It was not an immediate at-one-ment with the world order, but at-one-ment with God, which was made possible by the death on the Cross; and to any asking, " Is it worth while ? " S. Paul answers, " As the sufferings of Christ abound in us, so our consolation also aboundeth by Christ."

S. Mark viii. 34.

2 Cor. i. 5.

IV. We have seen that sin was a bondage from which we could not escape, and that Our Lord came to deliver us. But it is just because we are free men that we are also responsible for our conduct. We are called to live as free men should, "not using our liberty for a cloke of maliciousness," *i.e.*, as a pretext for bad conduct; " but as the servants of God." He asks from us a voluntary obedience.

1 S. Pet. ii. 16.

V. Lastly, we have seen that sin caused a separation between man and God, and that Our Lord came with God's gracious offer of reconciliation, but a perfect reconciliation means an at-one-ment in thought, desire and will. In Our Lord—Perfect God and Perfect Man, but One Christ—the at-one-ment of God and humanity is complete. He could say, " I and the Father are One." He also prayed for the whole Church, " that they all may be one; as Thou, Father, art in Me, and I in Thee, that they also may be one in Us, that the world may believe that Thou hast sent Me." In this unity among ourselves, in

S. John x. 30.

S. John xvii. 21.

this union with Our Lord, and in this at-one-ment with Him Who is all in all, God's purpose in creation is fulfilled and justified. It is because we have so imperfectly realised it, it is because of our unhappy divisions, that the world can still excuse itself from believing that the Jesus Who was crucified was sent by the Father for the world's salvation.

We conclude, in consequence, that those who respond to God's love have an individual work to do in union with the Redeemer and a corporate responsibility for making the Atonement, which is a reality with God, a reality in the world of men.

II. The Way towards At-one-ment with God

(A) *Discipline*

What have we to do in order that we may be progressively at one with Christ? The Mystics speak of the three ways of Purgation, Illumination and Unity, but although life is a progress with its goal at the gates of heaven, there are not three ways thither, but only one. Neither can we properly distinguish the way by three stages, purgative, illuminative and unitive, if we would be true to experience, for though it is true that we have to rid ourselves from sin, learn the truth and be united with Our Lord, these processes synchronise, or, at any rate, overlap one another.

In considering, then, the need of discipline, contemplation and love, we are only treating these subjects so that we may understand the way to atonement in an orderly fashion.

First of all let us be quite clear about the need for discipline.

Penitence, we have seen, does not and should not end with forgiveness, while forgiveness is only a stage towards the abolition of sin. Temptation persists in those who have been forgiven; and he who enlists on the side of Christ is committed to a stern conflict—the battle will rage most furiously with the foes within. He should not, however, resent the necessity for the struggle, for it is the way by which we attain to strength. We may have the Captain of Our Salvation at our side, and He was tempted like as we are, and felt the stress to be most terrible when He came to die.

So many, who have been delivered like the children of Israel from a cruel bondage, after a time forget its
Ex. xvii. 3.
Num. xi. 5.
Num. xiv. 2. miseries and only remember its dubious pleasures. They make good resolutions that they will not go back, and yet allow themselves to be enthralled by their undisciplined imaginations. When their innocence was lost, their eyes were opened, like those of the first Adam, to the mystery of evil and the fascination of
Gen. iii. 7. sin. They are still reluctant not to see and taste for themselves; but it is only through the eyes of the Second Adam, gazing upon them from the Cross, that they will learn the truth about sin, know it as God knows it, and turn from it with loathing.

How many Christians have to confess that their flesh still lusts against the spirit, so that they cannot do as they would but are at the mercy of wayward
Gal. v. 17.
Rom. vii.
14–17. impulses and satanic suggestions. They would like to be captains of their own souls, and masters of their fate; and they know that until they have attained to self-control they are not really free, and are not able to realise their sonship with God, or to offer Him a
Rom. xii. 1. reasonable service.

Lack of self-control is most noticeable to-day, and the reasons are not far to seek. An age that thinks it wrong to correct a child will not produce men capable of self-discipline. An age that has ceased to believe in heaven and hell soon ceases to regard life as a progress or as having a purpose. An age which proclaims one man to be as good as another must end by relinquishing all ideals. So men cease to be manly, and degenerate into discontented beings, drifting through life full of petulant complaints that somebody else does not " give them a good time."

If this be true, it behoves us to remember that the Cross is the symbol of our faith. Our Lord did not come into the world to please Himself, and His Rom. xv. 3. disciples should be capable of self-denial. He was made perfect by suffering, and His disciples cannot Heb. ii. 10. claim ease as their right. He died that He might purge our sins, but not that we should trust in His 2 S. Pet. i. 9. atonement, while altogether alien from His Spirit.

On the contrary, He was most emphatic about the lengths to which self-discipline might go. He speaks of a hand or a foot which may have to be cut off and cast away, or of an eye which may have to be plucked out in order that we may enter into life and escape the fire that never shall be quenched. We assent to S. Matt. v. 29, 30. S. Mark ix. 43–48. similar doctrine when propounded by a modern surgeon, and submit to an amputation which may save our life on earth; but we hear Our Lord's words with incredulous amazement, though He is speaking of something more important, of the life that is beyond and is for ever. We are no doubt right in not taking these bold figures of speech too literally, but we may yet see how there are places to which some man dare not go for his foot might slip, that there are things which he dare not handle, and sights which he should not contemplate if he would remain free from sin. There is then a call on him for renunciation, even though others in the same place may walk safely, or touch and see without offence.

But apart from such individual abstentions or definite penances, we all ought to lead a considered life, and that involves discipline. The Catholic Church tries to help men by appointing seasons for penitence and days of fasting, but how few of her children regard them. She also ordains ministers to hear confessions and set penances, but how few submit to her discipline. Having ceased to hear the Church, and trusting to their private judgment, too many have sought the easy way of self-indulgence and forgotten the steep road up to heaven. They certainly have no sympathy with S. Paul, who writes, " I buffet my body, and bring it into bondage : lest by any means, when I have preached to others, I 1 Cor. ix. 27. myself should be rejected."

But self-discipline may be perverted like all else that is good. Men in the past have come to look on it as an end in itself, and gloried in their corporal austerities and mortifications of the spirit, as if they provided indubitable signs of sanctity. Some Puritans also have refused for themselves and forbidden to others all the bright and beautiful things which God has given us, as though what was pleasant must needs be wrong. But Our Lord participated in all the innocent joys of men. There is a time for everything. He enjoyed our pleasures and endured our pain, giving God thanks for both.

We are not told to seek for crosses, but to take them up manfully when they come. We are told to have a

purpose in our lives, to have a standard of perfection
in view, and to take the consequences of pursuing
the one and maintaining the other. We cannot live
heedless lives if we would be at one with the God of
Order. To help us S. Paul urges the duty of self-
examination, and the New Testament is full of warnings that we should watch against occasions of falling.
We should keep some account of our acts and thoughts,
and should know whether or no we are getting the
better of particular sins. But let us regard them as
objectively as possible. Self-examination is not to be
confused with morbid introspection. It is possible
to be overmuch interested in ourselves, to weigh our
offences to a scruple and to analyse our motives with
such attentive curiosity that we are almost certain to
repeat the sins. Christians are not told to contemplate themselves but Jesus. Christianity is an
objective religion. It counsels us to lose ourselves in
others, as we seek to be at-one with the God Who is
all in all.

So we are exhorted to hasten forward, "looking
unto Jesus the Author and Finisher of our faith." He
it is Who has made the way possible by His death.
He it is Who inspires us to persevere. He sustains
us with His grace. He lifts us up when we fall.
With Him all things are possible; but He calls us to
follow in the way of the Cross. We can refuse to do
so if we like, and choose some other road which seems
to us more attractive; but, if we do so, we shall not
be at-one with Him, and hereafter it is possible that
we may find His atonement was not for us.

1 Cor. xi. 28.
2 Cor. xiii. 5.
S. Matt.
xxiv. 42.
S. Matt.
xxv. 13.
S. Matt.
xxvi. 41.
S. Mark xiii.
33.
S. Mark xiv.
38.

Heb. xii. 2.

III. The Way towards At-one-ment with God

(B) *Contemplation*

If self-discipline is the way in which we prepare ourselves for God's presence, and train ourselves for His service, attention, contemplation and recollection are necessary if we would both know Him and do His will. We have thought in the fourth chapter of how continuous was Our Lord's communion with His Father, and of how He was transfigured while He prayed. Men have to seek a like communion with Our Lord if they would continue His work and come to reflect His beauty.

There are many excellent people to-day, eager for service, who do not recognise this truth. They seek practical ends and are impatient of all that savours of the contemplative life. Like Martha they are " cumbered with much serving," and forget how "Mary chose the better part." The busy life is not wrong, far from it; but if we would do the Lord's work we must wait on His commands. He himself spent thirty years in a quiet home, and then especially prepared Himself for His work by a retreat of forty days in a solitary place. So also, when He gave His great commission to His Apostles, He told them that they must wait until they were " endued with power from on high." The time of waiting was not wasted, for they were " continually in the Temple, praising and blessing God."

Our Lord told us to love God; and He told us to love Him not only with our hearts but with our minds. Knowledge is necessary for right thinking, and thought is necessary for right action. We shall

S. Luke x. 38–42.

S. Luke xxiv. 49.

S. Luke xxiv. 53.

S. Matt. xxii. 37.

not help in the reformation of the world by hasty
and ignorant interference. So many of our philan-
thropic endeavours do more harm than good, because
we are led away by our feelings, and do not take the
trouble to think. So much of our thinking leads
nowhere, because we have insufficient knowledge of
God and man.

What, above all, is the crying need of to-day? Is
it not a new spirit? We want men with the gay
spirit of adventure who will welcome the obstacles
which are to be overcome. We want men who will
go breast forward up a way of sorrows and only
expect to find a cross upon the top. We want men
who will greet death, not with a curse, but with a
cheer, who will be able to say at the end like S. Paul, "I
have fought a good fight, I have finished my course,
I have kept the faith : Henceforth there is laid up for
me a crown of righteousness, which the Lord, the
righteous Judge, shall give me at that day."   2 Tim. iv.
7, 8.

Spirit, however, is only kindled by spirit, and if we
want the Spirit of Christ we must frequent His
company. We all know how a lively person will
change a dull party, which threatened to be a failure,
into a success. We know also how a born leader will
rally a wavering line upon the battlefield, so that it
charges, shouting in the face of death. The assurance
of Jesus being present has nerved weak women and
children to endure the tortures of martyrdom. His
Spirit has inspired them, and He came that we might
have life, and might have it more abundantly.   S. John x.
10.

When men would learn of Him, they are perhaps
first of all attracted by the Child in Mary's arms, for
He represents a love which they can easily understand.
They then follow the gracious teacher of Galilee and

ponder the stories in which He reveals God and life. But as they know more of the world's sorrows and disappointments, it is the Love which suffers that appeals to them with compelling power. It is the Love that expiates and atones which wins the free response,

And I must love Him, for He died for me.

Our Lord is the supreme Teacher and He teaches by example. If we trust Him as a Teacher and a Guide we cannot ignore His supreme act. None of His lessons are easy to learn, and a lesson that involves pain is very hard to master. We must not stand afar off, though we smite our breasts and lament the sins of others. True sympathy will bring us to the foot of the Cross, and then only shall we see His eyes and be pierced by the thought—" It is my sin that has caused Him to suffer."

S. Luke xxiii, 48.

If we would be receptive of His teaching, we must cultivate the habit of attention. Like S. John, we must be ready to mark and bear record. The soldiers were very near to Christ when He was dying, but they were intent on gambling for His clothes—the poor garments of a peasant. And is it not true that trifles distract us even in the brief periods which we dedicate to devotion. We have been near Christ, in His Presence, but our thoughts were far away, and the wonder of His message has not penetrated to our souls.

S. John xix. 35.

S. John xix. 23, 24.

He said so little upon the Cross. Most of the three hours was passed in silence. So in contemplation of Our Lord to-day we must expect to learn from the long silences, as well as from the seven words. It was His longsuffering perhaps which caused the Centurion to say, " Truly, this was the Son of God." We may

S. Mark xv. 39.

be brought to the same response when in the night of our souls we find that in His silence there is power.

Slowly, and by degrees, a man by contemplation learns; and what he learns becomes the matter of his meditation, until, in the presence of Our Lord, he turns his thoughts into prayers. It was so with the Penitent Thief, and we, like him, want, not only to _{remember}, but to be remembered. The old, old story is very beautiful; we would dwell on it again and again, but because of it we also look forward, and would seek the paradise of God. ^{S. Luke xxiii. 43.}

Mental prayer is a very difficult exercise, and it is perhaps more difficult to explain than to practise. The simple are puzzled when they are told that a good meditation involves an act of will by which thought, feeling and imagination are fused. On the other hand, many quite simple people attain to the heights and depths of spiritual knowledge which are hidden from the wise and prudent. They are more simple, more receptive and more direct in their seeking. They do not debate about themselves or analyse their psychological processes; and they are prepared to believe what the Holy Spirit says to them; and they see Our Lord, otherwise invisible, with the eyes of Love.

Some, like S. Paul, have had special revelations, and in a condition of ecstasy have been caught up to some third heaven, but S. Paul was very reticent about it and the Catholic Church has always discountenanced her children from either expecting or seeking such experiences. On the other hand, she encourages all to frequent her altars, and to believe in the reality of Our Lord's presence in the Blessed Sacrament. There we are to discern the Lord's Body. This is generally by an act of faith, though ^{2 Cor. xii. 2.} ^{1 Cor. xi. 29.}

many bear witness that, like the disciples at Emmaus, they have recognised His presence in the Breaking of Bread. Quite apart, however, from conscious verification of the truth, the faithful come forward to receive Him within themselves. With acts of faith and love they receive Him, but the virtue of the reception comes only from Himself.

S. Luke
xxiv. 30, 31.

Lastly, the devout communicant cultivates the spirit of recollection. He goes about his work and mixes in society and does not talk about his interior life. But the life that is in him cannot be hid. Men take knowledge of him that he has been with Jesus, and venerate or hate him accordingly.

Acts iv. 13.

Our Lord, in communion with His Father and in the power of the Spirit, accomplished the work which had been given Him to do, and offered an atonement for the sins of men. We, by contemplating His life and seeking His presence, enter into His Spirit, are united with Him and know in ourselves what the Atonement means.

IV. The Way towards At-one-ment with God

(C) *Love*

We must never forget that at-one-ment with God implies that we are conscious of His love for us and respond to it. There is no real unity between persons apart from love. But this truth raises difficulties in the minds of many sincere persons, who question themselves anxiously, asking, " Do I love God ? " We do wrong if we merely think of love in terms of emotion, for it lies deeper than our feelings. Love grows and love deepens, but there are certain conditions which are necessary.

First, it is obvious that Love by its very nature is expansive, and self-absorption is fatal to its existence. The self-centred can neither love truly nor make the best of themselves; and in seeking their own happiness they defeat their own object. They have not learnt the lesson of the Cross. There are so many to-day who are discontented with the world because it is so clearly not designed for their special convenience. The world, however, is big and they are small, and their business is to discover their special relation with it. When they begin to consider others rather than themselves, they find how many there are who excite admiration and how much beauty there is in the world. Perhaps, then they first know the inclination to give God thanks.

Secondly, a man finds that he is the inheritor of many potentialities, some of them evil and some of them good. He cannot by reasoning rid himself of the belief that he is a responsible being with a power of choice, though he may have only a limited power to accomplish. Should he deliberately choose the evil, or only pay an effortless homage to the good, he will never learn that what is called good is really good for him; and until he has made that discovery he will never love goodness for itself or the Good God. But if he chooses aright and seeks after righteousness, he will first feel the need of self-discipline and then he will be convinced of the necessity of grace. The grace that he receives will unite him with God in heart and will; and the more he consciously needs God, the more will he love Him, for in himself the power of God will be revealed.

U

Thirdly, if a man is to love God, he must needs have intercourse with Him, for it is impossible really to love a Great Unknown. This intercourse has on God's side been made possible by God's revelation of Himself in Jesus; and it is possible on our side by means of prayer.

We estimate our friendship with a fellow man, not only by our desire for his company, but by how much we can tell him when he is present. To an acquaintance we can talk about the weather, but we are lucky if we have a friend to whom we can confide the secrets of our souls. With some people we feel shy and constrained, and with some we can be perfectly natural. We may love, and yet fear that the beloved will discover our faults; but when we are conscious that love is returned, we are content that the beloved should see us as we are.

So in our intercourse with God we begin with set prayers and formal phrases, and then gradually venture on adding to them special petitions. We dare to confess particular sins, and commend to Him the fortunes of our friends. But how many interests of our lives do we never mention in His presence, and yet, if God is indeed the Father, He longs to hear from us, what He knows apart from us. He will listen to our momentary worries and the trifles that distract our lives. He would hear also of our pleasures, joys and hopes; they are as important as our sorrows and fears.

As children talk about themselves, their wants and what interests them, so men begin to pray and learn to pray, and feel that God hears, understands and answers, although His answers are often unexpected. But as we grow up in the spiritual life we are less inclined to talk about ourselves and want to pray about what interests God, and ask continually that His will may be done. So we become at-one with Him and share His mind. In the first stage we had confidence in His love for us; but in the second we are zealous in our love for Him.

All our prayers go up through Jesus Christ, Our Lord, and for His sake. Step by step we follow Him, until our prayers may come from some Gethsemane and yet be the prayers of faith. Strange as it may seem to outsiders, it is in the moments of bereavement and trial that Christians have the fullest assurance that God is Love. They see Our Lord at such times in His love for men, identifying Himself with them, enduring pain and expiating sin. With such amazing love God was well pleased— propitiated, if you like. He is also pleased when we show our willingness to work for others or to suffer for them; while we dimly begin to understand the connection between love and sacrifice, and come through sacrifice to glorify the God of Love.

Looking back over the last few pages, we may conclude that self-discipline cannot save us, for we do not live for ourselves alone; that contemplation Rom. xiv. 7. cannot save us, for we were intended for life and work and not merely to see and suffer, and that love can save us, but it is God's love, not ours, for even when God's love has been shown, our response is slow and fitful. And yet it is through our response, however slow, that we enter into the life of at-one-ment. It is then our love for God that constrains us to discipline ourselves; and it is God's love for 2 Cor. v. 14. us that invites us to the contemplation of His perfection. The three ways of the Mystics cross and recross one another. They are not three ways, but rather three strands that are twisted together—a Eccl. iv. 12. threefold cord which cannot be broken : it binds us securely to the Lord, Who for our sakes was bound.

V. The Way towards At-one-ment with God

(D) *Joy is the Assurance of Our Success*

We have described the pilgrim's progress, but what proof have we that he is on the right road, and how should we commend that road to others?

We reply that the religion of the Cross is the religion of joy, which sounds like a paradox until it has been verified by experience. Those conversant with saintly lives know that the true Christian is, like the true warrior or adventurer, never so happy as when in the midst of dangers, trials and difficulties. When others would curse God and die in despair, he is only living more intensely than at other times. The more exciting his surroundings the more cool and detached does he appear; and his undisturbed calm is sometimes misunderstood and sometimes irritates those who do not share in the secret of his interior peace.

We must not, however, confuse joy with pleasure. Pleasure comes to us from without and stimulates our senses, joy comes from within and is independent of our physical conditions or earthly circumstances. Pleasure falls on us like dew for our refreshment, but joy wells up within us like a fountain of water to refresh others. We need not despise pleasure, it is God's free gift, and for it we should give thanks;

but joy is the realisation of ourselves as part of God's creation. We should not seek for pleasure, for the search is vain. What once pleased us soon cloys, and perhaps becomes a craving for something which we no longer enjoy but cannot do without. The votaries of pleasure are always discontented, often bored, and sometimes know the disgust which comes of satiety. Joy, on the other hand, is life and liveliness. Of that we can never have enough, and it is the Christian who testifies to the fulfilment of Our Lord's purpose, " I am come that they might have life, and that they might have it more abundantly." ^{S. John x. 10.}

Joy is not inconsistent with suffering and may be the result of pain. So Our Lord explains " A woman when she is in travail hath sorrow, because her hour is come; but as soon as she is delivered of the child, she remembereth no more the anguish, for joy that a man is born into the world." So we are told of ^{S. John xvi. 21.} Our Lord, "For the joy that was set before Him," He " endured the Cross and despised the shame." ^{Heb. xii. 2.} The new creation and life of the regenerate issues from the Cross. S. Peter and S. John after they had been beaten by order of the Sanhedrin departed, rejoicing that they were counted worthy to suffer shame for Our Lord's sake. ^{Acts v. 40, 41.}

S. Paul had certainly no easy or pleasant life, but he was full of enthusiasm for his work, and absorbed in the importance of his message. When he boasted, ^{2 Cor. xi. 30.} it was of his infirmities, and the many things he had suffered for the sake of truth. Flogged and chained in a dungeon at Philippi, he could still sing, and he was ready and alert when the moment came to convert his jailer. The men he converted in Philippi ^{Acts xvi. 19–34.}

were themselves in turn doomed to suffering, but he wrote to them from another prison, " Rejoice in the Lord alway; and again I say, Rejoice."

Phil. iv. 4.

S. James writes, " My brethren, count it all joy when ye fall into divers temptations," and S. Peter writes, " If ye suffer for righteousness' sake, happy are ye."

S. James i. 2.

1 S. Pet. iii. 14.

Perhaps it may be suggested that so much exhortation only shows that some of the early Christians suffered from depression, and this may be true, for all had not an equal degree of faith. Some who were insensible to the glory of suffering had to be instructed in the value of discipline and correction, and so the writer to the Hebrews says, " Now no chastening for the present seemeth to be joyous, but grievous : nevertheless afterward it yieldeth the peaceable fruit of righteousness unto them which are exercised thereby."

Heb. xii. 11.

But allowing for all deductions, there is no doubt that joy has always been a characteristic of the Christian life. It has been shown in spirits which cannot be broken, and in the zeal of those who have been its propagandists. What had the early missionaries to offer enquirers?—Truth, freedom from sin, and, besides, the chance of martyrdom with the certainty of heaven. And what made such teaching attractive. Was it not the joy and happiness of the preachers? Their outward circumstances might be miserable but they already belonged to the eternal order and possessed by faith the blessings which they knew to be alone real.

All, indeed, are not heroic, many feel no adventurous impulse and are not aspirants for glory; and yet, none the less, show the interior joy which goes with a quiet spirit.   They are possessed by a peace which ^{S. John xiv.} the world can neither give nor take away, for they are at one with themselves and therefore at one with the God Who created them.   They can abide, confident that they are part of the eternal purpose, and children of an Almighty Father—in His arms they cannot be afraid.

But most men find their joy in work, that is in creative work, and it does not much matter if you create an epic or fashion a box to suit your private purpose.   It is the people who do not create but only copy who grow dull and tired.   Pursuing this thought the highest joy of all is to take part in the creative work of God the Supreme Artist.   In the beginning, we are told that the "morning stars sang together and all the sons of God shouted for joy."   Each of us [Job xxxviii. 7.] can co-operate with the grace of God until we become new creatures, each of us can go forth into the world and help forward the forces of redemption, hastening for the preparation of the day when God will make all things new.   That is the joy which no one can take from us, the joy of being at-one with God in His purpose and His work.

It was the Blood which was shed on Calvary which was for the salvation of the world.   It is the blood of the martyrs since which has been the seed of the Church.   It is through lives lived and laid down in His service that the creative work of God continues. It is through the gate of death that we hope to pass to a joyful resurrection.   But the promises of God are for this life also, and in doing His will, here and [S. Matt. vi. 33.] now, we enter into His joy. [S. Mark x. 30.] [1 Tim. iv. 8.]

VI. OUR WORK FOR OUR LORD IN THE WORLD

(A) *The Long-suffering Church*

We have hitherto been thinking of the interior life and noting its necessity if we would be at-one with God. We ought also to remember its necessity if we would be effective in our work for our fellow men. This latter point must not be forgotten; we have not been called of God and received His grace in order that we may save our own souls, but in order that we may minister to the souls of others. Our Lord did not live and die with the sole object of perfecting His own humanity. He lived for us and He died for our salvation; and we believe that His perfection is manifest in His love for His brethren. If then we would share in His life and His work, we must not be locked up in ourselves. Our religion does not only concern our souls and our God, but God, self and neighbour; and our religion has to be manifested in an imperfect Church.

There are plenty of unpleasantly censorious persons who delight in denouncing the sins of others. There are plenty of fanatics eager to legislate, and compel others to be good after their own pattern. There are plenty of impatient folk who quickly separate themselves from uncongenial surroundings, and would attain to Paradise before their time by restricting their society to their fellow " saints." But if we would do the Lord's work we must do it in His spirit. The Church as a whole and the individual members are alike called to longsuffering and patience, and these virtues are the more necessary as neither Church nor churchman may compromise with evil.

For more than three centuries the world hated the Church and tried to destroy it from without, and yet the Church grew in numbers and influence, obeying God rather than man, but diligent also in respect for the powers established, so far as was consistent with her own faith. Then the world joined the Church, men flocked into her. They heaped upon her privilege, riches and power; and so corrupted her from within. The friendship of the world was much more dangerous to her integrity than the hostility of the first centuries. The Church grew worldly; and immediately the worldly turned on the Church in scorn, asking, "Is your religion that of the Poor Man of Nazareth?"

There is an analogy between the Church of the Old Testament and the Church of the New. In both God's revelation has been in the keeping of imperfect men, in both there has been much evil but also splendid devotion, in both God has been working His purpose out, and in both it is man's duty to be loyal. Everything may have seemed lost in the days of Ahab, Manasseh or Ahaz, but there remained prophets who yet believed in Israel's mission, who trusted in the pious remnant, who were sure that the holy seed would yet bear fruit. So in the most corrupt days of the Christian Church, under the worst of Popes, there have still been men conspicuous as saints, besides the unknown thousands who did not bow the knee to any Baal. The precious seed has been preserved, for the Church which Jesus purchased with His own blood cannot die. Acts xx. 28.

The Church has always existed under a seeming disadvantage, for it is open to all who will come in, and Our Lord compared it to a drag-net which

S. Matt.
xiii. 47. should gather fish of every kind, bad as well as good.
Among the Twelve selected by Our Lord, one was the
traitor Judas; among the first converts at Pentecost
Acts v. 1–11. there were Ananias and Sapphira; among the firstfruits of missionary work in Samaria ʹwas Simon
Acts viii.
13–24. Magus. Ever since there have been tares among
S. Matt.
xiii. 29, 30. the wheat; and Our Lord forbids premature weeding.
If God be longsuffering and patient with us, so must
we be with one another. After all, the Church on
earth is not, and was not meant to be, a Church of
the Saved, but a Church for those who are being
saved. It does not exist as a club for the redeemed,
but is a great redemptive agency. It is like a school
that offers to educate all, bad as well as good; and
it dares to run the risk that at times the bad will
predominate.

The real dangers of the Church are to be found
not without but within her fold. She suffers, not
only from those who betray her, or from those who
disgrace her by their falls, but also from good people
zealous for her success, who are not in harmony
with her Spirit. There are those who would minimise
her claims and her faith, in the hope of inducing
those without to come in; and there are those who
would drive out all those within who do not agree
with themselves or conform to their requirements.
Some would broaden the basis of Church member-
ship until it stood for nothing in particular; and
some would narrow it until it became a select coterie
of persons who pronounced the same shibboleth with
the right accent.

We must remember that the Church exists for all
and is open to all; but the Church exists as a witness
to definite facts, as the Guardian of definite truths,

as the Guide to a definite way of life and in order
to uphold a definite morality. She cannot deviate
from her position without betraying the trust which
God has committed to her : and she is more likely
to help those without by maintaining her own
standard. Why should they come within, if her
faith is of so little importance that it can be accom-
modated to all comers? The present anxiety to
make the Church popular defeats its own object.
It shows lack of faith in her supernatural claim,
lack of dignity and also a lack of common sense.
An individual who is too anxious to court a new
acquaintance, and too eager to adopt his opinions
or echo his prejudices, naturally meets with the
peculiar scorn reserved for toadies. But what is
contemptible in an individual is more contemptible
in a Church with nineteen centuries of history behind
her—a Church which claims to represent the unpopular doctrine of the Cross and witness to the
Spirit of the Crucified.

Equally reprehensible are those who would limit
the Church to the measure of their own minds.
The best argument for the truth of our religion is
the response which Our Lord has met with from men
of many minds, of different temperaments and
varying needs. Yet there are fanatics in all parties
anxious to expel those who do not agree with themselves. The Church indeed propounds a faith, pre-
scribes a ritual and sanctions or forbids to her members
certain acts. She must do so or cease to be a Church
at all. But there are only twelve articles in her
Creed and any number of opinions about them.
It is most undesirable that we should all think alike,
and though some opinions may not be well grounded,

people are not to be expelled because they are muddle-
headed. There is one Ritual which is the social
bond, but the Ritual may be celebrated with more or
less ceremonial; and the existence of a Ritual which
unites all is not inconsistent with devotions which
unite some. A hard and rigid uniformity can only
end in formalism, and room must be left for life and
spontaneity in the Church. There are only ten
Commandments with the divine commentary of Our
Lord, and beyond them are a great number of moral
questions on which ethical teachers differ. We have
a right to strong opinions, but we have no right to
exclude those who differ from us. We all need much
more faith that " Truth is great and it prevails," we
all need much more of God's patience with the
perversity of men.

1 Esdras iv.
38.

Again, if we will not tempt people into the Church
by minimising her faith, we also should not be in a
hurry to drive people out because they are honest
enough to admit doubts. Some are naturally sceptical,
some are very sensitive on the subject of their own
sincerity, some are over-fond of exploration and
some are the victims of a misunderstanding. Let us
admit that people who proclaim every doubt that
crosses their minds are a great trial to the Church,
impair her witness and hinder her work; but their
very doubts often lead to the more confirmation of
her faith; and we have to remember the tenderness
of Our Lord with those who found it so hard to
understand His sayings. It is only when doubt
hardens into denial that an honest man is bound to
leave the Church; but even then it is better that
he should follow his conscience and go than that
he should be turned out. Heresy hunters make

heretics; and a man with a doubt is often driven to a denial by the controversial bitterness with which he is attacked.

Again the Church has to be very patient with sinners. She must indeed repel from communion, or even excommunicate, those who are living in open defiance of her moral law. It is for their sakes she does so, as well as for her own. But, for every defiant sinner, how many there are who constantly fall through carelessness, indifference or under the stress of some temptation; and the Church has to bear with them in their weakness, and make the best of their imperfect repentance.

How many there are likewise who cause more real scandal, because, notwithstanding their respectability, they are only known for their worldly, selfish and uncharitable lives. Many a man in his impatience with a bad priest, a formal presentment of religion and an unspiritual congregation has created a schism, but it would have been better if he had reminded himself that " Jesus Christ died for many imperfect people, of whom I am one."

If we are at-one with Our Lord, and would help others to a like at-one-ment, we shall need His Spirit of patience and longsuffering. We are members of His Body, the Church; and it is easy to be loyal to her so long as she is full of life, fervour and devotion; but the test of our loyalty comes when she seems dead, cold and formal. S. Paul reminds us, " when one member suffers all the members suffer with it "; and Christians should be ready to suffer with the evil in their own body, and to bear the same reproach as their Master, Who was laughed at as the friend of publicans and sinners.

1 Cor. xii. 26.

S. Matt. xi. 19.
S. Luke vii. 34.

We ought not to forget that it was because Our Lord identified Himself with men that he was able to offer to His Father a reparation for our sins; and that we, by refusing to dissociate ourselves from our fellows, may join in His work of reparation, bearing the reproach of the Cross in the hope of converting sinners.

VII. Our Work for Our Lord in the World

(B) *Intercession*

This idea of reparation is intimately connected with the work of intercession, which is felt to be a duty by all Christians, even when they are puzzled about its rational justification.

Under the Old Covenant we read of the urgent prayers of Abraham for the Cities of the Plain, of the prayer of Moses for the rebellious Israelites, of Solomon's great intercession at the dedication of the Temple, of Hezekiah's petition that Jerusalem might be delivered from Sennacherib, and of the confession which Daniel made on behalf of his fellow exiles. The Old Testament doctrine on the subject may best be illustrated by the fact that Samuel reassured the people who had rejected him by saying, " God forbid that I should sin against the Lord in ceasing to pray for you."

Such prayers were not only of a general character. David prayed for the life of his child. Elisha prayed for the Shunammite's son and also that his servant's eyes might be opened to see the angelic hosts. It is clear that these intercessions were not limited to spiritual blessings and did not aim merely

Gen. xviii. 23–33.
Ex. xxxii. 11 ff.
1 Kings viii. 22 ff.
2 Kings xix. 15 ff.

Dan. ix. 3 ff.

1 Sam. xii. 23.

2 Sam. xii. 16.
2 Kings iv. 33.
2 Kings vi. 17.

at spiritual influence. S. James, after telling us that
" the prayer of a righteous man availeth much," S. James v. 16.
offers by way of proof the petition, otherwise unre-
corded, of Elijah that it might not rain. S. James v. 17.

In the New Testament we read how the Noble-
man's son, the Centurion's servant, the man stricken S. John iv. 46–54.
with palsy, the lunatic boy, and the daughter of S. Matt. viii. 5–13.
the Syrophœnician were helped and cured by the S. Luke vii. 1–10.
intercession of others. So we learn that just as we S. Matt. xv. 1–28.
are dependent upon others for most of the material S. Mark vii. 26–30.
comforts which we enjoy, so we are dependent on
others for spiritual help, and that there is one law
that is operative both in the spiritual and material
world.

Our Lord Himself as Man has set us an example
of intercession. He prayed for Peter, that Satan
might not sift him like wheat, and He prayed for
His disciples that their faith might not fail. In His S. Luke xxii. 31–32.
great High Priestly prayer, He not only commended
Himself to the Father, but He pleaded His own
obedience on behalf of His disciples and for those
who should accept their teaching. On the Cross, S. John xvii. 9, 10
He went still further and prayed for His enemies, S. John xvii. 20.
" Father, forgive them, for they know not what they
do." His prayers were not only general but par- S. Luke xxiii. 34.
ticular, and at the grave of Lazarus He could thank
His Father that He had been heard and answered. S. John xi. 42.

By its very nature intercession is a priestly duty,
for by intercession we represent another before God.
Aaron was reminded of this duty, for every time he
entered the Holy Place he was to bear the names of
the tribes within his breastplate. Intercession is Ex. xxviii. 29.
also closely connected with sacrifice, for, when we
can make no claim, we must at least allege some

reason why we should be heard. The High Priest when He interceded for the people and made an atonement on their behalf, offered the living blood of the slain victims before the Mercy-Seat within the veil. So Our Lord has entered into heaven, the true sanctuary, with His own blood and there "ever liveth to make intercession for us."

Lev. xvi.
15 ff.
Heb. ix. 11,
12.
Heb. vii. 25.

This intercession is an abiding fact. By it the sacrifice once made is for ever being offered, and it is through the presence of the sacred humanity in heaven that the work done in time is eternally availing and efficacious. But we share in that humanity, we are members of His body, and we therefore share in His work. As Priest and Intercessor, He offers and perfects our prayers, for we only intercede through Jesus Christ, Our Lord. We have no especial sanctity as a claim for being heard, we have no sacrifice apart from His sacrifice to offer. It is as One with Him and in His Spirit that we approach God, and that not selfishly, but in aid of all for whom Christ died. "He died for all that we should not live unto ourselves," but unto Him, the Lover of Souls; and it is only "if we love one another" that "His love is perfected in us." There is no love for others without concern for their welfare; and that concern must find expression. There are many we can help in no other way except by prayer, and it is a help which no one can forbid or refuse.

Eph. v. 30.

Cor. v. 15.

1 S. John iv.
12.

Prayer to God is a duty owed by all but only fulfilled by some. Those who can pray—and it is hard work—should pray for those who through carelessness and ignorance cannot pray for themselves. Prayer for sinners is of the first importance. So S. John teaches us, "If any man see his brother sin a sin which is

not unto death, he shall ask, and he shall give him life
for them that sin not unto death. There is a sin unto
death : I do not say that he shall pray for it." ^{1 S. John v. 16.}
Why, it may be asked, is there the doubt about the
exception? Our prayers must be sincere; and so
we must have a real sympathy with the sinners for
whom we pray, as well as a lively sense of the dishonour done to God by their conduct. It is only
when we have both that we are at one with the Lord
Who offered to His Father on the Cross a reparation
for sin.

But it is not only for sinners that we should intercede. Our Lord prayed for His disciples and for their
work. So S. Paul imagines his Ephesian converts
" praying always with all prayer and supplication in
the Spirit, and watching thereunto with all persever-
ance and supplication for all saints; and for me, that
utterance may be given unto me, that I may open
my mouth boldly, to make known the mystery of the
Gospel." S. Paul goes further, for he regards the ^{Eph. vi. 18, 19.}
safety and security of the whole world to depend on
prayer. So he writes, " I exhort therefore, that, first
of all, supplications, prayers, intercessions and thanks-
givings be made for all men; for kings (even for Nero)
and for all that are in authority; that we may lead
a quiet and peaceable life in all godliness and
honesty." ^{1 Tim ii. 1, 2.}

Private prayer is good, but united prayer is better,
for it has Our Lord's promise, " That if two of you
shall agree on earth as touching anything that they
shall ask, it shall be done for them of My Father
which is in heaven. For where two or three are
gathered together in My Name, there am I in the
midst of them." It is natural therefore that when ^{S. Matt. viii. 19, 20.}

    x

we have Our Lord specially present with us in the Holy Communion we should offer our intercessions, helping one another and being helped to plead His Sacrifice before the Father's throne.

There are people who doubt the possibility of helping another by prayer, but they have no hesitation in asking a neighbour for his vote and influence when they want some position in this world. There are people who regard intercession as showing a meddle-some spirit; but no one condemns the man who, at his own risk, saves a suicide from drowning. There are people who talk of undue influence; but while there may be dangers in hypnotism or suggestion, or in the dominant will of a man who wishes to help his brother, there can be no danger in bringing the needs of another before the God of Wisdom and Love.

Intercession is based on our recognition of the solidarity of humanity. It derives its energy from our desire for other people's welfare, and our belief that God can do more than ourselves. It finds its justification in the blood which was poured out in sacrifice on Calvary, and is now offered in the heaven above.

VIII. OUR WORK FOR OUR LORD IN THE WORLD

(C) *Social Service*

We have thought how each man needs to discipline himself, and also how the Church needs to be schooled in patience. We have thought how by quiet con-templation we may learn of God, and then how, knowing Him, we may intercede for others. We have thought of the way of union in response to the

Love of God, and it remains to be seen how we must co-operate with the activities of that love in social service. Then, we shall understand the correspondence between the interior and exterior life and find that they are one.

There are, however, plenty of philanthropists to-day who care nothing about the love of God, although, through the Christianity which they reject, they are inspired with goodwill towards their fellows. They work hard, often feverishly, for the betterment of social conditions, and are impatient of those who insist on regarding the problems of amelioration from a spiritual and other-worldly standpoint. Pathetic is their belief in the value of voting and in the regenerative power of laws, and yet after a century of remedial legislation we have not produced a happy, or a united, or a contented population. Few are grateful for the gifts of a friend, and no one is grateful for the gifts of the State. They are at once accepted as rights, and soon held as of little account, for men only prize what they have earned for themselves.

Some remedial legislation has been good and more is to be desired; but it is not by committees and their well-intentioned regulations that men can be made happy. Legislation may prevent evil, but it cannot secure good; it may render men safe, but it can do nothing to redeem them.

Our philanthropists have often worked in the spirit of the Old Testament rather than of the New; they have thought more of the Law than of the Gospel; they have insisted more on rights than on duties, and on justice rather than on love. Our Lord showed us the only way, when He did not dispense His bounty from above, or organise a charitable scheme for the

world, but took the world as it was, and came to
S. Mark x.
16.
dwell among us. He took the children in His arms,
touched the leper, and spoke a word of love in the ears
S. Mark i.
40–42.
of the outcast. He was not indifferent to the world's
suffering or its temporal ills, but He was ready to
suffer with it, and He showed men that He cared.
He suffered with men, from men and for men, and in
suffering did not complain, for in Him suffering was
swallowed up by a consuming love.

Secondly, He taught what we are always forgetting, that it is the evil within men's hearts, and
S. Mark vii.
15.
not the evil without, which defiles. So in remedying
a social abuse we are only attacking a symptom;
it is sin that really matters, and it is sin that we so
often palliate or ignore. There is to-day much social
injustice in the world, but more misery is caused by
impurity, gambling and intemperance than by the
very worst of laws. Men want new hearts more than
new houses, men want a new spirit of love more than
an accumulation of comforts, men want the courage
to endure more than any anodyne from pain. They
must be brought to the One and only Redeemer, and
the best of social service is the proclamation of the
Cross.

Does that mean that the corporal works of mercy
may be despised? Far from it. The man who does
not practise what he preaches will not for long retain
his audience. I am not condemning the philan-
thropist, but am insisting first on the personal element
in all true charity and on personal relationships, and
secondly that all human misery is ultimately due to
sin, although only too often the innocent suffer for the
guilty as the Lord suffered upon the Cross.
Acts x. 38.
Our Lord went about doing good, and we cannot fail

to be attracted by His happy labours among the people
of Galilee. We picture His gracious Presence in the
midst of enthusiastic and responsive crowds. We too
may find that " it is more blessed to give than to
receive," that there is a joy in comforting the sad Acts xx. 35.
and in trying to raise the fallen. We should not be
wrong in saying, " Here is the happy life; and the
works of mercy bring their own reward."

We must not, however, forget that the service of
others ended in Our Lord's sufferings, and for them
also we must be prepared. Some, like S. James and
S. John, are a little too confident that they can drink
the Lord's cup and merit high places in His kingdom. S. Matt. xx.
They would like to die for king and country, or S. Mark x.
embrace martyrdom for the faith. Their imaginations
are aflame with heroism and they deem glory to be
its own reward. There is something that is noble in
such aspirations, but they are also too self-centred.
All are not naturally heroic, and all are not intended
for glory. Some, like S. Peter, fall through rashness
and presumption. There is virtue in being contented with a humble lot, in cheerfully doing little
things well.

In ordinary life it is a good thing to be a soldier or a
policeman, and to devote your life for the defence of
others; but the majority of men are called to unexcit-
ing work, and it is only when they do it that the
prosperity of the whole community is increased. So
it is possible to be God's servant, and a citizen of
heaven, and yet have only humdrum duties to perform. The world needs honest men in business; men
who will care for their families, be generous to their
employees, and considerate to their friends; men
who will remember that they have duties to their

equals, and how necessary it is that the many should maintain a Christian ideal if the few should be successful in saving the degraded. No man may neglect a Lazarus lying at his door, or pass by on the other side when a wounded fellow creature craves for his compassion, but everyone is not called on to spend his life in the organisation of charity, or in the sacrifice which rescue work entails. We must look up to and admire examples of heroic virtue, but we must not despise the day of small things, or think that little acts of courtesy and kindness are unworthy of our attention. We all need to pray that God will make our own vocation plain. We are not all called to the same work. Our work may be very humble, and yet we may be found faithful, "having made our calling and election sure."

S. Luke xvi. 19–31.
S. Luke x. 30–35.

If, however, we devote ourselves to help the wicked and the unfortunate, we shall only succeed if we start with the love of God or at least from a sense of the duty that we owe to Him. Otherwise we may soon be disgusted by man's ingratitude or discouraged by our own failure. We may also cease to care in any real sense for others, and seek our own preferment by the ostentation of our own good works.

If we are really working for God, we shall need Him more and love Him better as the years go by, for we shall enter more and more into His purpose and understand the value of His grace. Our love for God will grow with our love for man. As we work for sinners, so we shall come to care for them, and as we care for them we shall understand the forbearance of God. We shall also cease to condescend and become more humble before God and our fellows, for we shall discover in horrible surroundings splendid virtue, and learn how much good remains in those who are regarded as the offscouring of the world.

Lastly, there have always been a few whose work for others has been dominated by the thought of expiation. They are miserable at the unequal distribution of pleasures, and aghast at the callousness with which well-to-do people regard the misery of the poor. They are quite sure that the social system, by which some are comfortable, is responsible for the many who are not. They see the sins of their own class, and refuse to acknowledge the sins of any others, whom they excuse as the victims of circumstance. They cannot change the system, they can do little to alleviate the suffering, but they can sacrifice themselves. They can refuse to enjoy what is denied to others, and renounce the advantages to which they were born. They can identify themselves with those who are suffering, and offer in their own persons an expiation for the sins of their class.

They are sometimes morbid, dwelling on evil rather than good : their vision is somewhat distorted, and their plans for betterment are sometimes absurd; but they must be very near to the Saviour " Who being in the form of God . . . made Himself of no reputation, and took upon Him the form of a servant, and was made in the likeness of men : and being found in fashion as a man, He humbled Himself, and became obedient unto death, even the death of the Cross." Phil. ii. 6–8.

We may not agree with all their views, and with all the conclusions which they draw from them; we may doubt their wisdom and oppose their plans in the best interests of those whom they would serve; but we cannot doubt their spirit of sacrifice, or fail to see that

in sacrificing themselves they are akin to the Spirit
of Christ. As we recognise this, we are led in some
degree to understand how Our Lord offered Himself
as an expiation for the sins of men.

IX. Our Work for Our Lord in the World

(D) *Evangelisation*

We have spoken of the joy which comes of accepting
the Atonement—the joy of being at peace with God
and partaking of His creative work. But those who
have heard " the glad tidings of great joy " must be
like the Shepherds of Bethlehem and " make known
abroad " what they have heard. No one wants to
keep good news to himself, and this is the best of news
—" Peace on earth to men of goodwill "—peace with
God and peace with one another. This peace was
ratified upon the Cross and has to be proclaimed to
the ends of the earth.

Our Lord said—" Go ye into all the world, and
preach the Gospel to every creature," but His disciples
found His commandment hard to understand. They
were willing and eager to preach among the Diaspora
in all countries, but they had been so carefully
segregated by God for the education of their race
that many of them had come to look on all foreigners
as " common and unclean." They believed so
intensely that " Salvation was of the Jews," that they
forgot the promise made to Abraham that " in him
all the nations of the earth should be blessed." It
was only through a vision that S. Peter was induced
to go to the house of Cornelius, and it was only
through a fresh dispensation of the Spirit that he
admitted the household to baptism. He had sub-

Marginal references:
S. Luke ii. 10.
S. Luke ii. 17.
S. Luke ii. 14.
S. Mark xvi. 15.
Acts x. 14.
S. John iv. 22.
Gen. xxii. 18.
Acts x.
Acts xi. 4.

sequently to defend his conduct before the Church at
Jerusalem, and it was at first looked on as an exceptional occurrence, to be in no wise treated as a pre-
cedent.   Then Christians at Antioch began to speak
to Gentiles; and the perplexed Church at Jerusalem Acts xi. 19.
sent Barnabas thither to make enquiries, with the Acts xi. 22.
result that propaganda was permitted to all races. Acts xv.
But controversy soon arose whether converts should
be circumcised and compelled to keep the Law;
and a decision in favour of freedom was obtained from
the Council at Jerusalem presided over by S. James.
Still men argued that social customs need not be
affected by religious union, and Jews were unwilling
to break the caste laws which constituted them a
people apart.   This led to S. Paul's controversy with
S. Peter, which he reported to the Galatians.   Later Gal. ii.
S. Paul was able to assure the Ephesians that they 11–16.
who " being aliens from the commonwealth of Israel,
and strangers from the covenant of promise . . . are
made nigh by the blood of Christ . . . Who hath
broken down the middle wall of partition between
us."   He concludes triumphantly in writing to the Eph. ii.
Colossians that in the Church " there is neither Greek 12–14.
nor Jew, circumcision nor uncircumcision, Barbarian,
Scythian, bond nor free : but Christ is all, and in Col. iii. 11.
all."   Cf. Gal. iii.
                                                     28.
When once this principle of universality was
accepted all was clear.   " God had made of one blood
all nations of men "; and God had become man that Acts xvii. 26.
through the shedding of His own Blood all nations
might be redeemed.   Those who accepted that redemption were incorporated into the One Body or
Church, and had " One Lord, one Faith, one Baptism,
and One God and Father of all."   They were the new Eph. iv. 5.

men for whom all middle walls of partition had been cast down. They were to express this unity through mutual love, and by love to win those without, showing this love in returning good for evil. So Our Lord had taught : " Love your enemies, bless them that curse you, do good to them that hate you, and pray for them that despitefully use you and persecute you : that you may be the children of your Father which is in heaven; for He maketh His sun to rise on the evil and on the good, and sendeth His rain upon the just and on the unjust."

S. Matt. v. 44–45.

It was in accordance with these principles that the early Church went forth on her mission. She believed in the Atonement made on Calvary; and wanted not only that it should be known, but also that its method should be manifested. The lives of the saints are the true Epiphany, and reveal what God has done. In the brief space of thirty years the Gospel was carried from Jerusalem to Rome; and the Church was established in all the chief cities both on and off the route. We do not know the whole history of this wonderful expansion, for the Acts of the Apostles are almost confined to the activities of S. Peter and S. Paul.

The Church owes its origin to the Cross and flourishes through martyrdom. Men have not entered it because it teaches the highest ethical system, or because it has an organic structure capable of adaptation and growth, but because it witnesses to the fact that God loves men, became a man and died for men, rose again and offers men grace. Myriads have received that grace and can attest its power.

Some races have responded most readily to the moral appeal made by the suffering Christ; some have thought first of the victory over evil and their own consequent enfranchisement; and some looking up to God and down on sin have been penetrated with a conviction that sacrifice was a necessity, and have found salvation through cleaving to the Son of Man Who atoned. But the faith of all is concentrated on the Person of Jesus. It is through Him that they have found God without and within them. In finding Him they have found peace in themselves and begin to desire peace with one another.

But the work of converting men has to be done by men. Our Lord has made us labourers together with Himself; and how imperfectly His work has been 1 Cor. iii. 9. done by men is known to all. But we can never forget that Our Lord wants all races, and has commissioned men to win them; and we are condemned for our ingratitude if we are not zealous for His work. No atonement can be complete until it includes all; and we cannot hope fully to understand it until all nations have brought their peculiar gifts and endowments to the elucidation of the mystery and the illustration of its power. Our Lord waits, watches and longs for the souls of men. He waits also for His triumph, which must be deferred until the Gospel S. Mark xiii. 10. has been published to all nations. So in the Epistle to the Hebrews we are told that Our Lord " after He had offered one sacrifice for sins for ever, sat down on the right hand of God; from henceforth expecting till His enemies be made His footstool." Heb. x. 12, 13.

X. Our Offering to the Father

(A) *The Sacrifice of Praise and Thanksgiving*

Sin had caused a separation from God; but Our Lord not only offered an atonement for our sins, but also made Himself one with us. It is because we have been made one with Him that we share in His atonement, and it becomes ours. Believing this, we are bound to fit ourselves for God's presence and His joy, and to seek all means whereby we may grow in grace. Sharing in Our Lord's life we must also share in His labours for others, that all may be one in Him. But we must not forget His relationship with the Father, or the offering which He made. We also have our duty towards God, and must make our offerings, or we miss the whole purpose of the Atonement, which is that no one and nothing must be separate, but that God must be all in all.

God has made us for Himself, that is, capable of loving Him, reflecting Him, and knowing to some extent His perfection. When we consider Who God is and what we are, we can only approach Him in worship; and worship is a duty which we owe to Him and to ourselves. It is a duty owed to Him, but we also find that it is better to praise than to be praised, that it is only a pure enthusiasm which adds zest to life, and that adoration is not only a duty, but is also the fulfilment of our own existence.

The Psalmists felt this intensely. The Psalms are full of praise. The whole earth, sky and air suggest themes for exultant gladness, the history of the past and the great deliverances excite the voices of thanksgiving, and the goodness of God in the individual's life provokes gratitude, so that even "out of the deep," the Psalmist is still confident of His Mercy, Ps. cxxx. 1. and would celebrate Him "with Whom is plenteous redemption." Ps. cxxx. 7.

If men, so full of the beauty and terror of the world, could offer such praises to the Creator; if men, so alive to the awful holiness of God, could yet seek His face in adoration; if men could trust so entirely in His mercy upon such evidence as He had vouchsafed them; how much more should we, to Whom He has revealed Himself more perfectly, with psalms and hymns and spiritual songs, sing with grace in our hearts to the Lord? We not only look Eph. v. 19. up to God with admiration, but we look upon the Cross with gratitude; and when admiration is allied with gratitude the issue is love and joy.

Praise not only grows in volume but also in reality and intensity when it is offered in harmony with others; and it is only as a united family that we can properly celebrate the Fatherhood of God. We owe Him indeed the homage of our hearts, but we owe to Him also the proclamation of His goodness. It is for us to hallow His Holy Name. S. Matt. vi. 9.

The old Psalmist tells us how "his soul had a desire and longing to enter into the Lord's house," Ps. xlii. 2. and how he yearned to be "with the multitudes and such as kept holy day;" and we must not "neglect Ps. xlii. 4. the assembling of ourselves together," so that when Heb. x. 25. we have prayed "Thy Kingdom come" we can to S. Matt. vi. 10. some extent answer our own prayer by standing together with our brethren to acclaim the King.

And for what shall we praise Him? For all the wondrous works of creation, for His providence and care of ourselves, for all the blessings of this life and for hope of the world to come; but more especially do we praise Him for His revelation of Himself in Jesus, and for the redemption of the world through the Cross. That sacrifice was offered in darkness and consummated in pain, but we offer the same sacrifice in the morning light and celebrate it as a sacrifice of praise and thanksgiving.

Heb. xiii. 15.

XI. OUR OFFERING TO THE FATHER

(B) *The Pure Oblation*

We have thought of how Our Lord's sacrifice upon the Cross was the perfect fulfilment of all that the ritual of the Old Covenant had striven to express by symbols. The Blessed Sacrament of the Altar under the New Covenant represents all that He did and we should do. Then His sacrifice becomes our sacrifice, and in celebrating It we do not speak of It as a Sacrifice but as the Sacrifice, for in It the offering, which was made once for all, becomes available for us.

Rom. vi. 10. Heb. x. 10.

We must not forget Its intention. Some have been so concerned with the benefits which they individually receive in the Holy Communion that they forget how they have not only something to receive but also something to offer. Others have so insisted on Eucharistic adoration, and the devotions which may be properly offered to Our Lord, when present under the veils of bread and wine, that they have forgotten why He is there. Yet anyone who reads any Liturgy of the Catholic Church must be aware that all the prayers are addressed to the Father, and that the whole action consists in an offering made to Him, in union with the offering which Our Lord made upon the Cross.

First let us think of it simply as an offering. In the old days men brought the best of the flock or of the herd, or the firstfruits of the ground, and offered them to God and in His honour. So, we still place on the altar bread and wine with our alms and offerings. They are ours, but God gave them to us and we have made them our own. The corn has been turned into bread, the grapes into wine, and the metal has been minted. It is in the form that we use them that we consecrate them; not because God has need of them, but because we want them ourselves. Thus love finds its expression in sacrifice, and every sacrifice must cost the worshipper something, though it be only the two mites which make a farthing. 2 Sam. xxiv. 14. 1 Chron. xxi. 24.

Such offerings are like the presents which little children give to their parents out of the pennies which the parents have given to them. They are neither useful nor valuable in themselves, but they are very precious to the recipients. A mother treasures such love tokens even when the children have grown to be ashamed of their gifts. S. Mark xii. 42.

As they grow older, the children ask anxiously, "What does mother want?" and save their money for something which she will prize for its own sake. She marks their growing thoughtfulness, and happiness wells up like a fountain in a home where each is attentive to the wants of others, and not concentrated on his own desires.

But all the time what does the mother crave for? Is it not to hear her children praised, to be told of the good that they have done, or even of what they have suffered in order that others might escape?

In the spirit of a child the Christian asks, "What does God want?" He is not satisfied by the reply that he must "do justly, love mercy, and walk humbly," because that is his duty as a child of God, and he wants to make God a present. It was Our Lord, the Only begotten Son, Who knew the mind of the Father, and understands what is in the heart of man, Who gave us the Blessed Sacrament, saying, "Do this in remembrance of Me."

Micah vi. 8.

1 Cor. xi. 24.
S. Luke
xxii. 19.

We would give God something, and acts are superior to thoughts, and persons are more valuable than things. But there is only one Perfect Person, Who offered Himself wholly to the Father, and His offering was all the more glorious that it was made on behalf of others. His was the perfect offering, the one perfect act in the whole world's history. With it the Father was well pleased, and we can offer Him nothing better. So S. Paul teaches us, "As often as ye eat this bread, and drink this cup, ye do shew the Lord's death till He come."

1 Cor. xi. 26.

We show the Lord's death to the wicked world, proclaiming that through it is our hope of salvation; we show it forth to the angel hosts to prove how manhood may be crowned with glory and honour; but more especially we show it forth to the Father, that He may be once more pleased in hearing the praises of the Son.

But beyond this there is something that the God of Love longs for and we are diffident of offering. He says to each one, "My son, give Me your heart"; and we, knowing our sins and our imperfections, dare not approach Him with a gift that is soiled. But when we have Our Lord with us and in us, the One Mediator between the Father and ourselves, greatly

Prov. xxiii.
26.

daring, we offer Him "ourselves, our souls and bodies, to be a reasonable, holy and lively sacrifice." The offering is accepted for His sake, and it was for His sake that we were adopted into God's family.

XII. Our Offering to the Father

(C) *The Sufficient Satisfaction*

If we can only give ourselves to God, when we are mystically united with Our Lord's manhood, by a natural sequence of thought we pass from thinking of the Blessed Sacrament as an offering for God's honour to regarding it as an offering for our sins. We do not approach the throne of grace with excuses, but confessing our faults. We do not approach, trusting in our own righteousness, but in His merits. We argue that if the Sinless One is not ashamed to call us, sinners, His brethren, the all Holy Father Heb. ii. 11. will for the Son's sake acknowledge us to be His children. But there is, we have seen, no possibility of disagreement between Father and Son, and so S. Paul says, "God commendeth His love towards us, in that, while we were yet sinners, Christ died for us." It is, however, because He died and so Rom. v. 8. fulfilled the Father's will that we can be forgiven, for love had to be manifested before the fruits of love could be gathered in.

And what is our response? In the Blessed Sacrament we offer the death of Our Lord as the one Sin Offering. It is no mere commemoration of something which happened long ago, for the sacrifice which was once for all made in time is offered eternally in heaven where Our Lord exercises an unchangeable

Y

Heb. vii. 24. Priesthood. We do not rely on the abiding charm of a past act, but believe that " we have an Advocate with the Father, Jesus Christ the righteous : and He is the propitiation for our sins; and not for ours 1 S. John ii. 1, 2. only, but also for the sins of the whole world." Our Lord still works, is still living and is still in living relation with ourselves. It is we who are called to unite ourselves with Him in His work, and plead not only for ourselves but also for the whole world.

We cannot at present fully participate in the worship of the eternal order. We can only set forth Our Lord's death as it occurred in time. Yet, He, Who gave Himself wholly to us in His Incarnation, deigns to be with us in pleading the sacrifice, which is His own. He is ever the invisible celebrant behind the visible priest, as He is the invisible and immaculate victim beneath the veils of bread and wine. In offering the Broken Body and the poured-out Blood, we offer before God the evidence of our guilt, it is and should be our great confession; we offer also the evidence in which we trust for forgiveness. Man's guilt was patent when he slew the Lord of glory, and man's forgiveness was assured when the Lord of glory triumphed over death and rose to that new life in which we may share.

In the old days, when the worshipper made his sin offering, he sought for an unblemished victim, and hoped to identify himself with its life of innocence by shedding its blood and so setting that life free. In the Blessed Sacrament something much more real is effected, for we celebrate the sacrifice of a willing Victim Who offered Himself. It is not so much that we identify ourselves with Him as that He identifies Himself with us, and communicates to us the virtue of His nature that we may share in the vigour of His life.

So living in Him, we must share in His work. On the throne of Majesty, the True Mercy-Seat, He presents His blood for the sins of the world; and we too have " boldness to enter into the Holiest by the Blood of Jesus, by a new and living way, which He hath consecrated for us, through the veil, that is to say, His flesh." Heb. x. 19, 20.

And so to approach God's throne and so to plead the great Sin Offering for the living and the dead is " our bounden duty and service." The Christ is still suffering in His members, and still thirsting for a world that has not yet been won to the Love of God. So long as that is true, so long must the Blessed Sacrament be regarded as a Sin Offering; so long must we identify ourselves with the dolours of His Passion, and show visibly before all men the sufficient satisfaction of the Cross. In time and for particular needs we celebrate what is really an eternal fact of universal value.

XIII. Our Offering to the Father

(D) *The Peace of Communion*

It will be seen that the Blessed Sacrament can, like the Cross with which it is so intimately connected, be approached from more than one direction, and offered with more than one intention. But if we regard it as an offering, it is always addressed to God the Father. It is either an oblation in the Father's honour, or an impetratory sacrifice in which we set forth the Son's death for the world's sin, or 1 Cor. v. 7.

it is our passover sacrifice of thanksgiving, celebrated with the unleavened bread of sincerity and truth. As the action proceeds we remember how upon the Cross, Our Lord said first of all, " Father, forgive " and last of all " Father, into Thy hands I commend My spirit." We contrast also the opportunity offered to us of communion with His awful cry of dereliction. It comes home to us that there can be no terror equal to that of a man who feels himself forsaken of God and cast off from His communion.

S. Luke
xxiii. 34.
S. Luke
xxiii. 46.
S. Matt.
xxvii. 46.
S. Mark xv.
34.

In the last chapter we thought of the gift which we receive in the Holy Communion. In this we think rather of what we do. We hear a voice from heaven saying, " Blessed are they which are called to the marriage supper of the Lamb "; and when we rejoice in the gracious invitation we remember also that the Bride has made herself ready and that we, each one, must be clad in wedding garments. We can only rightly approach the Holy Table having repented and been forgiven. We remember that a wedding day presupposes a new life under new conditions, and we must be steadfastly resolved to lead such a life in union with Our Lord. We must also be in love and charity with our neighbours, for we are all to eat of the same food and drink out of the same cup, and discord should be impossible in the family life of the God Who is Love.

Rev. xix. 9.
Rev. xix. 7.

S. Matt.
xxii. 11, 12.

Above all we must not forget the occasion of the feast. We come to celebrate a victory over evil, a deliverance from servitude. We come also to celebrate a Peace made between God and man. We come to join in the new song of those who have been redeemed by the Blood of the Lamb out of every kindred and tongue and people and nation. We come

Rev. v. 9.

as those who have been appointed as kings and priests Rev. v. 10.
to reign on the earth. And as we sing of the triumph,
we are answered by the chorus in heaven of "ten
thousand times ten thousand, and thousands of
thousands," who proclaim that the Lamb Who was Rev. v. 11.
slain is "worthy of power, and riches, and wisdom,
and strength, and honour, and glory, and blessing." Rev. v. 12.
Moreover, every created thing in heaven, in earth
and under the earth, and in the sea unites in offering
homage to Him that sitteth on the throne and to
the Lamb. The Godhead is worshipped and with it Rev. v. 17.
that Humanity which was taken into Godhead at the
incarnation.

Is this merely the imagination of the exile in Patmos? It is more than that, for it is the expression
of his faith. In his loneliness he learnt the cosmical
extent of the new communion. He learnt not only
the hidden reward of earth's scattered saints, but
also how the harmonies of heaven are perfumed by
the odour of their prayers. He takes his details Rev. viii. 3, 4.
and images from the sacrificial and sacerdotal
worship which he knew, in order to make his thoughts
intelligible to those who knew it also, but all the time
his eye of faith is not dimmed. He has the substance Heb. xi. 1.
of things hoped for and the evidence of things not
seen as yet.

It may indeed be hard for one who frequents a
country church, with its unadorned worship and its
few communicants, to understand the raptures of
the apocalyptic seer. And yet the little band,
gathered about the Holy Table, locally represents
the concord of those who are at-one with God and
with their brethren. They have all come to meet
with Jesus and He is there; they are all united with

Him and together can sing *Gloria in excelsis*. The Priest officiating is a Priest of the Catholic Church, he follows the Church's order, and is himself a link with the Apostolic band. Each worshipper also is linked in thought, in hope and in love with others far away, living or dead, who belong to the same communion and serve the same Lord. The Priest sings, " Lift up your hearts," and they reply, " We lift them up unto the Lord." They rise beyond and out of their cramped surroundings to join in the *Sanctus* with the heavenly host. Our Lord provides for them the food of immortality, and they feast with Him. His blessing descends upon them—" the peace which passeth understanding." It is a peace which the world cannot give or take away. It is a peace with God, and an entrance into eternal life.

Phil. iv. 7.

XIV. ETERNAL LIFE HERE AND NOW

God dwelleth in eternity. For Him there is neither past nor future, but all things are present. He is not conditioned by anything which He has made. He is and does not change. It is on this changelessness of God that we should concentrate our thoughts, for living in a world of flux, we have a craving for abiding reality and ultimate truth.

We become pessimists if we contemplate life as a series of dissolving views, where nothing is permanent and nothing certain, where nothing can be preserved and nothing is worth while. We are grateful to scientists who find adaptation and law behind the phantasmagoria, but morally we are unsatisfied until we know that Truth, Beauty and Goodness do not depend on taste or fashion, but are attributes of the God who does not change.

If life depends on correspondence with environment, eternal life depends on our correspondence with the living and eternal God. So we read, " This is life eternal, that they should know Thee, the only true God, and Jesus Christ, Whom Thou hast sent." S. John xvii. 3. This knowledge is not merely intellectual and does not depend on understanding. We are to know God as a child knows his mother; and to rest in Him as a child rests in her arms. But we can only know Him through Jesus Christ Our Lord, Who in time revealed the eternal, and dying brought immortality to light.

Contemplating Our Lord, we shall not exaggerate the significance of ecstasy as a foretaste of eternity. Most people have at some time experienced such intense pleasure, such piercing pain, or such frenzied excitement, that memory was obliterated and there seemed nothing beyond : there was no realised environment, but only the exquisite moment. Are not such people in touch with eternity? Perhaps : but Our Lord was ever in constant correspondence with His Father, and therefore ever shared in eternal life, yet, except once on the Mount of Transfiguration, we read nothing of ecstasy. Moreover, in a state of S. Matt. xvii. 1-8. ecstasy men are passive; they suffer and do not S. Mark ix. 2-10. consciously act; and when they come back to them- S. Luke ix. 22-36. selves they are generally in a state of exhaustion.

Contemplating Our Lord, we shall not confuse survival after death with eternal life, or be over-concerned with psychical phenomena, or greedy for the reports of mediums, who at best are able to tell us of a continued existence on another plane.

Mediums, even when honest—and very frequently they are not—seem only to get in touch with earth-bound spirits, who are living on a lower level than the better class of men, and who are not sufficiently intelligent to communicate the conditions of their existence in a satisfactory manner.

For a Christian, eternal life is here and now. It is the gift of God, and we have received it, because of the atonement made by Our Lord upon the Cross. By Him we are reconciled with the Father, through Him we have communion with the Father, and in Him we have the revelation of the Father's love. We have no longer to seek after God; and in finding Him we " lay hold on eternal life." What is eternal life but union with God, the source of all life; and it should be clear that, so long as such a union exists, it is impossible for a man really to die.

1 Tim. vi. 12, 19.

Every time we are conscious of real communion with God we have a foretaste of eternity. Every time we obey the promptings of our conscience and do God's will rather than our own we are sharing in His life. Every time we judge anything according to the revealed standard of morality in defiance of expediency or fashion we adopt the eternal standpoint. The more we love, the nearer we are to God, until we can say with S. Paul, " I am persuaded, that neither death, nor life, nor angels, nor principalities, nor powers, nor things present, nor things to come, nor height, nor depth, nor any other creature, shall be able to separate us from the love of God, which is in Christ Jesus Our Lord."

Rom. viii. 38, 39.

XV. The Intermediate State

All saints have confessed that their communion with God is intermittent, and that often He seems to them very far away. All likewise confess that it is hard to relate everything to God, and to see the world with the eyes of eternity. They admit that they are to some extent self-centred, and therefore out of relation to eternal life. Like S. Paul they would say, " I count not myself to have apprehended : but this one thing I do, forgetting those things which are behind, and reaching forth unto those things which are before, I press toward the mark for the prize of the high calling of God in Christ Jesus." Phil. iii. 13, 14.

Our Lord has indeed proved that even in this life a man may be at one with God and share in eternal life, but even He felt straitened until His work in this world was accomplished. The larger life, with S. Luke xii. 56. grander opportunities and a wider vision, lies beyond. Here the good man must always expect to be surrounded, and to some extent thwarted, by hostile influences, to suffer rather than to triumph. This he will not complain of, but will rather rejoice, because the obstacles to be overcome are the proving of his manhood. Here he will find the stage for his great adventure, and it is not until the curtain is rung down that it can be said—he lived happily ever after.

This reminds us that whereas all men work for an end, no one ever considers an end apart from a new beginning. The boy looks forward to the end of his school life, because he will then go into a world of greater freedom and larger possibilities. The young man looks forward to the end of his courtship, and to the new life under new conditions which will begin with marriage. The workman hastens to finish his job, but he is calculating on the price he will be paid for it and how he will use the money. The artist, though he rejoices in his work, is irritable until it is done, but all the time he is anticipating the fame that will be his. So men must either look forward to death as a new beginning, or conclude that it is irrational. No one, however, who has been in touch with eternal life in this world or considers the analogies of nature can conceive of extinction. He can only be curious about the possibilities of existence while divorced from the body and awaiting resurrection.

Very little is told us about what will happen to those who die in a state of grace, and we have to remember that no two persons die in exactly the same spiritual condition. It is natural then to expect that all will not be treated alike, but that each will find himself in a position appropriate to his past. Our Lord told the Penitent Thief, " To-day shalt thou be with Me in Paradise," and we may be happy in the thought that death will entail no separation from Him. Again we shall be conscious, for Our Lord went and preached to the spirits which were in safe ward, announcing to them His glorious gospel of deliverance. Our memory will remain, and our concern for those we have left behind, for even Dives in the Parable was mindful of his five brothers, and recognised Lazarus in Abraham's bosom, although he had ignored him on his own threshold. Again, it will be a time of discipline, and so Our Lord, speaking in figurative language, said some would receive few stripes and some many. It must be a time of enlightenment,

S. Luke xxiii. 43.

1 S. Pet. iii. 19, 20.

S. Luke xvi. 19-31.

for how much will the best need to learn before he
is fit to enter heaven.   For some it will prove a time
of refreshment, light and peace, and for all it will
probably be a time of intense spiritual activity.   We
shall be able to learn, able to perfect our penitence,
able to pray.   We shall grow in sympathy and love
for others, for it is to a life of love and service that we
are called in heaven.   But, while discarnate, it is
inconceivable that we should act, and perhaps in the
intermediate state we may become free from those
conceptions of spatial relations and clock-time to
which we are accustomed; but time must have some
meaning for souls in the intermediate state, for they
still have something to hope for.   So S. John in Patmos saw the souls of the martyrs beneath the altar,
crying, " O Lord, how long ! "   Rev. vi. 9, 10.

XVI. The Beatific Vision

After the Great Assize, God will make all things
new, but the new heaven and the new earth will be   Rev. xxi. 5.
the result of all that has gone before, and the consummation of the ages will be also the beginning of
the life everlasting in the world to come.

As for ourselves, S. John says, " It doth not yet
appear what we shall be; but we know that, when
He shall appear, we shall be like Him, for we shall
see Him as He is."   In the days long ago, Our Lord   1 S. John iii. 2.
became one of us in order that we might be one with
God.   He died for us and rose again, that we might
rise to newness of life.   He came as the second Adam,
the head of the redeemed race, and we have been
incorporated into Him by baptism, and sustained by

His perfect humanity in His Holy Communion. So looking forward, we pray that we may grow like Him; and that, when He appears and calls us upward, we shall not be afraid of God, but find a Father Who is propitiated and in us is well pleased.

There have been mystics who have taught that eternal life will mean absorption into the infinite God, but this is not the Christian doctrine. The Christian's God, though immanent in all things, is none the less transcendent, and therefore the distinction between God and His creatures can never be done away. Secondly, Our God is love, and out of love created us that we might respond to His love, but we can only respond so long as we possess a distinct centre of consciousness. Thirdly, this belief in absorption is analogous with the heresy of Eutyches, who taught that the Manhood of Our Lord was swallowed up in the Godhead, as a drop of vinegar is lost in the ocean. But the Catholic Church teaches that the God from everlasting is Man for evermore, and that the two natures remain distinct in the One Christ. It is therefore in line with the ultimate assumptions of Christian theology, if we believe that for us eternal life will be the fulfilment of all that we mean by personality. Should we ever enjoy the Beatific vision, we shall not cease to be ourselves. On the contrary, we shall each apprehend the splendour of God in the light of what we have hoped, and because of what we have learnt, enjoyed and suffered. The very sins which God has pardoned will give us an individual understanding of His Mercy, and the bodies which He has redeemed and purified will provide fresh evidence for His praise.

If this conception be correct the eternal life enjoyed

by men will not be strictly timeless.   For as man is a
finite being and God is infinite, man can never know
God all at once but only by degrees and in succession.
Clock-time may be no more—as a measure it may
have no meaning for us; but simultaneity will not be
ours, as there will ever be more to see, to know and to
praise.   We are told "Eye hath not seen, nor ear
heard, neither have entered into the heart of man,
the things which God hath prepared for them that
love Him."   And these joys for men will flow from 1 Cor. ii. 9.
the fact that "God shall be with them and be their
God.   And God shall wipe away all tears from their
eyes; and there shall be no more death, neither
sorrow, nor crying, neither shall there be any more
pain : for the former things are passed away."   Rev. xxi. 3, 4.

But if men will know things in succession, in one
sense men will still experience change, and therefore
once more eternal life for men is not the same as
eternal life in God.   We can, however, think that
whatever changes we experience from without, our
condition will be unchangeable.   We shall be safe,
saved and free from the vicissitudes of fortune.   We
shall be at one with God, and able to rest in the love
which never tires.   Our life will know no decay, our
powers will not fail, our faculties will be perfected,
and there will no longer be any vacillation in our
purpose.   Secondly, eternal life means for us, that
we shall be in harmony with ourselves, with our
fellows, with the universe, with God, and able to
say Amen to all that is and give God praise.

So eternal life is attainment to a correspondence
with God which is only limited by our capacity.
To what we attain will depend on our past, for this
life has a meaning and a purpose, and eternity is its

explanation and fulfilment. It follows that as we are not now all alike, so we shall ever be different. Each man will have his own beatitude, and there is no equality in bliss. So S. Paul reminds us that " one star differeth from another star in glory," and Our Lord reveals that " In His Father's house are many mansions "; and He told us the parables of the Pounds and the Talents to show that all will not receive an equal reward. Yet in the life of heaven there will be no envy and no discontent. All will be full of joy, but all have not the same capacity for joy, and each will have his own contribution to make to the happiness of all. This thought of diversity in unity is in line with all that we know of God's creation; and the inequality of souls in heaven is a rational ground for believing that we shall enjoy a social existence. A life of reciprocal love will be possible, and each will be able to help the other, and all, in some way and to some extent, will reflect the perfection of that God in Whose image they were created.

1 Cor. xv. 41.

S. John xiv. 2.

S. Luke xix. 12–27.
S. Matt. xxv. 14-30.

This conception of a social life reminds us of how we say in the Creed, " I believe in the resurrection of the body." It is only through the body that we can communicate with others, or can act; and if in heaven we are to enjoy the fulness of life, we cannot be merely in a receptive and passive condition. But some find it hard to believe this doctrine.

We believe that the God from everlasting did not abhor the Virgin's womb, but took flesh and became man. We believe that the salvation of the world was won by the sacrifice of His Body upon the Cross. We believe that on the third day in the Body He rose again, " the firstfruits from the dead," and ascended into heaven. We believe that we are sustained by

His Body and Blood. We believe that His Spirit is working for the redemption of our bodies, and that our bodies may be temples of the Holy Ghost.

Matter, like spirit, was created by God; matter, like spirit, was redeemed by Our Lord; matter, like spirit, must also attain to its true manifestation in eternal life. It is true that at present we do not know the nature of either spirit or matter, the extent of their relations one to the other, or whether they are modifications of one thing. With our present knowledge we are bound to think of them apart, just as we must have two pictures of a shield which is gold on one side and silver on the other.

Again we recognise that the identity of our bodily life does not depend on the particles which inhere in it, for they are not the same from moment to moment, and we are always in a state of flux. From the womb to the grave the body changes, and yet is ever the same; but physics cannot help us to understand that mystery, and still less can it help us to understand how the σῶμα ψυχικόν is transformed into the σῶμα πνευματικόν. Yet S. Paul saw the necessity that "this corruptible (body) must put on incorruption, and this mortal (body) must put on immortality," before it can $^{1 \text{ Cor. xv.}}_{53.}$ be asserted that "death is swallowed up in victory."

The reason is obvious. We are composed of body and soul; and, though in this world the flesh often lusts against the spirit, we only enjoy the fulness of life when body and soul are in harmony. It is this fulness of life we desire and have been promised, and we have no wish to survive as ghosts and cannot look forward to an incomplete immortality. The fulness of life necessitates the ultimate salvation of body and soul.

We conclude that the redeemed will be the same though transfigured and glorified, and the consummation of their lives will be the glory of the Redeemer. His love will find its response and His sacrifice will not have been fruitless. He will celebrate His own triumph when He says, " Come, ye Blessed of My Father, and inherit the Kingdom prepared for you from the foundation of the world."

And the redeemed will answer, " We were far from God, and He brought us nigh : we were in the way of destruction and He delivered us."   And what is the end of the whole matter ?

1 S. John
v. 11.

> " God hath given unto us eternal life :
> And this life is in His Son."

MADE AND PRINTED IN GREAT BRITAIN.   RICHARD CLAY & SONS, LTD.,
PRINTERS, BUNGAY, SUFFOLK.